DISCIPLES OF THE WISE

DISCIPLES OF THE WISE

THE RELIGIOUS AND SOCIAL OPINIONS
OF AMERICAN RABBIS

By JOSEPH ZEITLIN, Ph.D.

TEACHERS COLLEGE, COLUMBIA UNIVERSITY
CONTRIBUTIONS TO EDUCATION, NO. 908

Essay Index Reprint Series

BOOKS FOR LIBRARIES PRESS
FREEPORT, NEW YORK

INTERNATIONAL STANDARD BOOK NUMBER:

0-8369-1859-2

LIBRARY OF CONGRESS CATALOG CARD NUMBER:

71-121517

PRINTED IN THE UNITED STATES OF AMERICA

DEDICATION

Reverently and affectionately is this volume dedicated to my mother, Esther Mathilde, who through the dignity of her life symbolizes the beauty of spirituality.

FOREWORD

A major task of organized religion is to determine the relevance of a body of historic belief, tradition and group testimony to contemporary problems and needs. The less authoritarian a particular religious body is and the wider the scope within it for individual judgment and pronouncement, the greater is the need, in a time of rapid social change, for taking stock of significant beliefs and opinions held by its leaders. The study here reported was such an undertaking. It involved a great amount of patient labor, as the reader will quickly discover.

The issuance of corporate pronouncements by religious bodies, of which there have been many in recent years, is a fruitful method of influencing public opinion. But it happens not infrequently that such declarations represent quickly formed judgments by not very durable majorities. They need the corrective of considered private judgments formed without group pressure. It might be worth while for religious bodies—and secular groups as well —to make provision for periodic opinion studies among their members both for guidance in group action and as a means of education with reference to emerging issues.

It is hoped that Rabbi Zeitlin's study, together with others that may be undertaken, will contribute to an understanding of the views of a group of influential religious leaders on certain questions of continuing interest. If it stimulates similar inquiries its value will be thereby enhanced.

F. ERNEST JOHNSON

ACKNOWLEDGMENTS

To the several hundred rabbis and theological students of the Reform, Orthodox, and Conservative wings of American Jewry, who so helpfully gave of their time in furnishing data for the present study, the author expresses his appreciation.

Gratitude is due especially to the sponsor of the study, Professor F. Ernest Johnson, who through the several years of preparation of the investigation was a source of inspiration, counsel, and encouragement.

The author also acknowledges his indebtedness to his co-sponsor, Professor Helen M. Walker, and to Professor Irving Lorge, for guidance given him in the statistical sections of the study.

Finally, the author wishes to express his appreciation to Professor Louis Ginzberg, Dean of the Jewish Theological Seminary of America, for reading the manuscript and offering a number of constructive suggestions.

CONTENTS

PART III

DISCIPLES OF THE WISE

NOTE

THIS INVESTIGATION *was conducted in the latter part of 1937. Hence all findings represent opinions of the rabbis at that time. Since then, major changes have occurred in the national and international scene. As a result, some of the opinions here presented may have sharpened; some may be entirely altered. In the light of the overwhelming changes which have taken place in recent years, the views held by the rabbis on certain issues prior to those changes are of particular interest. This is especially true of general social questions as compared with theological and strictly Jewish issues.*

It should be noted that wherever the word "attitude" occurs in the text it is used not in a technical sense but in the sense of opinion.

J. Z.

INTRODUCTION

THE PURPOSE OF THE STUDY

THE PRIMARY CONCERN of this study is to discover what American rabbis believe and preach with regard to a number of important questions in theology, problems in Jewish adjustment, and issues in social and economic reconstruction.

To the extent that this country is a democracy, it is important to study the forces which fashion public opinion, forces which play not only upon the community as a whole but also upon the specific religious and racial elements within it. A study of what American rabbis, or to use the Hebrew appellation *"Talmidé Hakamim"* (Disciples of the Wise), believe and preach is not solely a rabbinic concern, nor is it exclusively a Jewish concern; it is, rather, a matter vital to the entire American community.

Jews appear to constitute nearly four per cent of the general population of the United States.[1] The number of synagogue members appears to be between 300,000 and 350,000. Since each member is usually the head of a family, it may be assumed that between a million and a million and a half persons probably come within the direct influence of the synagogue and the officiating rabbis.[2] At certain times during the year the synagogue reaches a considerable number of Jews other than members and their families. The High Holiday[3] attendance at many synagogues far exceeds the membership roll.

In his capacity as preacher, the rabbi is potentially in a position to influence the views, attitudes, and mental habits of the congre-

---

[1] In 1927 the total number of Jews in the United States was estimated as 4,230,000, as indicated by an inquiry addressed by the American Jewish Committee to 4,000 representatives of Jewish communities. See Harry S. Linfield, *Jews in the United States*, p. 18. The sociologist, Lestchinsky, makes an estimate of 4,450,000 for 1935 but does not state the basis for his figure. See Jacob Lestchinsky, *Yiva Bleter*, Yiddish Scientific Institute, Vol. IX, p. 166.

[2] See Maurice J. Karpf, *Jewish Community Organization in the United States.*

[3] The High Holidays denote the days dedicated to the celebration of the religious New Year (Rosh Hashanah) and the Day of Atonement (Yom Kippur).

1

gational membership and of the other Jews who occasionally attend the services. Owing to the recent trend toward the establishment of congregational schools, the educative role of the rabbi is in the ascendant. Not infrequently he is recognized as the leader of the Jewish community and as a ranking representative of the larger community of which the Jewish community constitutes a part. Rabbis serve on the boards of Community Chests. Occasionally they serve on public school boards. Nationally, they participate with leaders of other faiths in projects and serve on committees and commissions concerned with public welfare.

Only fragmentary studies based on the beliefs of certain sections of the rabbinate are now available. The annual reports of the Central Conference of American Rabbis going back to the last decade of the nineteenth century reproduce resolutions and record votes of the Reform Rabbinate on certain matters of Jewish and general social importance. Only limited data are available for the Orthodox and Conservative wings of the rabbinate. There is, therefore, clearly a need for a systematic study of what rabbis believe and preach—a study which would embrace all three wings of the rabbinate. Such an investigation is attempted in this study.

AREAS OF THOUGHT TO BE EXAMINED

The beliefs and teachings of the rabbi touch on a wide variety of both Jewish and general thought and action. Primarily he is a teacher of the Jewish religion. But he is also concerned with the broader problems of Jewish life and customs, Jewish adjustment to non-Jewish environment, Jewish culture. Moreover, he is concerned with the contemporary tensions and problems in local, national, and world-wide human society and with the implications of the moral traditions of Judaism and the human race for a program for easing these tensions and finding a solution of these problems.

In the light of these considerations, this study was planned to ascertain what rabbis believe and preach within the following areas of thought: (1) theology, (2) problems of Jewish life and adjustment, (3) the social function of religion, (4) economic reconstruction, (5) education, (6) civil liberties, (7) peace and internationalism, (8) race relations, (9) sex equality and sexual morality.

The selection of issues within the fields of theology and problems of Jewish life and adjustment is based on an examination of
authoritative works on Jewish history, literature dealing with
contemporary lay and religious movements in Jewry, publications
voicing the views of American Jewry, and the Hebrew and Yiddish
press in general. The selection of issues in the area concerned with
the social function of religion is based on an examination of the
writings of contemporary liberal religious teachers and others
who have interested themselves in the social function of religion.
The selection of issues dealing with economic reconstruction, education, civil liberties, race, and sex, was influenced by the daily
press, by periodical literature, and by the literature devoted to the
discussion of the contemporary economic and social scene in general. The aim has been to choose not only problems persistent in
social thought, but also matters that are immediately important
and that are likely to afford a key to an understanding of the social
orientation of the rabbi.

PROCEDURE

Construction of a Questionnaire

One of the best methods available for such study is that of direct
inquiry addressed to individual rabbis. The mention of a few
considerations will suffice to make this point clear.

Judaism has no hierarchy and recognizes no body as authorized
to fix doctrines, attitudes, and modes of action. The rabbinate
and the Jewish community in general are divided in the United
States into three main sections—Reform, Conservative, and
Orthodox. These divisions differ considerably from one another
with reference to the nature and content of Judaism, the philosophy of Jewish adjustment to the world at large, and to some
extent also with reference to specific social issues. The reports of
the annual conferences of the rabbis proved invaluable in providing an orientation for the present study, suggesting issues in the
various areas and providing a background for interpretation of
data obtained by means of a direct inquiry addressed to the rabbis.

A questionnaire was prepared embodying important questions
within the areas indicated above. A first draft of the questionnaire

was administered to students of the Jewish Theological Seminary of America (Conservative), Yeshivath Rabbi Isaac Elchanan (Orthodox), the Jewish Institute of Religion and the Hebrew Union College (Reform). The instrument was then revised in the light of suggestions from the students and the helpful criticisms of a number of scholars, teachers, and other competent judges.

The Group Investigated

The American rabbinate can easily be classified into three principal wings, Orthodox, Conservative, and Reform. Virtually all the Conservative and Reform rabbis are affiliated respectively with the Rabbinical Assembly of America and the Central Conference of American Rabbis. Such unity of organization is lacking in the Orthodox rabbinate. About 400 Orthodox rabbis are affiliated with the Union of Orthodox Rabbis of the United States and Canada, and about another 100 with the Rabbinical Council of America. In general, the members of the Rabbinical Council are graduates of American colleges, have received their rabbinical training in the United States, and serve in English-speaking congregations. On the other hand, the large majority of the members of the Union of Orthodox Rabbis were trained in Europe and probably serve Yiddish-speaking congregations.

The questionnaire was distributed in the spring of 1937 among the members of the Rabbinical Assembly of America (Conservative), the Central Conference of American Rabbis (Reform), and the Rabbinical Council of America (Orthodox). No attempt was made to reach the affiliates of the other Orthodox rabbinical body.

In the study here presented, examination was made of the replies[4] of 108 Reform rabbis, or 30 per cent of a total group of 360; of 77 Conservative rabbis, or 31 per cent of a total group of 250; of 33 Orthodox rabbis, or 33 per cent of a total group of 100. In the first two groups mentioned, the number of respondents, provided the representativeness of their replies be established, may be said to give a fair picture of the current attitude of the *organized Reform and Conservative rabbinate*. However, in the case of the third group of 33 rabbis, it would be unwarranted to

4 Although more questionnaires were returned, only 218 were filled out in sufficient detail for the purposes of this investigation.

claim that their responses are characteristic of the Orthodox rabbinate of America. They constitute a sample of the membership of the Rabbinical Council in 1937, and include no representatives of the Union of Orthodox Rabbis of the United States and Canada with which the large majority of the Orthodox rabbinate is affiliated.

Treatment of Data

The data were analyzed so as to determine, in so far as possible—

With regard to beliefs:

1. How the total group of rabbis stand with respect to various issues in the different areas and with respect to significant ideas cutting across a number of issues.

2. How the different wings—Reform, Conservative, and Orthodox—compare with respect to these issues and ideas. Differences as well as similarities were studied.

3. How the positions of rabbis with respect to one issue are related to their beliefs with respect to another issue. (Cross-tabulation.)

4. The extent of coherence, non-coherence, and apparent inconsistency of the rabbis' beliefs.

With regard to preaching:

How the preaching emphases of the rabbis upon various broad issues compare, and what differences are to be noted among the three wings of the rabbinate.

Representativeness of the Sample

There is no way of establishing the degree in which the views, attitudes, and beliefs of the sample are representative of those of the entire American rabbinate. The percentage of replies was relatively large. The sample seems to contain approximately the same proportionate representation as exists in the total population of the rabbinate with respect to the characteristics of age, length of service, geographic distribution, income, etc. To what extent the questionnaire itself has been a selective factor cannot be known. But the possibility must be reckoned with that a greater proportion of protagonists of particular beliefs, opinions, and views, than of others chose to return marked questionnaires. No claim is made, therefore, that the distribution of views and beliefs in the group which was subject to the study is the precise index of that in the total rabbinic population. It is believed, however, that the study does present an approximate picture of currents of opinion in the American rabbinate.

Explanation of Terminology

It will be noted that the word "attitude" occurs in the title of the questionnaire and in a number of instances in the text. The word was used, as it is used colloquially, as being synonymous with "opinion" or "view" with reference to the issues raised.

PART I

INTRODUCTORY NOTE

THE TWO CHAPTERS *constituting Part I of the present study are devoted to an examination of the genesis of contemporary tendencies in rabbinic thought in so far as these tendencies are reflected in the records of historians, the writings of individual rabbis, and declarations, resolutions, and discussions of rabbinic bodies. No exhaustive study based on original sources was attempted in these two chapters.*

Chapter I is concerned with the views of the rabbis on the nature and content of Judaism, and the orientation of rabbis with respect to Jewish life and problems. Contrasts and similarities among the three wings of Judaism are presented in their context, and in terms of the changes which have occurred in Jewish and general life and thought since about the close of the eighteenth century. Chapter II discusses the positions which rabbinic bodies have formally taken, at various times, on economic and social problems since the beginning of the present century. The changing social philosophies of the rabbis were placed against the background of political, economic, social, and intellectual flux.

A word should be said to clarify the relation of the chapters in this section to Part III, which is devoted to an analysis of the questionnaire returns. The two chapters in the present section deal with changes in corporate, *more or less official views over an extended period of time. Part III (Chapters V–XV), is devoted to an analysis of what* individual *rabbis believed or preached at a particular time—the spring of 1937— when the questionnaires were distributed and filled out.*

The present section serves two purposes in the total plan of the study. First, these two preliminary chapters serve as a historical backdrop against which the current views of the rabbis become more intelligible. They afford an historic orientation to the contemporary beliefs and opinions of the American rabbis, and a basis for determining the extent of agreement and divergence between the contemporary (1937) views of individual rabbis and the corporate views of rabbinic bodies of earlier times. Second, the material embodied in the two introductory chapters has proved helpful in mapping out the areas for the questionnaire study and in formulating a large number of specific issues for inclusion in the questionnaire. Moreover, the discussion of the results of the investigation serves as a background for an understanding of contemporary beliefs and preaching emphases.

CHAPTER I

TRENDS IN CONTEMPORARY JUDAISM

SECTION I

JUDAISM IN THE PRE-EMANCIPATION PERIOD

THE EMPHASES of the three wings of present-day Judaism—Reform, Conservative, and Orthodox—cannot be adequately understood unless they are presented against a background of the pattern of Jewish life and thought which endured, largely unchanged, until about the end of the eighteenth century. Up to that time Jewish life and thought were conditioned by two interlinked factors: (a) the Jews did not constitute a part of the communities in which they lived; (b) the Jewish intellectual and spiritual outlook remained substantially medieval in spirit until about the middle of the nineteenth century.

The following aspects of the medieval outlook are singled out for the purpose of sketching briefly the outline of pre-Emancipation Judaism.[1]

The Concept of a Religious Civilization

The medieval thinker conceived civilization as an organic unity of which religion was the actuating principle. Thus Catholicism was not merely a set of religious beliefs and practices, but also a number of principles which actuated the arts, the economy, the social organization, and the politics of the Middle Ages, and which integrated these diverse aspects of life into a unitary Catholic civilization. The advent of modern times was characterized, among other things, by the separation of the various aspects of life from

---

[1] The brief sketch of pre-emancipation Judaism here presented is based on a number of authoritative works on Jewish history, including: Heinrich Graetz, *History of the Jews;* Salo W. Baron, *A Social and Religious History of the Jews;* Margolis and Marx, *History of the Jewish People;* Simon Dubnow, *Dibre Yeme Yisrael, b'Dorot ha-Aharonim.* The works of Mordecai M. Kaplan, *Judaism as a Civilization* and *The Meaning of God in Modern Jewish Religion,* also proved useful.

the binding force of religion and the relegation of the latter to
the distinct sphere of the inner life.

Supernaturalism

The natural order of the world was conceived as inferior to and
dependent upon the supernatural, divine order of reality. The
modern era begins with an insistence on the self-sufficiency and
perfection of the natural order of reality.

Static Concept of Reality, Truth, and Revelation

In the medieval view, the ultimate source of the highest truth is
divine revelation, which is unchanging. Truth is therefore attained by a process of looking back to the original custodians of
revelation rather than by moving forward through the process of
discovery. Modern thought places emphasis upon the need for
the discovery of new truths.

On the eve of Jewish emancipation in the middle of the nineteenth century, Judaism still bore the earmarks of medieval
ideology. Judaism was conceived as an organic civilization rather
than as a separate department of life. The Jewish people, the
Jewish scheme of life and values, and the Jewish religion were
conceived to be one and inseparable.[2] The faith of the Jews was
conceived as the foundation of Judaism, as a pattern of life. The
content of the Jewish faith was conceived as the reason for the
Jewish way of life—Judaism as the way itself. A number of
medieval Jewish philosophers formulated creeds, but these creeds
never achieved the nature of dogmas binding upon all Jews.[3]
The relation between religious faith and religious practice was so
intimate as to make the two indistinguishable from each other.
As will be pointed out in the introductory note to Chapter V, the
theological beliefs of the Jews were implied in their way of life
rather than explicitly stated.

The Torah, oral and written, was believed to solve all con-
ceivable problems of intellectual and practical life.

[2] In the language of Jewish mysticism, "Three Entities are inextricably bound
together: The Holy One Blessed Be He, The Torah, and Israel." *Zohar*, Vol. III,
p. 73a.

[3] On the creeds formulated by Jewish thinkers in the Middle Ages see Husik, *History of Medieval Jewish Philosophy*, especially Cresca's Creed, pp. 392 ff., the Maimo-
nidean Creed, pp. 409 ff., and Albo's Creed, pp. 410 f.

An examination of the history of Jewish tradition will reveal definite innovations and even contradictions between earlier and later strands in the religiously sanctioned traditional pattern of Jewish life. However, the new was always conceived to be implied in the old. As the Talmudists expressed it, "Whatever a competent scholar is likely to discover in the future is a part of the Torah which was delivered to Moses on Mount Sinai."[4]

Because of this static concept of the true and the good, the intellectual activity of the Jews in the pre-Emancipation and pre-Enlightenment period exhausted itself in interpreting preceding strands of the Jewish tradition. When confronted with a novel problem, the task of the traditional Jew is not to look for a novel solution, but to interpret the Torah to discover what implication it carries for presenting the solution. In consequence, the rabbi limited his function to mere exposition.

The process of absorption of Jews into the political life of the Western nations as well as the impact of modern thought constituted a challenge to the traditional view of Judaism as a distinct and organic civilization and to its medieval aspects. The divisions of present-day Judaism in Western Europe and the United States into the Reform, Conservative, and Orthodox wings represent different answers to the question of what constitutes the optimum adaptation of Judaism to the demands of modern life and thought.

SECTION II

REFORM JUDAISM

Origin and Development of Reform Judaism in Germany

Intellectually, Reform Judaism is a protest against and a radical departure from the traditional orientation described in the above paragraphs. Traditional Judaism was nationalistic. It was conceived as the Jewish way of life. To Reform Judaism, a rational system of beliefs aiming at a universal faith is the essence of Judaism. In the traditional view Judaism was essentially static; to Reform it is developmental.

From its origin to the present time, Reform Judaism has been

---

[4] Palestinian Talmud, Tract Peah, Ch. II, p. 17a.

a movement of the classes rather than of the masses. Seligmann, the historian of the Reform movement, enumerates the occupations of people who participated in laying its foundations. He lists bankers, merchants, manufacturers, professional people, scholars, and the like, but fails to mention artisans, storekeepers, peddlers, etc. These latter groups admittedly did not participate, yet they constituted the majority of German Jewry.[5]

What the rich and prominent Jews at the time of the emergence of Reform Judaism wanted was to participate fully in the cultural, political, and economic life around them, and to avail themselves of the opportunities afforded by the newly born liberal capitalism. They desired: (a) to be admitted into full citizenship and to be accepted socially, (b) to identify themselves with the new streams of thought, (c) to salvage within the framework of these aspirations as much of Judaism as possible.

These goals of the Jewish upper middle class had a profound influence in shaping the ideological content of Reform Judaism. It is in the light of these aims that the distinctions between *national* Judaism and *universal* Judaism, the spirit of Judaism and its particular expressions—"prophetic Judaism," "developmental Judaism," "ethical Judaism," and "legalistic Judaism"—which figure so prominently in the pronouncements of Reform Judaism, are to be understood.

When the matter of the political emancipation of the Jews came up in the French Constituent Assembly, two questions arose: (a) Are the Jews a nation or a religious community? (b) Do Jews have Jewish characteristics by virtue of their "nature," or because of the peculiar environment in which they live?[6] The issues figured not only in the discussions of the revolutionary constituent assembly and in the sessions of the Jewish notables convoked by Napoleon,[7] but also in the deliberations of German statesmen and intellectuals with regard to the Jewish problem.

In contrast with the "classes," the masses rejected emancipation. They considered themselves Jews nationally, culturally, and reli-

---

[5] Caesar Seligmann, *Geschichte der Jüdischen Reformbewegung von Mendelssohn bis zur Gegenwart.*

[6] For the issues which figured in the discussions about Jewish emancipation in revolutionary France, see Simon Dubnow's *Dibre Yeme Yisrael b'Dorot ha-Aharonim,* Vol. I, Ch. I. [7] *Ibid.* See also Heinrich Graetz, *History of the Jews,* Vol. V, pp. 486 ff.

giously, and had no desire to become anything else.[8] They feared
that their mode of living and their culture would be endangered
by enfranchisement.[9] While the Jewish bourgeoisie in Paris made
it clear that they understood that emancipation would involve
the abrogation of Jewish autonomy, the masses appealed for its
retention. In Holland the masses, through their representatives,
declared themselves against emancipation when the matter was
brought up before the legislative body.[10] In Hungary, as late
as the 'forties, rabbis on behalf of their communities publicly declared that they had no desire to be enfranchised.[11]

While no causal relationships between the trends in early Reform Judaism and the central emphases of the Enlightenment can
be established, it is probable that the latter influenced the former.
The ideas of the Enlightenment were a part of the social situation
at the time of the birth of the Reform movement. Social adjustment of the Jewish bourgeoisie would therefore include adjustment of Judaism to these ideas. Moreover, the emphasis of the
French Enlightenment, in contradistinction to the traditional
philosophy which it combated, was the ideological basis of social
change in general and of Jewish emancipation in particular.

The philosophers who identified themselves with the French
Enlightenment rejected the relics of medieval traditionalism,
authoritarianism, and mysticism, and saw in reasoned experience
the sole road to truth. By their zealous defense of the "rights of
man" the philosophers of the Enlightenment combated the older
notion that a man's birth, station, and religious identification are
a valid index to the treatment to which he is entitled. That such
an intellectual climate fostered the origin of the Reform movement, which looked toward the political, social, and cultural
emancipation of the Jews, can be readily understood.

At this point it is pertinent to consider some of the probable
influences of the Enlightenment upon the Reform ideology. It is
not improbable that the Reform movement owes much of its pronounced rationalistic outlook to the spirit of the Enlightenment,
which recognized self-evident ideas and clear-cut sense impressions

8 *Ibid.*, Vol. V, pp. 454 ff.
9 Simon Dubnow, *op. cit.*, Vol. II, p. 88.
10 Heinrich Graetz, *op. cit.*, Vol. V, pp. 454 f.
11 Simon Dubnow, *op. cit.*, Vol. II, p. 88.

as the sole criteria of truth, rejecting emotionalism and sentiment as obstacles to human progress. Thus, Rabbi Jacob S. Raisin, in describing Reform Judaism, sees in it a continuation of the rationalistic strain that earlier was in evidence in the writings of Maimonides and Saadia.[12] Rabbi Emil G. Hirsch insisted that Judaism is basically a religion of reality, and deplored spiritualistic accretions.[13] Until recently Reform identified the essence of Judaism with a number of clear-cut and rational articles of faith.

Another characteristic of the period in which Reform came into being was the negative attitude toward the historic past. The old life, based on emotion accompanying custom and habit, must be thrown overboard in order to facilitate the creation of a new heaven upon a new earth. Probably this fact accounts in part for the attitude of the Reform Jews toward Talmud and *Shulḥan 'Aruk* and the body of customs and laws that grew up in the course of many centuries of Jewish history—an attitude which ranged from indifference to out-and-out hatred.

Reform Judaism reflects the faith of the French Enlightenment in the power of environment to transform the life of the individual and the group. Essentially the impulse behind the emergence of Reform Judaism was the conviction that by abrogation of the Talmudical law and by Jewish participation in the social, political, and cultural life of the country of residence, the peculiar characteristics which differentiate Jew from Gentile would disappear.

While the Reform movement taught such transformation of Judaism as would enable Jews to avail themselves of new political, economic, and social opportunities and place their thinking in line with the progressive intellectual currents of the time, it also aimed to salvage Judaism. Conversion among the wealthy Jews was taken as a matter of course. Having become fashionable, apostasy spread to the economically and culturally lower strata of Jewry.

The pioneers of Reform felt that the solution lay in lightening the burden which Judaism imposed,[14] in adapting Judaism to the needs and spirit of the time, in beautifying Jewish observances, and in emphasizing the moral implications of Judaism.

[12] Jacob S. Raisin, *Reform Judaism Prior to Abraham Geiger*, in *C.C.A.R. Year Book*, Vol. XX, pp. 197–245. Charlevoix, 1910.

[13] Emil G. Hirsch, *My Religion*.

[14] Dubnow, *op. cit.*, Vol. I, Ch. II.

By the middle of the nineteenth century there developed, as a result of the process of adjustment, a set of new notions concerning Judaism. To a large section of the upper-class German Jews, Judaism could no longer be a civilization, a culture, or a complete way of living. But faith in "ethical monotheism" could be retained. Judaism could no longer be a national religion. It could, however, be universalistic, expressing hope in the redemption of mankind through the good offices of a "priest people." New ceremonials were devised, and also a new liturgy, in which Hebrew was reduced to a minimum and the nationalistic contents were entirely eliminated. The ideology of Judaism was made to fit the thought-patterns of the advanced thinkers.

Thus we find Holdheim arguing that everything in historic Judaism that has a bearing on the Jews as a political entity must be abrogated; combating rabbinism because of its nationalistic concept of Judaism, and repudiating belief in a personal Messiah and hope of the return to Zion. In its official declaration the Reform congregation of Berlin in 1845 states in part: "We cannot pray sincerely for an earthly Messianic dominion which is to lead us to the home of our ancestors out of the fatherland to which we cling with all the bonds of love . . ."[15]

German idealism, which assumed a position of intellectual dominance in Germany in the middle decades of the nineteenth century, greatly aided in the fashioning of the Reform creed. Not only was this philosophy hospitable to the formulation of the Reform creed, but it presented ideas which could be embodied in that creed and serve as its intellectual justification. German idealism came to be a spiritual, evolutionary philosophy of history and of reality in general.

By the beginning of the nineteenth century the evolutionary approach to the study of language, literature, and art became a dominant characteristic of intellectual Germany. The application of the evolutionary approach to the study of the Jewish past resulted in the *Wissenschaft des Judenthums*. By the thesis that Judaism is an organically evolving historical process, this movement afforded a Jewish validation to Reform.

A further impulse to the formulation of the Reform doctrine

[15] David Philipson, *The Reform Movement in Judaism* (1931), p. 233.

was supplied by the progress of the Reform movement itself. As the nineteenth century advanced, more and more congregations were changing their religious practices in line with the Reform attitude. But as yet this attitude had not been formulated into an ideology. The revisions in faith and the transformation of practices differed with the different congregations and rabbis. Some of the participants in the movement were impatient with what they thought to be too much hedging and compromise; others found evidence of too sudden and too drastic a break with the Jewish tradition. It was felt that a set of common principles and common observances which would avoid both extremes could be of great help in consolidating the gains and hastening the progress of Reform Judaism. The formulation of these principles and practices was the task of the rabbinical conferences which took place in Brunswick, Frankfort, and Breslau in 1844, 1845, and 1846 respectively, and of the Leipzig and Augsburg Synods held in 1869 and 1871.

The first conference, held in Brunswick, gave indication that henceforth Judaism was to be a religion divorced completely from the autonomous Jewish historic experience, that Judaism was to be denationalized.

The two succeeding conferences continued the process of the emasculation and universalization of Judaism. The distinction of form and spirit, universal versus national, was applied to the question of the retention of Hebrew in the prayers. The result was that Hebrew was found not to be "objectively necessary." The Rabbis recognized, however, the subjective necessity of retaining some Hebrew elements in the ritual, at least for the present.[16]

The most important decision of the third conference, held in Breslau under the presidency of Geiger, was the removal of the "fences" or the regulations instituted by rabbis in the past for the purpose of protecting the main features of Sabbath observance.[17]

The need for a renewed effort to consolidate the forces of Reform Judaism and to clarify its position resulted in the convening of the Leipzig Synod in 1869 and the Augsburg Synod in 1871, following a lapse of twenty-five years since the Breslau conference.

16 Philipson, *op. cit.*, pp. 164 f.
17 *Ibid.*, pp. 212 f.

The Leipzig Synod was devoted exclusively to settling questions of ritual. Toward the close of the Augsburg Synod a platform was accepted in which is to be found the first explicit authoritative formulation of Reform Judaism. The following is a quotation from the Augsburg declaration of principles:

> . . . Judaism has passed through many phases of development, and in them has unfolded the *inmost being* more and more. . . . The spirit of the true knowledge of God and of pure morality is filling more and more the consciousness of mankind. . . . Judaism joyfully recognizes in this phenomenon an approach to those aims which have at all times guided its course through history.
>
> The *essence* and *mission* of Judaism remain *unchangeable* in themselves, but the mighty change which is taking place constantly . . . has called forth an urgent necessity for reorganization of many of the forms of *Judaism.*[18]

Here we have for the first time an official formulation of the creed of Reform Judaism. The Hegelian strain in this creed is obvious. Judaism is conceived as an objective idea which develops dialectically by an inner necessity.

Reform Judaism in America

Reform Judaism was introduced in America by the influx of German Jewish immigration in the middle decades of the last century. The history of the movement in this country is roughly divisible into three periods.

The first period was marked by the rapid growth of individual Reform congregations from Germany. During this period the various Reform congregations and rabbis were bound together only by a common sentiment. As yet there was no clear common platform; there were no institutions for the training of rabbis, and no agencies for the implementing of a common policy. This period ends somewhere in the 'seventies, when the organizing genius of Isaac M. Wise began to make itself felt on a wide scale.

The second period is marked by the establishment and growth of the institutions of Reform Judaism—the Hebrew Union College, the Central Conference of American Rabbis, and the Union of American Hebrew Congregations—and by the formulation of the creed of Reform Judaism. In the formulation of its creed,

18 Quoted by Philipson, *op. cit.*, pp. 324 f.

Reform Judaism in America continued the tradition of the German conferences and synods. During this second period, all definitions of faith of the Reform rabbis were marked by the rationalistic approach, the negative attitude toward the past, the distinction between the eternal spirit of Judaism and its changing forms, the identification of the eternal spirit of Judaism with a few ethical precepts, the denationalization of Judaism and the open disavowal of fellowship in Jewish nationality, the rejection of Palestine as a focal point in Jewish values, the minimizing of the role of Hebrew in Jewish life and worship, and the liquidation of the Jewish pattern of life in favor of a Jewish spiritual religion.

Changes in the composition of the Jewish population in America during the last decades of the nineteenth century and the pre-war period of the twentieth, the events that followed World War I, and the transformation of the intellectual climate resulted in the emergence of the third phase of Reform Judaism. The leaders and members of the early Reform movement were virtually all German Jews. They had no strongly nationalistic Jewish attachments. The only link which they recognized was the religious one. The wave of East-European immigration brought to America large masses of Jews whose culture and pattern of life were distinctly Jewish. These immigrants had a vital feeling of peoplehood and nationhood. To them Palestine was a focal point of aspiration. With the continued arrival of East-European Jews, Zionism was becoming an increasing force in American Jewish life. The mentality of large sections of East-European Jewry was shaped by the mystic and emotional approach toward God, toward Judaism, toward the world, and, generally speaking, toward the life of Hasidism as contrasted with the rationalistic outlook of the Reform movement.

The characteristics of the third period in Reform Judaism are the return of the feeling of peoplehood and of appreciation of the place of national elements in the scheme of Judaism, the retreat from extreme rationalism toward greater emphasis on ritual and mysticism, and the emergence of social realism.

As a matter of course, organized agencies of Reform Judaism, referred to earlier, continued to be part of the movement. The first of these to be organized was the Union of American Hebrew

Congregations, established in 1873 by Isaac M. Wise. According to the 1937 annual report of the Union, about 290 temples, with a membership of approximately 53,000, are affiliated with the organization.[19] The Union conducts extensive educational, publishing, and organizational ventures. Its contributions are the main source of income of the Hebrew Union College. This institution opened its doors in 1875. Its first graduating class consisted of four rabbis. Since its establishment it has ordained 411 rabbis.[20]

The Central Conference of American Rabbis was organized in Detroit, in 1889. Isaac M. Wise served as president of the Conference from its founding until his death in 1899. From its inception the Conference has served as the sounding board of the Reform faith.

The Pittsburgh Conference of 1885 declared religion to be "an attempt to grasp the Infinite." Revelation was affirmed as the basis of religion. But the concept of revelation embodied in the Pittsburgh Declaration differed radically from the traditional conception. Revelation was freed from anthropomorphisms, and was conceived as a continuous process which is identical with the intellectual, spiritual, and moral evolution of mankind. This concept of revelation served as the basis for a definition of attitude toward the teachings of the Bible. A distinction was made between the spirit of the Bible, which is eternal and has a claim on the everlasting loyalty of the Jews and of mankind in general, and the letter of the Bible, which expresses the primitive ideas and national experience of Jews and therefore has no present-day claim on man's loyalty. The anthropomorphic elements of the biblical God-concept as well as the legalistic portions of the Bible were rejected. "We hold that all such Mosaic and rabbinic laws as regulate diet, priestly purity, and dress, originated in ages and under the influence of ideas entirely foreign to our present mental and spiritual state." "Only such ceremonies as elevate and sanctify our lives" are declared to be valid. "We accept only as binding . . . the moral laws" of the Jewish tradition.

The creed rejects contemporary Jewish nationalism. "We consider ourselves no longer a nation, but a religious community and

[19] *Annual Report of the Union of American Hebrew Congregations*, 1936–1937, p. 12.
[20] *American Jewish Year Book*, 1936–1937, p. 636.

therefore expect neither a return to Palestine nor a sacrificial worship under the sons of Aaron, nor the restoration of any of the laws concerning the Jewish state." The Jewish people live for the realization of the mission of Judaism, which is identified with the ushering in of the Messianic age—an age of universal acceptance of the Jewish God-concept and the application of the moral principles of truth, justice, and peace among all men.

For a number of decades the Pittsburgh Declaration was accepted as expressing authoritatively the position of Reform Judaism in America. The changes in the composition of the Jewish population which have taken place in America since the Pittsburgh Declaration, the newer orientations and concepts in the physical, psychological, and social sciences, and the transformations in the pattern of Jewish and general social life which followed World War I, called for a reformulation of Reform's position. At the 1936 meeting of the Central Conference of American Rabbis, a series of "Proposed Guiding Principles of Reform Judaism" was presented. "The changes that have taken place in the modern world and the consequent need of stating anew the teachings of Reform Judaism" are given as the prime consideration for this draft.

The 1885 Declaration of the Conference can be taken as articulating the spirit of American Reform in the second phase of its development, while the 1936 Declaration represents the central convictions of this wing of Judaism in its third phase. Taken together they illustrate both continuity and change.

An attempt to put concrete cultural content into Judaism is evident in the 1936 Declaration of principle. The Declaration is free from the negativism with reference to Jewish institutions, ritual, and ceremonies which characterized the philosophy of its earlier version. "The vitality of Judaism depends upon the preservation of the religious year, the Saturday-Sabbath and the Holy Days."

Furthermore, this Declaration takes a much friendlier attitude toward the national aspects of Judaism. It revokes the previous anti-Zionist stand of Reform Judaism. It sees in Palestine "not only a haven for the oppressed but also a center of cultural and spiritual life." The "guiding principles" do not, however, consider the national elements of Judaism as of primary significance. "We maintain . . . that our character as an eternal people is based upon the Torah."

Like earlier pronouncements, the 1936 Declaration also holds to the principle of continuous revelation. "The Torah, both written and oral, enshrines the perpetual light of Judaism, the ever-growing consciousness of God, and the ripening of self-knowledge of the Jewish people." The Torah is conceived as the evolutionary spirit which animates and expresses itself in ever-changing forms as human intelligence and morality progress. Loyalty to the Torah is the essence of Judaism, but such fealty does not impose the obligation of belief and observance of all details of Jewish tradition. The older distinction between spirit and letter clearly remains.

The 1936 pronouncement reaffirms the belief in the earlier doctrine of the mission of Israel. "The mission of Israel expresses our undying will to live a life of ethical and religious creativeness. Israel will endure as long as its destiny will be bound up with the destiny of faith, brotherhood, freedom, justice, love, truth, and peace."

Like earlier declarations, this one identifies the essence of Judaism with the striving for moral progress. "Judaism aims at the elimination of misery and suffering, of poverty and degradation, of tyranny and slavery, of prejudice, ill-will and warfare."[21]

SECTION III

CONSERVATIVE JUDAISM

Loyalty to Jewish tradition distinguishes Conservative Judaism from Reform Judaism. Whereas the Reform rabbis show a tendency to regard much of the Jewish heritage as a body of forms that have outlived their purpose and as the external shell of the inner and eternal spirit of Judaism, Conservative Judaism sees in the customs, ceremonies, and laws which have come into being during the course of Jewish history the very essence of Judaism. Conservative Judaism agrees that Judaism is a dynamic evolution-

[21] All quotations are from the Central Conference of American Rabbis, "Guiding Principles of Reform Judaism," *Year Book*, 1936.

ary process and that it must be adapted to contemporary needs, but denies that that evolutionary process is one of abrogation of tradition and of movement to an abstract idealism.

Conservative Judaism has been accused by representatives of both the Reform and the Orthodox point of view as lacking in a basic orientation. This is probably true if by orientation is meant a series of clear-cut principles. It is not true, however, that there is nothing distinctive about Conservative Judaism. The bifocal aspect of its approach—including both traditionalism and adaptation—is its distinguishing feature.

Conservative Judaism originated in Germany as a reaction to Reform's drastic break with Jewish tradition.[22] Its pioneer was Zachariah Frankel, who was deeply imbued with the developmental approach toward culture and institutions which in Jewish scholarship expressed itself in the *Wissenschaft des Judenthums*.

Frankel's philosophy of Judaism is expressed in the phrase "positive historical Judaism." He never offered a precise definition of what he meant by these words. Professor Louis Ginzberg believes that the best explanation of Frankel's concept of Judaism is that "Judaism is the religion of the Jews."[23] Judaism is a religion of deed rather than a theological doctrine. The test of whether a law, practice, or ceremony is an essential part of Judaism is not whether it fits in a theological formula, but whether it has come to be accepted by the Jewish people in the process of its historic experience. The origins of the elements of Judaism have nothing to do with their validity. Judaism is hospitable to a number of explanations of its nature and origin, but it insists on the preservation of its content. Thus conceived, Frankel's view of Judaism insists on the preservation of the uniqueness of Jewish conduct and observance in adapting Jewish thought to the ever-changing general ideas of mankind, and at the same time leaves scope for intellectual freedom.

The most far-reaching event in the history of Conservative Judaism in America was the founding of the Jewish Theological Seminary of America in 1886. Since its establishment it has graduated 317 students.[24] Well-nigh all its alumni serve Conservative

---

22 See article by Frankel in *Jewish Encyclopedia*, Vol. V.
23 See chapter on Frankel in Louis Ginzberg's *Students, Scholars, Saints.*
24 *American Jewish Year Book*, 1936–1937.

congregations. Dr. Solomon Schechter, president of this institution from 1901 until his death in 1915, exercised a profound influence on Conservative Judaism in America.

The United Synagogue of America, organized by Schechter in 1913, now counts approximately 220 congregations and has a total membership of about 50,000. Conservative rabbis—about 250 in number—are organized in the Rabbinical Assembly of America.[25]

Conservative Judaism has since its inception concerned itself mainly with a practical program of perpetuation and development of the Jewish tradition. To quote one of its leaders:

> As a result of common influences we are united on the following platforms: (1) We look upon Judaism as a developing religion and culture and assume that this development whether in institutions or thought can be traced and accounted for. (2) We encourage various schools of interpretation which seek to harmonize modern thought with Jewish beliefs. (3) We support the rebuilding of Palestine as a Jewish homeland. (4) We support and actively participate in the propagation of Hebrew, the tongue as well as the literature, in the school as well as in the synagogue. (5) We desire the perpetuation and growth of our ceremonial. (6) We shall attempt to organize the various Jewish groups for the purpose of improving Jewish domestic law.[26]

Like Orthodoxy and Reform, Conservatism sees in revelation the basis of Judaism. A precise definition of what revelation means to the Conservative rabbis is lacking, however, and there is no doubt that there is considerable difference of opinion among them as to the meaning of revelation. Similarly, are there differences within the ranks of the Conservative rabbinate regarding the nature of God and the physical efficacy of prayer.

The positive attitude toward traditional Jewish law is the quality that most distinguishes Conservative Judaism from Reform. To the Reform rabbis the Jewish law represents a phase which Judaism has outlived. Only the moral spirit behind the legal forms is eternally valid. Conservative Judaism sees in both the form and the spirit of the law the very essence of Judaism. There is, however, considerable difference of opinion among Conservative rabbis as to the degree of adjustment of the Jewish law to the needs of the time.

[25] *Ibid.*
[26] Max Kadushin, *Proceedings of the Rabbinical Assembly,* 1927, pp. 65 f.

Differ as Conservative writers may regarding the manner and degree in which the law may be changed, interpreted, and adapted to the needs of modern life, they all agree that the life of the Jews is to be molded by the law, and that the law which is to function in modern life must be a continuation of Biblical and Talmudic law. Conservative Judaism stands for flexible legalism and rabbinism. Domestic relations have traditionally been regulated by Jewish law, and Conservative rabbis feel that this area of life cannot be surrendered to the state. Marriage and divorce fall within the sphere of religious legislation. In consequence, the Rabbinical Assembly has greatly concerned itself with the attempt to clarify that part of the Jewish law which has bearing on domestic relations and problems in the light of modern conditions and present-day needs.

With respect to other Jewish institutions, Conservative Judaism, too, would hew close to the line of Jewish tradition. Conservative rabbis advocate Sabbath observance in the manner and the spirit in which it has been observed during past centuries of Jewish life. Conservatism also looks upon the observance of the dietary laws as an essential part of Judaism.

That the synagogue is the central institution of Jewish life all wings of Judaism agree. Synagogue ritual must be sanctioned by tradition. Hebrew has always been and is to remain the language of Jewish worship. While Conservative rabbis welcome the tendency toward making the synagogue a social center, they do not see its main function in social activities. The primary task of the synagogue is the perpetuation and dissemination of Jewish tradition, law, and culture. The synagogue should aim to become again a Beth Ha-midrash—a house of study.[27]

If by religion is meant a *belief* with respect to the nature of and an attitude toward the "real" and the "good," it can be said that the religion of the Conservative rabbis of today has as an essential part of its content Jewish nationalism and Jewish culture.

The Jewish people is conceived by Conservatism as an end in itself. It does not live, as in Reform Judaism, for the sake of a

[27] See the articles on the Synagogues in the *Proceedings of Rabbinical Assembly*, 1928, pp. 28–52; especially "The Status of the Synagogue in Jewish Life" by Rabbi Abraham J. Levy; "Inadequacies in the Status of the Synagogue Today" by Rabbi Israel Goldstein; and "Synagogue Attendance" by Rabbi Alter F. Landesman.

mission, however worthy the mission may be. As Rabbi Louis Finkelstein put it:[28]

We cannot accept the formula that Israel lives only for its mission of monotheism. . . . Great as monotheism is . . . greater still as are the ethics of Israel, there may be still other creations of the spirit of this people.

Hebrew is not merely the language of Jewish worship; it is the language of the Jewish people. The unique creativeness of the Jewish spirit must find expression in this language. Quoting again from Dr. Finkelstein:

Ours must be the task of restoring the pristine sanctity . . . of Hebrew as a language of prayer for the Synagogue and as the medium of instruction in our religious schools. We will have to create a reading public for books, as we cannot ignore the terrible plight of Hebrew literature in America.

Palestine is likewise an ultimate.

We want to see Palestine rebuilt; we have for it too an intuitional, unreasoning, and mystic love. We want to see Palestine rebuilt as the spiritual center of Israel. . . . But aside from its help in maintaining the spiritual integrity of our dispersed communities we look on Palestine as we do on the Torah—as an ultimate, a thing that is good in itself. . . . We should like to persuade its present generation of colonists and workers that the interests of their people demand their observance of the Torah, and the interests of Truth their recognition of God. And yet if our arguments should prove of no avail, we, unlike all other religious groups who accept Zionism, are willing to trust the future to God and to His people.

SECTION IV

ORTHODOX JUDAISM

In matters of practical conduct the similarities between the Orthodox and the Conservative attitudes outweigh the differences. Both Orthodoxy and Conservatism see Judaism not as a mere creed but as a design for living. Both accept the authority of Jewish tradition and law. Both are opposed to abrogation, changes, and amendments of the law, and both believe that the law must be

---

[28] All quotations from Rabbi Louis Finkelstein's paper, "The Things that Unite Us," in the *Proceedings of Rabbinical Assembly*, 1927.

constantly interpreted. With respect to the degree and manner of interpretation, however, there are differences of opinion.

In the Conservative view, the law has a double sanction—utilitarian and transcendental. The law is an expression of an eternal ideal and spiritual reality which transcends changing opinions and values, but at the same time its purpose is to enrich human life in a human sense. It follows that, whenever it is clearly established that a particular law no longer functions in the advancement of life, it is not the law which is called into question but rather its interpretation, and a new interpretation is indicated as necessary. In the Orthodox view, the utilitarian sanction of the law is subsidiary to its transcendental sanction. Ultimately the law is good in itself rather than good for men. It is the responsibility of the Jew to be so fashioned by the law as to accept the law as good for him. The Conservative rabbi is thus willing to interpret the law so as to introduce fairly significant changes in conduct; the Orthodox rabbi would countenance only minor changes.

To the end of reinterpreting the law in the light of modern needs, there are those among the Conservative rabbis who favor the setting up of a rabbinic body to deal with this matter. The Orthodox rabbinate does not see any immediate possibility of the establishment of a body with legal authority sufficient for such a far-reaching undertaking. They therefore favor the literal adherence to the law as traditionally interpreted.

In respect to intellectual orientation, the differences between the Orthodox and Conservative wings of the rabbinate are considerable. The latter group recognizes the need of accommodating the age-old faith of the Jews to the framework of modern thought. The Orthodox world view, on the other hand, conforms less closely to the scientific orientation. Modern Orthodoxy does indeed "accept" science, but probably in a restricted sense. The distinction is made between scientific truths, which are relative, and religious truths, which are ultimate.

What modern Orthodoxy apparently does is to permit science and traditional faith to lie side by side without making any effort at integration. It would seem that belief in an infinite God who nevertheless has anthropomorphic attributes, and belief in an afterlife and in rewards and punishments, are essential to Orthodoxy.

For several decades immigrants from Eastern Europe constituted the mainstay of Orthodoxy in America. With the cessation of immigration and the advance of Americanization, some of the Orthodox leaders recognized the need of giving Judaism a new garb. In the course of time some of the Orthodox synagogues introduced the English sermon.

Perhaps the most important institution in modern Orthodoxy is its rabbinical training school—the Rabbi Isaac Elchanan Theological Seminary and the Yeshiva College which is conducted under its auspices. The chief aim of this theological school is to train rabbis for Orthodox congregations. It was established in 1896, and since that date has graduated 167 students.[29] The Yeshiva College aims to give secular training to prospective rabbis and to others. It recognizes that general culture must supplement Jewish tradition in the education of the modern Jew. The following is an excerpt from the statement of aims of the Yeshiva College: "It seeks to strengthen in the minds of its students this abiding consciousness and the high ideals of the spiritual heritage of the Jewish people and to develop intellect and character through the pursuit of those humanizing studies by which life is enriched."[30] Note, however, that the "spiritual heritage of the Jewish people" and the "humanizing studies" are viewed as separate and apart.

The Hebrew Theological Seminary of Chicago is another training school for the Orthodox rabbinate. It was established in 1922, and since its establishment has graduated 52 students.[31]

The rabbis who represent the point of view of modern Orthodoxy are organized in the Rabbinical Council of America. This body was established in 1923, and at the time this study was undertaken had a membership of about 100. Another group of Orthodox rabbis is known as the Federation of American Orthodox Rabbis. This is a rather loosely organized body which consists largely of representatives of the older Orthodoxy. It claims to have about 400 members, but it is difficult to obtain any precise data with respect to membership, activities, and platform.

It will be the aim here to gather the views of spokesmen of

[29] *American Jewish Year Book*, 1936–1937.
[30] *Yeshiva College Catalogue*, 1936–1937.
[31] *American Jewish Year Book*, 1936–1937.

modern Orthodoxy on the issues which they consider important. The sources of these views are *The Jewish Library*, edited by Rabbi Leo Jung, and *The Orthodox Union*. *The Jewish Library* consists of a series of papers whose purpose is to disseminate the Orthodox point of view and to make it attractive to contemporary Jews. *The Orthodox Union* is the official organ of the Union of Orthodox Jewish Congregations of America.

The Orthodox view of the Bible and the concept of revelation differ from those of Reform and Conservatism. To the Reform rabbinate, the Bible is a record of the growing moral and intellectual insight of the Jewish people. Conservative rabbis apparently differ as to the sense in which the Bible is true. To Orthodox rabbis, the Bible is true in an absolute sense. It is more than experienced truth, reasoned truth, or inspired truth; it is divine truth. Revelation is supernatural; its source is not the human spirit but divine activity. The truth of revelation and of the Bible holds for all areas of life.

Orthodoxy holds that science is an instrument for attaining relative truth. Its findings have no decisive bearing on the final truths which religion reveals. When science ceases to formulate the regularities of sense-phenomena and attempts to present an ultimate view of reality, it goes beyond its legitimate bounds.[32]

Orthodoxy sees Judaism as an unfolding pattern of life. Talmudic Judaism and the Judaism of the codifiers are viewed not as an addition to but rather as a development of what has always been in Judaism. Full observance of the regulations of the *Shulḥan ʿAruk* is mandatory upon Jews.

There is, furthermore, a difference between the attitudes toward Palestine of the Orthodox and Conservative rabbis. To the latter, the rehabilitation of Palestine is an end in itself. While the Conservative rabbi would like to see Jewish life in Palestine fashioned in the mold of Jewish tradition, he is inclined to leave that to the Jews who live in Palestine. Orthodoxy, however, insists on the creation of a traditionally patterned mode of life in Palestine. At Zionist Conferences representatives of Orthodoxy have repeatedly raised the issue of observance of the Sabbath and dietary laws in Jewish settlements in Palestine.

[32] Moses L. Isaacs, Faith and Science, *The Jewish Library*, Second Series.

CHAPTER II

SOCIAL JUSTICE AND THE RABBIS

THE PRECEDING CHAPTER dealt with the corporate positions expressed at various times in the writings of individual rabbis and in declarations of the various rabbinic bodies on issues concerning Jewish religion, life, and problems. The present chapter is concerned with the corporate views of the several wings of the rabbinate on the political, economic, and social issues which have developed since the beginning of the twentieth century and which concern the community as a whole, regardless of religious affiliation. Changes in basic orientation will be noted and explained in the light of the changing social situation. Most of the material upon which this chapter is based consists of declarations, resolutions, and discussions of rabbinic bodies.

SECTION I

THE SOCIAL JUSTICE PROGRAM OF THE REFORM RABBINATE

Judging from the annual reports of the Central Conference of American Rabbis, the issues of political, economic, and social life are chief concerns of the Reform rabbinate, probably because of its adherence to the concept of the Messianic Mission of Israel.

The annual reports contain declarations, resolutions, and discussions concerning basic philosophies of social organization, just distribution of national income, labor organizations and collective bargaining, unemployment, public works and relief, housing, social insurance, the protection of the rights of religious minorities, interracial relations, academic freedom and civil liberties, international relations, the World Court, the League of Nations and international arbitration, recognition of Russia, disarmament and the nationalization of the manufacture of munitions and armaments, democracy, fascism, and communism, marriage, prohibition, birth control, etc.

In its attitude toward the inherited social and economic order as a whole and toward specific problems and issues which are involved, Reform Judaism has attained considerable maturity since the beginning of the twentieth century. In the early part of the century it showed no indication of questioning the soundness and the morality of an economic system which is based on private ownership of the means of production and on the quest for private profit. Nor did it show any evidence of the realization of the intimate relationship between the economic and moral aspects in the life of the individual and society. On issues concerning the relations between labor and capital the Reform rabbinate pursued the rigorous principle of justice, and declared itself "neutral."

In the years following World War I, and particularly during the years of the economic crises, the Reform rabbinate has experienced considerable growth in its social philosophy. Considering the reports of the Commission on Social Justice, resolutions, and discussions from 1931 to the present, it would seem that the contemporary Reform rabbinate is very much in doubt about the basic justice of our social order. The rabbis seem to question the ability of a *laissez faire* economy to provide a decent living for the masses. The prevailing method of distribution of wealth is brought under criticism. From the position of neutrality in the conflict between labor and capital, the rabbis have moved toward a decidedly pro-labor bias.

The years of crisis and depression have contributed considerably to the growing social maturity of the Reform rabbinate. A realistic approach to social issues and greater pro-labor and pro-collectivist bias begins to be noticeable in the 1931 report[1] of the Commission on Social Justice, starting with the recognition that the cause of the crisis lies in the failure of wages to keep up with the volume of production. The Commission came out clearly for the right of labor to organize, and committed itself to patronizing only those employers who accept the principles of collective bargaining. It recognized unemployment as the "most pressing social problem," amounting to a major moral issue. To the end of coping with this problem, recommendations were made for an intensified public

[1] Report of Commission on Social Justice, *Year Book of Central Conference of American Rabbis*, 1931.

works program to be covered by increased taxation in the higher brackets, Federal relief, and compulsory unemployment insurance.

The 1932 report shows an even greater swing in the direction of basic criticism of the economic order.[2] The Commission found something fundamentally wrong with a social system which permitted a rise in dividends to occur simultaneously with a decline in wages, and expressed doubt as to whether an economic system which is primarily motivated by the desire for profit can ever "achieve a satisfactory sense of responsibility." This basic criticism of capitalism was adopted by a vote of 59 to 16.[3] The Commission proceeded to express the need for a fundamental reconstruction of our social organization—a reconstruction which would make it possible for the masses to partake of a decent life. The advocacy of such reconstruction was declared to be an important function of the Jewish ministry. "It is our duty to evaluate economic schemes from the ethical point of view."

The 1933 report reflected the mood of the nascent New Deal.[4] The vote on the recommendation of the Commission to approve the Roosevelt program fairly represents the early division of the Reform rabbinate on the New Deal. The recommendation was adopted by a close margin of 33 to 26.[5] The report expressed regret on the slow progress of legislation looking toward the abolition of child labor and the establishment of social security. It denounced the lowering of standards of wages by employers.

Perhaps one of the most significant pronouncements of the Commission on Social Justice was the one issued in 1934.[6] It finds our social order, which permits 80 per cent of the population to live below the level of minimum decency, morally unacceptable. The report points to the bankruptcy of *laissez faire* economic institutions and the need for radical reconstruction of the economic system along collectivistic lines. The principles of cooperation and service must displace competition and the quest for private profits as bases for economic organization. The Commission recommended redistribution of wealth, clearly recognizing that this

[2] *Ibid.*, 1932.

[3] Report of Committee on Resolutions, *Year Book of Central Conference of American Rabbis*, 1932, p. 104.

[4] Report of Commission on Social Justice, *op. cit.*, 1933, pp. 57–63.

[5] Report of Committee on Resolutions, *op. cit.*, 1933, p. 112.

[6] Report of Commission on Social Justice, *op. cit.*, 1934.

implies the setting up of social standards appropriate to both minimum and maximum incomes. As a point of departure it recommended a steeply graduated taxation scale. The report also endorsed the socialization of banking, transportation, and communication. It criticized the N.R.A. on the score that it did not sufficiently safeguard the rights of workers. As a method of coping with unemployment it recommended, besides direct relief, the limitation of hours of labor, elimination of child labor, an intensified program of public construction, and the inauguration of a system of unemployment insurance.

The problems of peace and war and of international relations in general also are matters of deep concern to the Reform rabbinate. In its attitudes to these problems the Reform rabbinate reflected the views and opinions of large sections of the population irrespective of religious affiliation in the early and middle 'thirties. It was held by many that America's entry into World War I was a mistake, and there was deep disappointment with the peace that followed. There was a tendency to see the principal cause of war in the economic rivalries of powerful industrial and financial groups. Profits, and especially the profits of armaments manufacturers, were viewed by many as the principal motivation of war. World War II did not yet seem imminent. There was a tendency among religious people to pose the problem of war between nations and the participation of the individual in armed conflict in terms of absolute moral categories, and to forget the contingencies which might make war necessary to secure moral values.

The Central Conference has on a number of occasions declared its opposition to war on absolute moral and religious grounds. A 1931 resolution in part declared: . . . "It is in accord with the highest interpretation of Judaism conscientiously to object to any such participation."[7] The 1936 conference reiterated this position and called upon the government to grant Jews the right to refuse military service as conscientious objectors.[8]

In consequence of their rejection of war on moral grounds, the conscientious objectors found strong support for their cause

---

[7] Report of Committee on International Peace, *op. cit.*, 1931.
[8] *Op. cit.*, 1936, p. 74.

among the Reform rabbis. Thus the Conference protested in 1931 the refusal of admission to citizenship of conscientious objectors.[9]

By overwhelming majorities the Conference, on a number of occasions, passed resolutions against compulsory military training. It supported investigations of the munitions industry and legislation looking toward "taking profit out of war." It pointed out many times the need for keeping a vigilant eye on the cinema and other opinion-forming agencies which sometimes depict war in a favorable light.

The Conference repeatedly urged American participation in the World Court, and committed itself in favor of early entry of the United States into the League of Nations. Pending such entry, the Conference advocated cooperation with the League, especially against Japan and Germany.

The Central Conference advocated a program of disarmament for the United States and American participation in schemes for international disarmament. At various times it urged reduction of the American armament budget, admonished the government against naval construction up to treaty limits, and recommended that America assume the initiative in calling a conference looking toward world disarmament.

The proceedings of the Conference showed evidence of the recognition of the intimate relation between economics and the incidence of war and peace. Thus, in 1934, the Committee on International Peace began its report with the statement that the problem of peace is bound up with social and economic justice.[10]

The Central Conference concerned itself to a considerable extent with the safeguarding of civil liberties. In 1935 it urged the United States Senate to investigate the status of civil liberties in this country, and in the subsequent report it commended the La Follette investigation for revealing infringements against civil liberties by industry.[11] At least on one occasion the Commission on Social Justice came out in defense of the principle of academic freedom by requesting the reinstatement of a professor who obviously had been discharged because of "radicalism."

In view of the minority status of the Jews it is not surprising

9 Report of Committee on International Peace, op. cit., 1931.
10 Report of Commission on Social Justice, op. cit., 1935, 1936.
11 Ibid.

that the Central Conference felt deeply on the question of interracial relations. As far back as 1920 it advocated the enactment
of the Federal anti-lynching law. In subsequent conferences the
rabbinate protested strongly against anti-Negro terrorism, and
condemned conditions which render it difficult for Negroes to
obtain civil and economic justice. In 1935 it advocated the extension of citizenship to Orientals.[12]

The Conference expressed devotion to the principles of religious
liberty and the complete separation of Church and State. It protested not only the discrimination against Jews but also that against
Catholics. For a number of decades its Committee on Church and
State relentlessly combated attempts to introduce the Bible and
other religious matter into the public school curriculum. It repeatedly voiced objection to Christmas celebrations in the public
schools. In 1932 it warned against the introduction of religious
training under the guise of character education, and objected to
the plan to release children during public school hours for religious training, "as an effort which seeks to link up religious education with the public schools."[13]

The Committee also opposed compulsory Sunday observance
laws. In one state it was influential in eliminating the question of
religion from applications for teaching jobs in the public schools.
In keeping with the principle of rigid separation of Church and
State, the Central Conference expressed its opposition to the
Jewish people participating in politics as Jews.[14]

SECTION II

THE SOCIAL JUSTICE PROGRAM OF THE CONSERVATIVE RABBINATE

The social justice record of the Conservative rabbinate covers
a much shorter period of time than that of the Reform wing. The
Conservative rabbinic body began publication of its annual reports
in 1928. The Conservative reports devote proportionately greater
space to Jewish matters. Consequently there is much less material available for a study of the position of the Conservative rab-

12 *Ibid.*, 1935.
13 Report of Committee on Church and State, *op. cit.*, 1932.
14 *Ibid.*, 1934.

binate on matters of social practice than for the Reform rabbinate. It would be a mistake, however, to assume that the Conservative wing is less keenly interested than the Reform wing in social and economic problems. As a matter of fact, diagnosis of the ills of contemporary society and the proposed social programs of the Conservative group may give the impression of being more fundamental than those of the Reform group. The Conservative body has stated in unambiguous terms that certain aspects of our inherited social order are in contradiction to the highest ethical principles of Judaism.

In its first report, rendered in 1932, the Committee on Social Justice of the Rabbinical Assembly lists as its objectives[15] the formulating and publicizing of the attitudes of the Rabbinical Assembly toward the question of social justice; calling relevant information to the attention of members of the Rabbinical Assembly; the encouragement of members of the Rabbinical Assembly to conduct research and study in the fields of social justice; the bringing about of a friendly relationship between Jewish labor groups and the Synagogue; the establishment of agencies for the adjudication under Jewish auspices of disputes between Jew and Jew.

The thinking of the Conservative rabbis on the facts and problems of contemporary society and the proposals made for society's reconstruction resulted, in 1934, in the Pronouncement on Social Justice. The foreword to the Pronouncement states: "Not all of the members subscribe to all the positions taken in this Pronouncement. It does, however, represent the preponderant and authoritative attitude of the rabbis affiliated with the Rabbinical Assembly of America."*

The Pronouncement has, indeed, two impressive characteristics: (1) It makes an attempt to ground its social philosophy in the ethical tradition of Judaism. The rabbis present not merely their own social philosophy, but also what they consider the implications of Judaism in the task of social reconstruction. (2) It is explicit on particular social problems and presents a basic approach to the

---

[15] Report of Committee on Social Justice, *Proceedings of Rabbinical Assembly,* 1932.

* This and the quotations following are from the Pronouncement on Social Justice. The subsequent discussion is based entirely on this Pronouncement.

entire contemporary economic structure. It rejects private ownership and production for profit as morally wrong, and advocates collective ownership of productive wealth through a democratic process of transition.

Guided by the consideration of the moral worth of individuality, the Pronouncement "calls upon society to protect individuals against economic and social oppression." In the economic sphere it advocates minimum-wage and maximum-hour laws, collective bargaining, and the elimination of child labor, and it disapproves of company unions and "all arbitrary efforts to prohibit strikes either by legislation or by judicial injunction or by the denial of the right to peaceful picketing and any attempt to restrict by 'yellow dog contracts' or by any other way the freedom of labor to organize in defense of its interests."

The Pronouncement finds the price-and-profit system to be contrary to the principle of the brotherhood of man. "We hold an individualistic profit inspired economy to be in direct conflict with the ideals of religion. We maintain that our present system, based as it is on acquisition and selfish competition, is a practice of the denial of human brotherhood . . . our system of individualism has degraded human character. It has appealed to the most selfish instincts in man. It has been tried and found woefully wanting." The Pronouncement looks "to the ultimate elimination of the profit system as the basis of our national economy."

Under the caption "The Social Use of Wealth," the Pronouncement declares that "Judaism teaches . . . that God intended the world's resources to be used in the interests of mankind." The Pronouncement looks upon the phenomenon of concentration of wealth as "an unjustifiable expropriation of the great masses of mankind." It therefore calls upon the State "to use its power of taxation to correct the gross inequity of the distribution of wealth." In the meantime, the declaration favors government regulation of industry. There are, however, a number of economic resources which "society cannot be content with the effort to regulate" but must actually own in the near future. These resources are: (*a*) the instruments of banking and credit; (*b*) the means of transportation and communication; (*c*) the sources of power such as water, coal, oil, gas, and electricity.

The peace program promulgated in the Pronouncement sweepingly supports the rights of the conscientious objector. "We recognize the right of the conscientious objector to claim exemption from military service in any war which he cannot give his moral assent to, and we pledge ourselves to refrain from any participation in it." It voices its opposition to the teaching of military science and tactics in the high schools, colleges, and the universities. It calls for the leadership of the United States in an international disarmament program, conscription and use without profit of all industrial resources in the event of war, and nationalization of the arms and munitions industry.

It may be noted, in conclusion, that the Pronouncement is opposed to dictatorships "whether of the right or of the left," both as an end in itself and as a method of social reconstruction. It looks upon democracy as an essential feature of the good society. It contends, however, "that the failures of political democracy are due in large measure to its corruption and abuse by private economic interests." It is convinced that the methods of democracy and education are equal to the task of reconstructing society along desirable lines.

SECTION III

THE SOCIAL JUSTICE PROGRAM OF ORTHODOX JEWRY

To judge from the materials available, organized Orthodox Jewry has not greatly concerned itself either with defining its position on important contemporary issues or with formulating implications of Judaism in present-day social problems.

At the 1933 Conference of the Union of Orthodox Jewish Congregations of America, a Social Justice Committee was set up. The Conference declared that such a committee was necessary "in order that the influence of religious teaching as prescribed by our Torah may direct and stimulate the forces of social betterment and improve human relations."[16] The Committee undertook the formulation of a policy expressing the attitude of Orthodox Judaism on current social and economic problems. The areas to which it was to give its immediate attention were industrial relations, religious

[16] *The Orthodox Union*, December, 1933.

and social discriminations, and international peace. Sub-committees were appointed to study each of these fields. It appears, however, that the Committee did not accomplish very much. There is hardly any reference to its activities in the subsequent issues of *The Orthodox Union*—the official organ of the Union of Orthodox Jewish Congregations.

Though the Union of Orthodox Jewish Congregations from time to time has issued statements on social problems, it has never formulated a set of principles for the appraisal of society or developed a plan for social reconstruction. There is, therefore, no documentary basis for determining the social sympathies of Orthodox Jewry.

A perusal of the issues of *The Orthodox Union* which are available reveals that organized Orthodoxy has supported "forward looking policies . . . to outlaw wars and the establishment of a five day work week." The advocacy of the latter stems from a desire to safeguard the Sabbath rather than from general social considerations. In 1935 the Union condemned with even-handed justice both Fascism and Communism.[17] A year earlier it had extended support to the Legion of Decency in its campaign against alleged immoralities on stage and screen.[18]

Over and above the general issues on which the Orthodox official leadership has taken a stand, its interests are centered in Jewish problems. It has declared itself a number of times to be against the discrimination practiced against Jews, but it has not generalized its position to embrace other minority groups.

[17] *Op. cit.*, June, 1935.
[18] *Ibid.*

PART II

INTRODUCTORY NOTE

OF THE TWO CHAPTERS *included in this part of the present study, one is devoted to a consideration of some social aspects of the rabbinate and the other to the personnel of synagogue Jewry.*

The significance of the study is postulated on the assumption that the rabbinate is an influential factor in shaping the ideas and attitudes of at least the synagogue Jewry. Such questions as who the rabbis are, and what background, general education, and Jewish training they bring to the task of teaching and preaching, are intimately related to their social function. Of equal importance in connection with the influence of the rabbinate are the size, distribution, and economic composition of synagogue Jewry.

CHAPTER III

THE PERSONNEL OF THE RABBINATE

THIS CHAPTER will present the aspects of the rabbi's background brought out in the questionnaire results. These include (1) place of birth; (2) age and length of service; (3) secular education; (4) rabbinic training; (5) economic status; and (6) marital status and size of family. In describing the general setup, fundamental differences among the three wings with respect to these characteristics must be determined for the light they may throw on divergencies among the wings on the issues presented in the questionnaire.

CHARACTERISTICS OF THE RABBIS

Place of Birth

Table I summarizes the information submitted by the rabbis concerning the countries of their nativity. For the entire group 60 per cent are natives of the United States; 27 per cent were born in Eastern Europe; and about 11 per cent come mainly from Western Europe. The significance of these figures is evident if the facts of Jewish immigration and the distribution of Jews in Europe are considered. While no statistics are available, it is the impression of older rabbis that in the years prior to World War I the overwhelming majority of even the Reform rabbinate consisted of immigrants. The Americanization of the rabbinate in this country is accounted for by the cessation of immigration to America and the development of American institutions for the training of rabbis. Should these factors continue to operate, the American rabbinate will in a decade or two consist entirely of native-born men. That a much larger number of the European rabbis were born in Eastern Europe than in Western Europe may be accounted for by the fact that the East European countries were the main centers of Jewish population and also of Jewish learning.

TABLE I

PERCENTAGE DISTRIBUTION OF RABBIS BY PLACE OF BIRTH

	Reform	Conservative	Orthodox	All Rabbis
Total group	108	77	33	218
Number not responding	11	8	5	24
Place of Birth		Percentage		
United States				
New England and Middle Atlantic	30.9	34.8	10.7	29.4
Western and Midwestern	27.8	7.2	3.6	17.0
Southern	4.1			2.0
United States (not further specified)	13.4	10.1	7.1	11.3
Total United States	76.2	52.1	21.4	59.7
Canada	1.2	5.8		2.7
Eastern Europe	11.3	36.3	57.2	26.8
Western Europe and Miscellaneous*	11.3	5.8	21.4	10.8
Total other countries	23.8	47.9	78.6	40.3
Total all countries	100.0	100.0	100.0	100.0

* Miscellaneous refers to rabbi born in Mogavor, Morocco.

Differences among the wings are striking, as the following statistics will demonstrate. Approximately three quarters of the Reform group are native Americans, as against approximately one half of the Conservative and one fifth of the Orthodox. Of this American-born section the birthplaces of the Reform rabbis are distributed throughout the United States, with the number in New England and the Middle Atlantic States only slightly greater than that in the western and midwestern States. On the other hand, the Conservative and Orthodox show a concentration in the New England and Middle Atlantic regions, where about 70 per cent of the Jews in the United States are located.

The distribution of the foreign-born in each wing is also of interest. In the Reform wing there are about the same number from Eastern as from Western Europe, whereas in the Conservative and Orthodox groups the East-European-born are several times as numerous as the West-European-born. It should be remembered that the process of Jewish emancipation and assimilation made rapid progress in the countries of Western Europe, whereas in the East European countries legal and cultural obstructions to freedom of relations between Jews and non-Jews prevailed. On the basis of place of birth, then, it would seem that the Reform rabbinate is more representative of American life than the other two groups, and that the Conservative and Orthodox groups represent more strongly Jewish experience, tradition, and culture.

Age and Length of Service

Tables II and III present the frequency distributions of the age and period of service of the rabbis.[1] The average age and length of service were computed from the raw data. The average ages of

TABLE II

FREQUENCY DISTRIBUTION OF RABBIS BY AGES

	Reform	Conservative	Orthodox	Total
Total group	108	77	33	218
Number not responding	3	2	1	6

Age in Years	Frequency			
Less than 25		1	1	2
25–29	22	19	6	47
30–34	25	27	12	64
35–39	16	15	5	36
40–44	14	6	3	23
45–49	5	3	2	10
50–54	5	1	1	7
55–59	6	2	1	9
60–64	5	1		6
65–69	4			4
70–74	2		1	3
75 and over	1			1
Total	105	75	32	212

[1] A variance ratio test was applied to the data in Tables II and III separately. A definite interdependence was found between the ages of the rabbis and the wings with which they are affiliated. The same interdependence was found for length of service.

The calculated $F = 10.18$. At the 5% and 1% levels of significance respectively F was 3.89; 3.87 and 6.76; 6.72 for appropriate degrees of freedom. Therefore F is definitely significant.

Similarly, a variance ratio test applied to length of service and wing yielded a calculated F of 5.98. At the 5% level of significance F was 3.04; 3.02. At the 1% level of significance F was 4.71; 4.66. Therefore F is definitely significant.

TABLE III

FREQUENCY DISTRIBUTION OF RABBIS' LENGTH OF SERVICE IN RABBINATE

	Reform	Conservative	Orthodox	All Rabbis
Total group	108	77	33	218
Number not responding	2	3	1	6
Length of Service in Years	Frequency			
1–5	30	30	7	67
6–10	27	24	11	62
11–15	12	10	4	26
16–20	12	4	5	21
21–25	3	2	2	7
26–30	6	1	1	8
31–35	7	2	1	10
36–40	4	1	1	6
41–45	2			2
46–50	3			3
Total	106	74	32	212

Reform, Conservative, Orthodox, and the entire group respectively are 40.0, 34.3, 36.2, and 37.4 years. The average periods of completed service in these groups are 14.3, 8.9, 12.3, and 12.1 years. The rabbis who responded to the questionnaire are thus seen to be fairly young men. Among the three wings the only differences which are statistically significant[2] are those between the Reform and the Conservative rabbis on both age and length of service, showing for the entire group that the Reform membership are definitely older on the average and have longer average periods of service than the Conservative group.

By subtracting the average length of service from the average age, the average age at which the rabbis entered service is obtained. The figures for Reform, Conservative, Orthodox, and the entire group are respectively 25.7, 25.4, 23.9, and 25.3 years. None of the differences among the several pairs of averages are significant.[3]

[2] Students t test was applied to the differences of pairs of averages on age and length of service for appropriate degrees of freedom. For age: At the 5% level of significance $t = 1.96$; the computed t was 3.82. Therefore the computed value is significant. For length of service: At the 5% level of significance $t = 1.96$; the computed t was 3.69. Therefore the computed value is significant.

[3] The same test was applied as in footnote 2. The critical value of t at the 5% level of probability was 1.96. None of the computed values equalled or exceeded the critical value. Hence none of the computed t's are significant.

Thus on the basis of the group studied it cannot be said that the average age of entry into the rabbinate varies substantially among the three wings.

Secular Education

Table IV presents the picture of the formal secular education of the rabbis. Only earned degrees received from lay institutions were counted; honorary degrees and academic degrees received from rabbinical training schools were omitted. The minimum level of educational attainment in the rabbinate is thus represented by the Bachelor's degree.

TABLE IV

PERCENTAGE DISTRIBUTION OF RABBIS BY HIGHEST EARNED DEGREE

	Reform	*Conservative*	*Orthodox*	*All Rabbis*
Total group	108	77	33	218
Number not responding	4	5	6	15
Highest Degree Received	*Percentage*			
No degree			3.7	0.5
Bachelor	67.3	63.9	55.6	64.5
Master	18.3	26.4	29.6	22.7
Doctor	14.4	9.7	11.1	12.3
Total	100.0	100.0	100.0	100.0

Differences among the three wings with respect to formal education seem to be minor. No basis was found for assuming an interdependence between the educational attainments of rabbis and the wing of the rabbinate with which they are affiliated.* Thirty-five per cent of the entire group who answered the questionnaire have attained advanced degrees.

On the basis of Table V the most popular subjects in undergraduate study are philosophy and psychology, with 38 per cent of the entire group indicating these as their choice. Other popular fields are history, economics, and sociology, with a 26 per cent

* As shown by Chi-square test. Assuming no relationship between degree and wing, Chi² = 3.154. For appropriate degrees of freedom Chi-square with a 50% probability equalled 3.357. Therefore the hypothesis of no relationship is not rejected.

TABLE V

PERCENTAGE DISTRIBUTION OF RABBIS BY SUBJECT
OF UNDERGRADUATE AND GRADUATE MAJOR

	REFORM		CONSERVATIVE		ORTHODOX		TOTAL	
	U.	*G.*	*U.*	*G.*	*U.*	*G.*	*U.*	*G.*
Total group	108	108	77	77	33	33	218	218
Number not								
responding ...	18	71	18	44	11	19	47	134
Subject				*Percentage*				
Literature,								
English,								
Language	27.8	8.1	18.6	9.1	13.6	7.1	22.8	8.3
Philosophy,								
Psychology ...	41.1	18.9	33.9	15.2	36.4	28.6	38.0	19.0
Science and								
Mathematics ..	2.2	2.7	5.1		9.1	7.1	4.1	2.4
History,								
Economics,								
Sociology	21.1	21.6	32.2	36.3	31.8	14.3	26.3	26.2
Education	1.1	8.1	6.8	12.1	9.1	21.4	4.1	11.9
Semitics	3.3	5.4	3.4	12.1			2.9	7.1
Religion	2.2	29.7		6.1		14.3	1.2	17.9
Law		5.4		9.1		7.1		7.1
Music	1.1						0.6	
Total	99.9*	99.9*	100.0	100.0	100.0	99.9*	100.0	99.9*

* These do not total 100.0% because of the rounding off of figures.

following, and literature, English, and language, with 23 per cent. This is the order of popularity in the Conservative and Orthodox wings. The Reform rabbis give English, literature, and language as their second choice, and the social sciences as third.

In graduate study the social sciences take first place, but with only 26 per cent of the rabbis majoring in this field. In this division the major fields are more numerous, including education and religion in addition to the three popular undergraduate fields mentioned. Differences among the wings become more acute, the Reform showing greatest interest in religion and giving second place to the social sciences; the Conservatives with the social sciences predominating and philosophy following; while the Orthodox rank philosophy first and education second. Religion is a subject of major interest only to the Reform group. Apparently Conservative and Orthodox rabbinical candidates are not interested in religion as a separate field of study. This difference may be accounted for by the early view of Reform that Judaism is a distinct department of life, as contrasted with the traditional view that Judaism is the Jewish pattern of life.

Rabbinical Training

The Jewish Theological Seminary is the only training school for the Conservative rabbinate in the United States. Until about a decade ago, when the Jewish Institute of Religion was established by Rabbi Stephen S. Wise, the Hebrew Union College was the sole training institution of the Reform rabbinate. While the Reform rabbinate on the whole still carries the stamp of the Hebrew Union College, and the Conservative rabbinate that of the Jewish Theological Seminary, the Orthodox rabbinate is rather a mixed group with regard to the factor of rabbinical training. The outstanding training school for Orthodox rabbis is the Rabbi Isaac Elchanan Theological Seminary, in New York City. The Chicago Hebrew Theological Seminary, training schools abroad, and private ordainment seem to contribute a sizable proportion of affiliates to the Orthodox rabbinate.

Table VI presents information with regard to the training schools of the rabbis who replied to the questionnaire. On the basis of the figures it seems that the ideology of the Jewish Theological Seminary and the type of training it offers qualify some of its graduates for service in Orthodox congregations of the type included in this study. Of these, 1 out of every 7 fills a post in an Orthodox congregation, and about 1 out of every 3 Orthodox rabbis reporting is a graduate of this institution. Graduates of the Hebrew Union College and the Jewish Institute of Religion more frequently select Reform congregations, and graduates of the Jewish Theological Seminary predominate in Conservative synagogues.

Brief comment is here presented regarding the courses of study offered by the four more important training schools, since differences in their curricula may account in part for differences in the positions of the three wings on religious and social issues.

The Hebrew Union College is the older of the two Reform rabbinical schools, and, as already indicated, has contributed a large

TABLE VI

FREQUENCY DISTRIBUTION OF RABBIS CLASSIFIED BY SCHOOLS IN WHICH THEY
RECEIVED THEIR RABBINIC TRAINING

	Reform	Conservative	Orthodox	Total
Total group	108	77	33	218
Number not responding	3	1	5	9

School of Rabbinic Training	Frequency			
Hebrew Union College, Cincinnati	90	5		95
Jewish Institute of Religion, New York City	15	1	1	17
Jewish Theological Seminary of America, New York City		68	11	79
Yeshiva–Rabbi Isaac Elchanan, New York City		1	13	14
Hebrew Theological Seminary, Chicago		1	3	4
Total	105	76	28	209

majority of the membership of the Reform rabbinate. The avowed
aims of this institution are the preservation of the "eternal" and
unchanging principles of historical Judaism, maintenance of "un-
broken continuity" between present-day Judaism and the past,
and "adaptation" of Judaism to requirements of present-day life.
The most important subjects in the curriculum, listed in descend-
ing order of the total time prescribed for their study, are: Bible,
the Talmud, Homiletics and Midrash, History, Theology, and
Philosophy. The developmental approach is pursued in presenting
the religious heritage of the Jews. This is most marked with reference to the Bible and the Talmud. The time devoted to the study
of the Talmud appears to be insufficient for conveying an adequate
knowledge of this vast literature. The study of philosophy seems
to be limited to those aspects which have a bearing on the Jewish
creed. Comparatively little attention is given to neo-Hebraic
literature. It should be noted that the Hebrew Union College
offers courses in Jewish education and the social studies. The
latter aim at acquainting students with contemporary social prob-

lems and the techniques for their investigation and solution.[4]

The training offered by the Jewish Institute of Religion differs in important respects from that of the Hebrew Union College, since the course of study of the Jewish Institute of Religion is calculated to convey a sense of Jewish nationality and to elicit an interest in the present-day life, culture, and problems of the Jews. Emphasis is placed on recent Hebrew prose and poetry. In history, social and economic trends of contemporary Jewish life receive attention. The course in Jewish music includes, in addition to ritual music, that recently created in Palestine. Like the Hebrew Union College, the Jewish Institute of Religion offers courses in social service and Jewish education.[5]

The Jewish Theological Seminary was established "for the perpetuation of the tenets of the Jewish religion." Features that distinguish it from the institutions of Reform Judaism are adherence to tradition and a commitment to the preservation and further development of rabbinic Judaism. To be admitted to the Seminary "applicants must be . . . loyal adherents of [Jewish] observance, such as the Sabbath, holy days, daily prayers and dietary laws." On the basis of year-hours devoted to study, the Talmud and Halakah (Rabbinic Law) are by far the most important subjects in the curriculum of the Seminary. Considerably more time is devoted to the study of the Talmud and Codes in the Conservative institution than in the Reform training schools. Other important subjects in the order of the emphasis they receive are Bible, Jewish History, Midrash and Homiletics, and Medieval Hebrew Literature. In this Seminary no formal provisions are made for modern Hebrew literature, Jewish education, and social service, although beginnings are being made in this direction.[6]

Any attempt to describe the course of study offered by the Yeshiva is rendered difficult by the fact that the institution does not publish a catalogue. On the basis of personal acquaintance with the course of study and through conversations of students, a number of observations can be offered.

Requirements for admission are rigid with respect to Jewish knowledge and observance. To enter the Yeshiva one must be

4 Hebrew Union College, *Catalogue*, 1936–1937.

5 Jewish Institute of Religion, *Course of Study*, 1936–1937.

6 Jewish Theological Seminary of America, *Catalogue*, 1936–1937.

an observing Jew and must show ability to read the Talmud without assistance. Familiarity with the Bible and with Hebrew is assumed. Unlike the institutions of Reform and Conservatism, the Yeshiva does not demand completion of a collegiate course as a prerequisite for admission. A department for secular education is provided by the College.

There is no formal definition of the course of study which students must complete for ordainment, nor is the time required for completion specified. The main subject of study is the Talmud. Upon attaining a fairly extensive knowledge of Talmudic literature students proceed to the study of Codes, with special emphasis on dietary laws, domestic relations, and ritual. Ordination (Semika) takes place when the student has a mastery of the special branches of Codes. There is no formal provision for the study of the Bible, Hebrew language and literature, Midrash and philosophy, or Jewish education and social service. The content and method of study in the Yeshiva are entirely devoid of the historic and developmental approach which is characteristic of instruction in the Hebrew Union College, the Jewish Institute of Religion, and the Jewish Theological Seminary.

Economic Status

Table VII summarizes the information submitted by the rabbis concerning their annual income. In computing averages, incomes

TABLE VII

FREQUENCY DISTRIBUTION OF RABBIS ACCORDING TO ANNUAL INCOMES

	Reform	Conservative	Orthodox	Total
Total group	108	77	33	218
Number not responding	4	3	4	11
Annual Income	*Frequency*			
Below $2,500	21	13	7	41
$2,500 to $3,999	35	32	13	80
$4,000 to $5,999	20	20	7	47
$6,000 to $10,000	22	8	2	32
Above $10,000	6	1		7
Total	104	74	29	207

reported below $2,500 were figured as $2,000, which was considered a reasonable guess by rabbis familiar with conditions prevailing in poorer communities. The income bracket of $10,000 and over was figured as $10,000. On the basis of these somewhat arbitrary assumptions the averages in the Reform, Conservative, and Orthodox wings and for the entire group appeared to be respectively $4,728, $4,108, $3,698, and $4,362. The median annual incomes were: Reform, $3,829; Conservative, $3,625; Orthodox, $3,365; the entire group, $3,672. Taken as a whole, the rabbinate

TABLE VIII

FREQUENCY DISTRIBUTION OF RABBIS ACCORDING TO MARITAL STATUS

	Reform	Conservative	Orthodox	Total
Total group	108	77	33	218
Number not responding	1	2	1	4
Marital Status		*Frequency*		
Single	18	17	5	40
Married	83	58	27	168
Widowed	5			5
Separated	1			1
Total	107	75	32	214

TABLE IX

FREQUENCY DISTRIBUTION OF RABBIS ACCORDING TO NUMBER OF CHILDREN IN FAMILY

	Reform	Conservative	Orthodox	Total
Total group	108	77	33	218
Number not responding	12	15	5	32
Number of single men	18	15	5	38
Number of Children in Family		*Frequency*		
0	24	12	0	36
1	30	12	6	48
2	16	16	9	41
3	5	6	4	15
4	3	1	3	7
5				
6			1	1
Total	78	47	23	148

thus constitutes a part of the economically comfortable element in society. Both with respect to average and median salary, the Reform rabbinate ranks first.

Marital Status and Size of Family

Tables VIII and IX summarize the rabbis' reports concerning their marital status and the number of children in their families. The Conservative group shows the largest proportion of unmarried individuals, probably to be accounted for by the fact that members in this wing are on the average five and a half years younger than the Reform rabbis and about two years younger than the Orthodox rabbis.

The averages for the number of children in the rabbis' families are: Reform, 1.14; Conservative, 1.40; Orthodox, 2.35; and for the entire group, 1.41. The Orthodox rabbi's family thus included on the average about one child more than the Conservative or Reform rabbi's family.

CHAPTER IV

THE AUDIENCE OF THE RABBIS

THIS CHAPTER discusses the size, geographic distribution, place of birth, and economic status of the membership of Jewish congregations, as well as the quality of Jewish-Gentile relations obtaining in the places where the synagogues are located. Again, as in Chapter III, the important consideration will be differences among the three wings in regard to these characteristics. Features of the group as a whole will also be noted.

NUMERICAL STRENGTH OF THE SYNAGOGUE

Some attempt at an estimate of synagogue membership and the number of congregations of that year is included in the *American Jewish Year Book* for 1937. The membership is placed between 300,000 and 350,000. Inasmuch as the members are heads of families, the Year Book gives the estimated number of those who are associated with the synagogue as between 1,000,000 and 1,500,-000.[1] Figures collected by H. S. Linfield concerning religious bodies in connection with the United States Census place the number of Jews in the United States in 1937 at 4,831,180 and the number of congregations at about 3,700.[2]

The 1937 Year Book describes the strength of the Conservative and Reform wings in terms of number of synagogues and size of affiliated membership. For the Reform group a total of 290 synagogues is reported, all affiliated with the Union of American Hebrew Congregations, having a total membership of about 50,000. The Conservative group claims a total of 250 synagogues affiliated with the United Synagogue of America, and 250 non-affiliated, with a total membership of 75,000. No separate figures are given in the Year Book for the Orthodox congregational mem-

[1] Maurice J. Karpf, "Jewish Community Organizations in the United States," *American Jewish Year Book*, 1937–1938, p. 47.
[2] H. S. Linfield, *American Jewish Year Book*, 1940, p. 181.

bership. Nevertheless it seems certain that the numerical strength of Orthodoxy, measured by number of synagogues and size of associated membership, far exceeds the joint strength of both the Reform and the Conservative wings. After deducting the total number of Reform and Conservative synagogues, 790 in all, from Dr. Linfield's figure of about 3,700 synagogues in the United States, the number of Orthodox synagogues would appear to be about 2,900. Again deducting membership figures for the first two wings from the 300,000 to 350,000 total membership given above, the result is 175,000 to 225,000 heads of families associated with Orthodox congregations.

It will be realized from data already discussed that only a small proportion of the general Orthodox congregations are served by rabbis who have received their training in America. Only these Orthodox rabbis and their congregations come within the sphere of the opinions reported in this document.

GEOGRAPHIC DISTRIBUTION OF CONGREGATIONS AND MEMBERSHIP

A comparison of the geographic distribution of the congregations and congregational membership with that of American Jewry would throw light on the relative influence of the synagogue and the rabbi. Such comparison can be only partial. Available data make it possible to form a fairly accurate picture of the geographic distribution of both congregations and congregational membership of the Conservative and Reform wings and of the total population of Jews in the United States. This information is summarized in Table X. The office records of the United Synagogue provided data for those Conservative congregations which are affiliated with that body, and the 1937 report of the Union of American Hebrew Congregations gives complete figures for the Reform wing. For the Orthodox wing the data were obtained from a list of the Union of Orthodox Jewish Congregations. No information is available concerning the numerical strength of these congregations; no generalizations are possible on the basis of such limited data.[3]

[3] Dr. Linfield's figures on the distribution of Jews in the United States by states in 1937 are given in the *American Jewish Year Book* for 1940.

Table X reveals the extent of concentration of the Jewish population in the Northeastern States. Roughly, the distribution of

TABLE X

PERCENTAGE DISTRIBUTION OF JEWISH CONGREGATIONS, CONGREGATIONAL MEMBERSHIP AND TOTAL JEWISH POPULATION IN THE UNITED STATES BY GEOGRAPHIC LOCATION

| | CONGREGATIONS | | | MEMBERSHIP | | ALL JEWS IN THE UNITED STATES |
	Reform	Conserva-tive	Orthodox	Reform	Conserva-tive	
Number....	267[a]	249[b]	108[c]	54,270[a]	48,825[b]	4,831,180[d]
Location			*Percentage*			
The North						
North East	26.8	71.1	75.9	39.2	70.4	71.0
East North Central..	21.6	12.9	9.5	25.4	16.2	15.6
West North Central..	7.3	5.6	.9	5.8	5.1	3.7
Total North ..	55.7	89.6	86.3	70.4	91.7	90.3
The South						
South Atlantic..	13.9	5.2	4.6	5.7	2.1	2.0
East South Atlantic..	11.5	.4	1.8	6.9	.5	1.4
West South Central..	11.9	1.6	5.5	9.4	1.5	1.8
Total South ...	37.3	7.2	11.9	22.0	4.1	5.2
The West						
Mountain	2.1	0.8	0.9	1.2	0.9	.7
Pacific ..	4.9	2.4	0.9	6.4	3.3	3.8
Total West ...	7.0	3.2	1.8	7.6	4.2	4.5
Total United States ...	100.0	100.0	100.0	100.0	100.0	100.0

[a] From *Year Book of the Union of American Hebrew Congregations,* 1937, p. 12.
[b] From 1938 records of the United Synagogues of America.
[c] From a list of the Union of Orthodox Jewish Congregations. No membership data available.
[d] From *American Jewish Year Book,* 1940, p. 181.

the Conservative congregational membership parallels that of the whole Jewish population. In the North East and East North Central States the percentage ratio of members of Conservative congregations to the total membership in the Conservative wing is identical with the percentage ratio of Jews in these regions to the total Jewish population. In other regions the percentage of Conservative synagogue membership varies but slightly from the total percentage. No figures are available which permit an accurate comparison of the geographic distribution of the membership of Orthodox congregations with that of United States Jewry. Nevertheless, the fact that 75.9 per cent of the known Orthodox congregations are located in the North East region, as revealed in Table X, indicates a probable concentration of Orthodox Jewry in that area.

In the case of Reform Jewry, however, the parallel between Jewish population and congregational membership is not maintained. The North East, where more than two thirds of the Jews in the United States reside, accounts for only a little over one third of Reform's congregational membership. The percentage of Reform Jewry in all other regions is, on the other hand, in excess of the percentage of Jewish population in these regions.

With respect to the comparative influence of the various wings of the rabbinate, the data above point to the conclusion that Conservative and Orthodox rabbis are in a better position to make themselves heard in the centers of Jewish population than Reform rabbis; but that, on the other hand, the wider distribution of Reform rabbis over the country probably adds to their importance as a factor in shaping non-Jewish opinion.

PLACE OF BIRTH OF JEWISH CONGREGATION MEMBERS AND THEIR PARENTS

The rabbis were asked to indicate whether the main body of the membership in their congregation are foreign born, American born of foreign parentage, or American born of American parentage.[4] Table XI summarizes the responses. For the total group of congregations, 80 per cent are reported as having the dominant

[4] See Section IV of questionnaire: "The bulk of the membership of my congregation are . . ."

element native born of either foreign or American parentage. Of course there is no way of judging how accurate the reports of the rabbis are. The recency of Jewish mass migration to America which commenced during the latter part of the nineteenth century accounts for the paucity of congregations in which the dominant element consists of second-generation Americans.

TABLE XI

PERCENTAGE AND FREQUENCY DISTRIBUTION OF CLASSIFICATION OF 200 CONGREGATIONS BY RABBIS' ESTIMATES OF NATIVITY OF LARGEST PROPORTION OF MEMBERS AND THEIR PARENTS

	RABBIS' ESTIMATES OF NATIVITY OF CONGREGATIONS							
	Reform		*Conservative*		*Orthodox*		*Total*	
Place of Birth	*No.*	*%*	*No.*	*%*	*No.*	*%*	*No.*	*%*
Foreign born	5	5.1	23	32.4	11	36.7	39	19.5
American born of foreign parents ..	66	66.6	47	66.2	19	63.3	132	66.0
American born of American parents	28	28.3	1	1.4			29	14.5
Total	99	100.0	71	100.0	30	100.0	200	100.0

The reports of the rabbis indicate a number of interesting differences among the various wings. In the Reform wing only a very small number of rabbis—one out of twenty—reported that the dominant element in their congregations is foreign born. For the Conservative group the proportion is almost a third, while in the Orthodox wing it is over a third. On the other hand, reports that the dominant element is American born of American parents come from a little more than one quarter of the Reform rabbis. There are no such reports in the Orthodox group and only one in the Conservative. However, in the category "American born of foreign parents," the three wings are almost identical, about two thirds of the rabbis in each giving this classification for the dominant element of their congregations. On the basis of the reports of the rabbis it appears that Reform congregational membership includes relatively the largest proportion of Jews of American antecedents. These reports are, in most cases, no more than mere guesses. They are corroborated, however, by the general impression of observers of the different wings of Jewry.

If the degree of removal from Europe be taken as an index of Americanization, Reform Jewry is considerably more Americanized than either Orthodox or Conservative Jewry. The Reform service, the rabbis, and their ideology seem to have been more successful in the past in reaching Jews who have strong roots in America than have the Conservative and Orthodox wings; by the same token the Reform rabbis have been less successful in attracting the immigrant Jewish masses. It may also be that membership in the Reform congregation is a badge of distinction usually chosen by the wealthier and more completely Americanized Jews. The plausibility of this view is greatly reinforced by an analysis of the distribution of membership of the various types of congregations by income and occupation, which is presented in the next section.

ECONOMIC STATUS OF SYNAGOGUE JEWRY

In attempting to obtain a picture of the economic status of synagogue Jewry, the rabbis were requested to assign rankings in accordance with order of representation in the congregation of various income and occupational groups.[5] These data appear in Table XII.

Admittedly the estimates assigned by rabbis to various income groups are based on their impressions and not on accurate information. Moreover, the tabular data give no direct information concerning the composition of synagogue Jewry as a whole. Nothing is known of the size of membership of the different congregations nor of the proportion of a particular income group to the total membership. Nevertheless, some information concerning the economic status of synagogue Jewry can be deduced from the data. The overwhelming majority of Jewish congregational membership seems to consist of people with incomes adequate for a decent livelihood—$2,000 to $4,999 per year, and of the moderately well-to-do—$5,000 to $10,000 per year. The number of congregations assigned incomes below $2,000 in the congregational membership is small indeed.[6]

[5] See Section IV of questionnaire: "Rank the income groups in your congregation . . . etc." "Rank the occupational groups in your congregation . . . etc."
[6] See first ranking for all congregations for income groups of less than $2,000 per annum.

On the basis of the rabbis' reports, the enjoyment of a favorable economic status is more common in the Reform constituency than in either the Conservative or the Orthodox. In the Reform wing the $5,000 to $10,000 income group[7] is reported to be almost as

TABLE XII

FREQUENCY DISTRIBUTION OF CONGREGATIONS BY RABBIS' RANKINGS ASSIGNED TO FOUR INCOME (PER ANNUM) GROUPS IN MEMBERSHIP

	Reform	Conservative	Orthodox	Total
Total group	108	77	33	218
Number not responding	17	8	6	31
Rank of Four Income Groups	*Frequency*			
Less than $2,000				
1st ranking	3	8	6	17
2nd ranking	9	15	12	36
3rd ranking	14	15	2	31
4th ranking	31	13	2	46
No response	34	18	5	57
Total	91	69	27	187
$2,000–$5,000				
1st ranking	49	49	16	114
2nd ranking	25	12	7	44
3rd ranking	13	5	3	21
4th ranking	0	0	0	0
No response	4	3	1	8
Total	91	69	27	187
$5,000–$10,000				
1st ranking	35	9	4	48
2nd ranking	42	34	5	81
3rd ranking	11	21	16	48
4th ranking	0	0	0	0
No response	3	5	2	10
Total	91	69	27	187
Above $10,000				
1st ranking	4	3	2	9
2nd ranking	10	4	2	16
3rd ranking	42	20	4	66
4th ranking	18	14	11	43
No response	17	28	8	53
Total	91	69	27	187

[7] $5,000 to $10,000 income group refers to congregations composed mainly of this income group. This terminology will be used in referring to all statistics found in Table XII.

numerous as is the $2,000 to $5,000 group, while the highest income group, that above $10,000, is thought to be more numerous
than the lowest one, i.e., below $2,000.

In the Conservative and Orthodox wings, however, the $2,000
to $5,000 group is evidently more numerous than the $5,000 to
$10,000 group. While the two classes of income under $2,000 and
above $10,000 respectively are presumably small in these two
wings, the former seems to be somewhat more numerous than the
latter.

It should be noted, however, that the Orthodox congregations
which come within the purview of the present study probably
have a membership which is better established than the average
Orthodox congregation. Orthodox synagogue Jewry as a whole
is probably in poorer circumstances than is indicated by the figures
of Table XII. The fact remains, however, that the Conservative
rabbis, the locally trained Orthodox rabbis, and especially the
Reform rabbis speak to the comfortably off, moderately rich, and
fairly rich, and to but few poor Jews. The most likely inference
is that people whose income barely reaches or even falls below the
sufficiency level[8] are not affiliated with congregations in large numbers. This conclusion will be further borne out by an analysis
of the congregational membership by occupational groups.

Table XIII summarizes the data submitted by rabbis concerning
the prominence of various occupational groups in their congregational membership. Seven categories were used in the questionnaire, to correspond to the seven income groups listed: industrial, clerical, professional, managerial, proprietary, commercial,
and agricultural groups. The same difficulties that obtain with
respect to income distribution prevent an accurate picture from
being drawn of the occupational distribution of American
Jewry, because of the fact that not all the rabbis had the same
conception of some of the occupational categories listed.

Nevertheless, as in the case of income distribution, some little
information can be gathered from the tabular data. The proprietary group apparently comes first. One hundred eleven, or
about 59 per cent, of the rabbis reporting on the occupational distribution of the congregational membership, assign this group first

---

[8] A level which merely provides for the basic necessities of life.

TABLE XIII. FREQUENCY DISTRIBUTION OF CONGREGATIONS BY RABBIS' RANKINGS
ASSIGNED TO SEVEN OCCUPATIONAL GROUPS IN MEMBERSHIP

	Reform	*Conservative*	*Orthodox*	*Total*
Total group	108	77	33	218
Number not responding	15	9	5	29
Rank of Seven Occupational Groups	*Frequency*			
Industrial				
1st ranking	0	2	2	4
2nd ranking	0	4	0	4
3rd ranking	2	0	2	4
4th ranking	2	2	3	7
5th ranking	4	9	3	16
6th ranking	17	14	6	37
7th ranking	2	0	1	3
No response	66	37	11	114
Total	93	68	28	189
Clerical				
1st ranking	2	1	0	3
2nd ranking	9	5	1	15
3rd ranking	9	7	6	22
4th ranking	14	10	2	26
5th ranking	21	11	4	36
6th ranking	1	5	2	8
7th ranking	0	0	0	0
No response	37	29	13	79
Total	93	68	28	189
Professional				
1st ranking	6	0	0	6
2nd ranking	26	15	4	45
3rd ranking	22	28	7	57
4th ranking	14	9	7	30
5th ranking	12	4	5	21
6th ranking	0	1	0	1
7th ranking	0	0	0	0
No response	13	11	5	29
Total	93	68	28	189
Managerial				
1st ranking	4	0	0	4
2nd ranking	16	15	5	36
3rd ranking	31	11	4	46
4th ranking	14	9	3	26
5th ranking	4	4	1	9
6th ranking	3	0	3	6
7th ranking	0	0	0	0
No response	21	29	12	62
Total	93	68	28	189

TABLE XIII (*Continued*). FREQUENCY DISTRIBUTION OF CONGREGATIONS BY RABBIS' RANKINGS ASSIGNED TO SEVEN OCCUPATIONAL GROUPS IN MEMBERSHIP

Rank of Seven Occupational Groups	Reform	Conservative	Orthodox	Total
		Frequency		
Proprietary				
1st ranking	60	39	12	111
2nd ranking	10	11	8	29
3rd ranking	8	4	0	12
4th ranking	6	2	3	11
5th ranking	3	0	1	4
6th ranking	0	1	0	1
7th ranking	0	0	0	0
No response	6	11	4	21
Total	93	68	28	189
Commercial				
1st ranking	21	26	14	61
2nd ranking	27	16	8	51
3rd ranking	10	7	1	18
4th ranking	9	4	0	13
5th ranking	3	2	0	5
6th ranking	0	2	1	3
7th ranking	0	0	1	1
No response	23	11	3	37
Total	93	68	28	189
Agricultural				
1st ranking	0	0	0	0
2nd ranking	1	0	0	1
3rd ranking	1	1	0	2
4th ranking	1	0	0	1
5th ranking	1	1	1	3
6th ranking	4	0	1	5
7th ranking	11	12	2	25
No response	74	54	24	152
Total	93	68	28	189

place, and an additional 29, or slightly over 15 per cent, give it second place. Next in order is the commercial group, which is followed by the professional group. Only six congregations rank this last-mentioned group first, but many rabbis assign it second or third ranking. In 108 cases the professional group is reported by the rabbis as occupying first, second, or third place numerically, and in only 30 cases is this group not represented at all, or slightly represented. The managerial group trails behind the professional group, but is decidedly higher in order than the group of clerical employees.

It is obvious that people who are engaged in agriculture are practically unrepresented in the congregational membership. The representation of industrial workers is almost as negligible. Of the 189 rabbis reporting on the occupational status of their congregational membership, 114, or 60 per cent, imply that the representation of industrial workers is so small as not to deserve any ranking, even on a seven-point scale. These data seem to warrant the conclusion that the preponderance of membership of Jewish congregations belongs to the proprietary, commercial, and professional groups. The remainder is made up chiefly of managerial and clerical employees; farmers and industrial workers are practically absent.

The figures for occupational distribution reinforce the conclusion that synagogue Jewry is not economically representative of the American population. The following figures are given by Sogge in regard to the occupational distribution of the gainfully employed population in the United States in 1930.[9]

Occupational Group	Per Cent
Industrial wage-earners	37.9
Farm laborers	9.0
Farmers	12.4
Servants	4.1
Lower salaried	14.6
Professionals	7.9
Proprietors and officials	8.7
Unclassified	5.4

The discrepancy between the total of 21.4 per cent of farmers and farm laborers in the wage-earning population of the United States and the almost total absence of such workers in synagogue membership is adequately accounted for by the smaller number of Jews engaged in agricultural occupations. In the 1927 study of the Jewish population Dr. Linfield places the number of Jews who live in rural areas at 109,600, or 2 per cent of the total Jewish

[9] From T. M. Sogge, "Industrial Classes in the United States," *Journal of American Statistical Association*, XXXVIII, June, 1933, p. 199. Later figures that are comparable to the data of the present study are not available.

population, and not all these are engaged in agricultural pursuits.

The economic peculiarities of American Jews do not, however, account, except in a minor degree, for the exceedingly small representation of workers and the preponderance of those whose income is derived from ownership of property, from commercial pursuits, or from professional practice. No doubt the commercial, proprietary, managerial, and professional classes are more numerous among Jews, and industrial workers less numerous than they are in the American population as a whole. Nevertheless, the largest single occupational group among Jews, as among non-Jews, is that of industrial workers. In 1934 B. Charney Vladeck estimated the number of Jews engaged in the needle trades and a few minor industries as 350,000.[10] Assuming that the ratio of gainfully employed persons among Jews is the same as that in the general population—nearly 40 per cent—and placing the Jewish population in America at about 4,800,000, there are in America about 1,920,000 Jews engaged in gainful occupations. Vladeck's figures thus indicate that industrial workers probably constitute about 18 per cent of gainfully employed Jews. Yet Vladeck's figures are not sufficiently inclusive. Esther Kinzler's study of the occupational distribution of Jews in New York City points out that of the gainfully employed (male Jews) about 30 per cent are industrial workers, about 40 per cent correspond to the mercantile, proprietary, and managerial groups, 12 per cent are clerical workers, and about 8 per cent are professional and semi-professional.[11] Probably the proportion of workers is higher among New York Jews than for Jews in the country at large. Hence the percentage of industrial workers among American Jews engaged in gainful occupations appears to be between 18 and 30.

It is probably true that the rabbis tend to color their reports by undue emphasis on the members of good economic status, since the latter are probably influential in synagogue affairs. However, it is clear that Jewish industrial workers in the United States are many times as numerous, and the professional, managerial, and

---

10 B. Charney Vladeck, "The Effect of the New Deal on Jewish Labor Proceedings," *National Conference of Jewish Social Service*, 1934, p. 15.

11 Esther Kinzler, *Some Aspects of Occupational Declaration of Jews in New York City*. Thesis, Graduate School for Jewish Social Work, 1935.

proprietary classes are, on the other hand, decidedly less numerous than their indicated proportions in the synagogue membership. The conclusion that the synagogue membership is selective, that it fails to attract workers and appeals primarily to the economic middle class and upper classes, seems to be decidedly justified.

RELATIONS BETWEEN JEWS AND GENTILES

Table XIV summarizes the rabbis' appraisals of the relations between Jews and Gentiles in their communities and their reports concerning the presence or absence of a community chest in which Jews and non-Jews participate.

TABLE XIV

CLASSIFICATION OF COMMUNITIES ACCORDING TO THE REPORTED RELATIONS BETWEEN JEWS AND GENTILES AND THE PRESENCE OR ABSENCE OF COMMUNITY CHESTS

	Reform	*Conservative*	*Orthodox*	*Total*
Total group	108	77	33	218
Number not responding*	12	6	5	23

Quality of Jewish-Gentile Relations	*Classification by Community Chest*							
	Yes	*No*	*Yes*	*No*	*Yes*	*No*	*Yes*	*No*
Good	33	33	17	26	5	9	55	68
Indifferent	2	24	10	18	4	10	16	52
Bad		4						4
Total	35	61	27	44	9	19	71	124

* Not responding either on quality of relations or on community chest, or on both.

In the light of the returns, it would appear that in most of the communities reported in the study rabbis consider that the relations between Jews and non-Jews are good. Of a total of 218 responses, 23 failed to describe the quality of the relations between Jews and Gentiles in their communities. Of the 195 remaining, 123, or 63 per cent, stated that relations are good; 68, or 35 per cent, that relations are indifferent; 4, or 2 per cent, that relations are bad.

Of the total number responding on this item, a greater proportion of Reform rabbis than either Conservative or Orthodox report good relations. The percentage of rabbis indicating good relations are: in the Reform group, 69 per cent; in the Conservative group, 61 per cent; in the Orthodox group, 50 per cent. On the other hand, the few cases of bad relations are all reported by Reform rabbis.

Of the 218 rabbis who replied to the questionnaire, 71 reported the existence of community chests in their communities. The percentage of reported community chests is considerably greater in communities with reported good relations than in communities that reported indifferent relations. No community chests are reported from the communities where relations are bad. By application of a statistical test[12] it was found that the reported Jewish-Gentile relations were significantly related to the presence or absence of community chests.

Working on a community chest may influence a rabbi's estimate of the situation. The data, at any rate, seem to warrant the conclusion that either the community chest is a factor in promoting good relations, or that the existence of good relations helps to promote the establishment of a community chest, or both.

---

[12] A Chi-square test was applied to the totals of the data of Table XIV. Assuming no relationship between presence or absence of community chest and relations with Gentiles, Chi-square equaled 9.93. Since Chi-square for appropriate degrees of freedom with a one per cent probability equaled 6.635, the hypothesis is definitely rejected.

PART III

INTRODUCTORY NOTE

THE QUESTIONNAIRE *which served as the instrument of investigation in this study covers a variety of subjects. The propositions and multiple-choice statements presented deal with theology, philosophy of Jewish life, the social function of religion, objectives and methods of social reconstruction, peace and internationalism, civil liberties, education, race, and sex. In the following pages a chapter or a section of a chapter will be devoted to an analysis of the beliefs of rabbis in each of these areas, with a view to ascertaining their position on the issues listed.*

PARTICULAR ISSUES. *These will be presented for the group as a whole as well as for the separate wings—Reform, Conservative, and Orthodox. The peculiar beliefs of each wing will be noted as well as the beliefs in which all three show the greatest agreement.*

GENERAL ISSUES. *The reactions of the rabbis to some of the particular issues presented in the questionnaire are probable indications of their position with regard to broader issues not stated, but implied in the formulation of the particular issues. Thus, the attitude of a rabbi with respect to what is changing and what is unchanging in relation to the nature of God, the nature of the Bible, the attitude of Judaism toward scientific doctrines which appear to contradict the Bible, immortality, etc., is a probable indication either that he leans toward a naturalistic position with regard to religion, or that he is inclined toward a supernaturalistic philosophy. Similarly, the responses to a number of particular propositions with respect to Jewish life are helpful in indicating whether or not a rabbi identifies himself with the Jewish nationalistic point of view. In other areas, too, a number of propositions which have a common idea can be found.*

PATTERN OF BELIEFS. *An attempt will be made to discover what beliefs accompany one another and to what degree they do so. The patterns of belief will be studied for the group as a whole. Differences which obtain between the wings will be noted only in a few important instances.*

*The references "Reform rabbis," "Conservative rabbis," and "Ortho-
dox rabbis" designate rabbis who serve in Reform, Conservative, and
Orthodox congregations respectively. No attempt has been made to
discover whether the rabbis identify themselves personally with the
views of the particular wings of Judaism with which they are associated.*

*In presenting the positions of the rabbis on particular issues, repeti-
tion of figures and percentages of those who hold these positions will
be avoided, so far as possible, by use of the following terminology:*

(1) Negligible minority designates a minority of 1 to 9 per cent.
    Minority   designates a minority of 10 to 19 per cent.
    Sizable minority   designates a minority of 20+ per cent.

(2) Dominant group   designates the view of the largest group when that group
                                       falls short of a majority.

(3) Majority   designates a majority of 50 to 64 per cent.
    Large majority   designates a majority of 65 to 79 per cent.
    Preponderant
    Predominant
    Predominating   } designates a majority of 80 to 89 per cent.
       majority
    Virtual agreement   designates a majority of 90 to 99 per cent.
    Unanimity   designates 100 per cent.

*The following procedure was employed in the analysis of the atti-
tudes of rabbis toward general issues: The questionnaire was examined
for groups of propositions the reactions to which give probable indication of how the rabbis stand with respect to certain broad and significant issues. Charts were then drawn up to indicate what positions
with respect to general issues the responses to specific issues imply.
Finally, the total responses to all propositions in a particular group
were analyzed in terms of percentages of responses indicating the two
diametrically opposed positions with respect to the broad issue. Com-
putations were made for each wing as well as for the entire group.*

*It is by no means suggested that the charts constitute certain indica-
tions of how rabbis stand on general issues such as naturalism, Jewish
nationalism, collectivism, etc. The connotation of these terms implied
in the chart appears to be justified on the basis of their use in relevant
literature and ordinary discourse. At any rate, the statement that a
certain percentage of the responses are "naturalistic," or "Jewishly
nationalistic," etc., whenever it occurs in the text has a meaning only
in so far as the responses to the items included in the respective charts
are indicative of these general attitudes.*

*Patterns of beliefs were investigated through the method of cross-
tabulation. Thus the rabbis who affirm, deny, or question the proposi-*

tion that "Judaism must remain forever hostile to science which tends to destroy faith in the literal truth of the teachings of the Bible." (1–I)* were classified with respect to their positions on the proposition, "Belief in the actual occurrences of miracles recorded in the Bible is indispensable to Judaism" (2–I). By means of such intertabulation it is possible to discover to what extent the belief that Judaism must be hostile to science goes hand in hand with the belief in the actual occurrence of miracles as recorded in the Bible, and vice versa.

In studying the patterns of beliefs, selection was of course necessary. The questionnaire raises 130 issues. Mathematically, a great many combinations of beliefs are available for study, but not all the possible combinations are equally meaningful. Thus the rabbis' attitudes on the question of socialization of industry are meaningfully related to their positions on the issues of a farmer-labor party; whereas their beliefs with regard to Sabbath observance and the sit-down strike do not appear to be so related. A list of 250 important combinations of items was drawn up, and of these 150 were analyzed.

In most cases Section I of the succeeding chapters is devoted to the analysis of rabbis' positions on the specific issues raised in the questionnaire as well as to underlying general issues, while Section II is concerned with the analysis of patterns of thinking on the basis of connections found in responses to pairs of related propositions.

The analysis of positions on individual issues and of patterns of thought which constitute the content of Chapters V–XII is followed by a chapter devoted to an examination of the degree of consistency which is revealed in the thinking of the rabbis. Thus, Chapter XIII follows to a large extent the pattern of responses set forth in Section II of Chapters V–XII. In both divisions the degree of connectedness of pairs of responses for the group as a whole is indicated. However, Chapter XIII is more comprehensive than the earlier chapters in two respects. It presents composite measures made up of a number of pairs of responses on related propositions, thereby showing degrees of consistency for the entire group of rabbis on the general issues covered in the previous chapters. It also goes beyond the results of Section II of Chapters V–XII, by giving analogous findings for the three wings of the rabbinate separately as well as for the entire group. Chapter XIV attempts to discover the varying frequencies with which rabbis preach and teach the views they hold in the different areas of thought.

* Arabic and Roman numerals refer to items and sections in the questionnaire respectively.

CHAPTER V

THEOLOGICAL VIEWS OF THE RABBIS

SECTION I

THE PLACE OF THEOLOGY AND THE POSITION OF THE RABBIS

The Place of Theology[1]

In a study of the beliefs of Christian ministers, a chapter on their theological views is most appropriate, for in Christianity there is a definite and well-defined system of theology in which dogma and articles of faith occupy a position of primary importance. Therefore the discovery of the beliefs of these Christian ministers is of real significance.

In a study of the beliefs of rabbis and Jewish ministers, however, any chapter on theology ought to be offered with reservation and apology. The student who is acquainted with Jewish religious tradition knows that in Judaism dogma *per se* is virtually non-existent.

Kohler, the distinguished authority on Jewish theology, observes that Judaism differs from Christianity on these three points:

First, in Christianity, articles of faith formulated by the founders and heads of the Church are conditions of salvation. Judaism does not know salvation by faith in the sense of Paul, the real founder of the Church.

Second, Christian theology rests on a formula of confession, the Symbolum of the Apostolic Church, which alone makes one a Christian. Judaism, however, has no such formula of confession which renders a Jew a Jew.

[1] This description of the place of dogma in Jewish theology is based upon a number of authoritative treatises on Judaism, including: Kohler, Kaufmann: *Jewish Theology;* Schechter, Solomon: *Some Aspects of Rabbinic Theology;* Finkelstein, Louis: *Role of Dogma in Judaism;* Reprint from *The Thomist,* Jan. 1943, *The Maritain Volume;* Husik, Isaac: *A History of Medieval Jewish Philosophy;* Ginzberg, Louis: *Students, Scholars and Saints*—The Religion of the Pharisees; Finkelstein, Ross, Brown: *The Religions of Democracy.*

Third, creed is a *sine qua non* of the Christian Church. To disavow is to cut oneself loose from membership in the Church. Judaism is quite different. The Jew is born into the faith, and even after renunciation he is considered an apostate Jew.

Theology never had for the Jews that focal interest which it had in Christianity. Though Catholicism emphasized the essentiality of works to salvation, it also insisted on the supreme importance of correct faith. One's salvation depended not only on partaking of the sacraments of the Church, but also on the affirmation of the official dogmas of the Church. One's eternal destiny was conceived to depend not only on punctiliousness of observance, but also on whether one affirmed or negated this or that verbal proposition. Protestantism went even further, by pronouncing the doctrine of salvation by faith only.

In contrast, Judaism never produced an authoritative set of propositions, acceptance of which was universally deemed essential to membership in the congregation of Israel or to salvation. It is true that a number of medieval Jewish philosophers formulated creeds and that Maimonides' formulation came to be embodied in the prayer book. But these creeds never achieved the nature of dogma binding on all Jews. When Maimonides formulated his thirteen articles of faith, they were immediately challenged.

It was not so much the correctness of the propositions that was in question as their mandatory nature. Thus there was objection to making the belief in the incorporeality of God a condition for membership in the congregation of Israel, although those who voiced the objection probably shared Maimonides' belief in the incorporeality of God. Albo reduced the thirteen articles of faith of Maimonides to three; other authorities to five or six or more. Isaac Abravanel and David ben Zimra utterly disapproved any attempt to formulate articles of faith.

Apparently identifying religion with creed, Mendelsohn went so far as to assert that Judaism is not a revealed religion, but rather a revealed code. The Hebrew word *emunah*, which comes closest to being synonymous with faith, denotes reliance upon and adherence to God, rather than a formal acceptance of creed. The Jews believe in general ideas of theology, rather than in particular ones. The reduction of the thirteen articles of faith to three meant that the several articles that pertained to the understanding of the Godhood were combined in one. Similarly, several articles pertaining to revelation were reduced to one, as was done in the case of those that dealt with reward and punishment. A rigid dogmatic creed was unacceptable to the Jewish people. Moreover, the general theological ideas which Jews believe in are more implied in the Jewish way of life than statable in a series of verbal propositions.

It is natural to ask what the Jews believed. Prefatory to an answer, it should be pointed out that although there is no biblical or rabbinic precept in Judaism which teaches "thou shalt believe," there are, nevertheless, leading principles of faith. A knowledge of the religious thought of the Jew is to be derived from the spirit of his literature as a whole rather than from formal doctrines alone. Professor Louis Ginzberg, the foremost Hebrew scholar of our time, in his essay, "The Religion of the Pharisee" (see note 1), indicates that true understanding of the religion of the Jews at the time of the rise of Christianity can be gained from those sources "which express the religious consciousness of the bulk of the nation or Catholic Israel." Again he says: "The most characteristic feature of the rabbinic system of theology is its lack of system. With God as a reality, revelation as a fact, the Torah as a rule of life, and the hope of redemption as a most vivid expectation, one was free to draw his own conclusions from these axioms and postulates in regard to what he believed."

Schechter in *Some Aspects of Rabbinic Theology* makes an interesting observation. He tells us that a great English writer has remarked "that the true health of a man is to have a soul without being aware of it; to be disposed of by impulses which he does not criticise." Dr. Schechter goes on to say: "In a similar way the old rabbis seem to have thought that the true health of a religion is to have a theology without being aware of it; and thus they hardly ever made—nor could they make—any attempt towards working their theology into a formal system, or giving us a full exposition of it."

Dr. Finkelstein offers the view that the religious concepts of Judaism are expressed in "propositions in action" rather than in verbal propositions. Judaism demands of its adherents a devotion to the way of life given in a system of commandments and laws. Although adherence to the commandments is mandatory, their interpretation in verbal propositions affords much scope for variety of views. This makes for fluidity of religious concepts.

Jews do not distinguish between Judaism as a set of beliefs and Judaism as a total pattern of living.

What the Jews believe is implied in their practice of the Torah rather than explicitly stated. The beliefs of Judaism have constituted the reason and emotional motivation of Judaism as a way of life. They have served this purpose and yet remained for the most part inarticulate. Always the emphasis has been on the superstructural deed and not on the foundational creed.

This background provides sufficient orientation for a review of the opinions and beliefs of the rabbis in theological matters. This may help to account for the disparity of beliefs not only among the three wings of Judaism, but even within the several groups of the rabbinate which subsequent analysis of the views of the rabbis will reveal. The great divergence of opinion among the rabbis, however, may actually indicate nothing significant in the matter of religious observance and the way of life of one rabbi as compared with another.

The views of the rabbis concerning religion, God, prayer, the nature of the Bible, sin and salvation, immortality, the adequacy of the Torah, naturalism and supernaturalism, are presented because religious readers are likely to be interested in the views of rabbis on these matters.

The reader must bear in mind that the succeeding sections of the present chapter do not aim to present a realistic picture of significant differences among the several groups of the American rabbinate, but deal rather with religious theory, an area in which wide differences of views are legitimate from the Jewish point of view.

The Position of the Rabbis

The views of the rabbis will be considered under nine headings: (1) nature of religion—is it changing or unchanging? (2) concept of God; (3) authorship and nature of the Bible; (4) function of prayer; (5) sin and salvation; (6) immortality; (7) adequacy of the

Torah as a guide to the moral perplexities of today; (8) Sabbath observance; (9) naturalism *vs.* supernaturalism.

This last-named topic is a composite of all the previous ones except (7) and (8). It is based on the key provided in Chart I of the Appendix (p. 214), which indicates for most of the items in this chapter the significance of alternative responses in terms of the general issue of naturalism *vs.* supernaturalism. Thus the object finally is to determine the positions of the several wings as well as of the entire group on this general issue. These topics relate mainly to the metaphysical and personal aspects of religion. In Chapters VI and VII the place of religion in the scheme of Jewish life and the social function of religion will be considered.

Nature of Religion—Is It Changing or Unchanging?

Is religion a phase of human evolution which is bound to disappear with time? If not, are religious standards of conduct subject to change and reconstruction, or are they unchanging?

*Rabbis are unanimous in rejecting the view that "as a result of man's growing intelligence and changes in his aspirations and desires religion will disappear." By implication they are unanimous in agreeing that religion as an institution is abiding. There is diversity of opinion on exactly what in religion is abiding. About one out of every six rabbis in the group as a whole believes that *religious standards are not subject to change and reconstruction though their application may be.* The preponderant majority, however, agree that "even fundamental religious standards of conduct must be continually reconstructed." To four out of every five rabbis the primary element in religion is apparently the very process of evolution, change, and reconstruction of the content of religion.

There is decided difference of opinion on the issue of what is changing and what is unchanging in religion between the Reform and Conservative wings, on the one hand, and the Orthodox wing

---

* In all cases, the questionnaire item pertinent to any particular discussion in Chapters V–XII is referred to in parentheses immediately following the statement, an Arabic numeral indicating the item, and a Roman numeral the section of the questionnaire in which it occurs. Where the item is paraphrased in the discussion so that its meaning is somewhat changed, italics are used. Where the same wording is given as appears in the questionnaire, quotation marks are introduced.

on the other. In the former two groups there is virtual agreement, bordering on unanimity, that fundamental religious standards are subject to change—the naturalistic response—whereas about 77 per cent of the Orthodox rabbis believe that religious standards of conduct are unchanging (6–II).

Concept of God

The rabbis were asked to choose the concept which to them best expressed the nature of God. It should be noted that the choice of a single best expression does not rule out the possibility that a rabbi's concept of God is enriched by other characterizations. Presumably, many of the rabbis who state that God should primarily be conceived as the sum of forces which make for intelligence, goodness, and beauty still believe that God is also in some sense a Creator. Although the data do not thus permit of the formulation of a precise conclusion about the concept of God which the rabbis hold, the differences expressed in terms of "best expression" are worthy of note.

It would appear that the God-concept of the preponderant majority of the rabbis is free from anthropomorphism and the notion of first cause. Only two rabbis in the entire group of 218 define God as a first cause, and only one out of every seven, as literal creator of the universe—the two supernaturalistic responses. The remainder believe that the nature of God is best expressed as: (a) "the sum total of forces which make for greater intelligence, beauty, goodness; (b) the unitary creative impulse which expresses itself in organic evolution and human progress; (c) the symbol of all that we consider good and true." The first of these three views of God is by far the dominant one.

With respect to the God-idea, no appreciable difference can be seen between the Conservative and Reform wings. These two groups differ, however, from the Orthodox group, a majority of whom think of God primarily as a creator. In both the Conservative and the Reform wings this concept of God which best expresses the views of the rabbis is held by only about 8 per cent of the respondents.*

* See item 5, Section II, of questionnaire.

Authorship and Nature of the Bible

The fundamentalist, literalist, or traditional view of the Bible has but little support in the group under investigation, and that little is practically concentrated in the Orthodox wing. Stated another way, the Reform and Conservative wings are unanimous in accepting what may be termed the "modernist" view of the Bible, whereas the Orthodox wing is divided between the modernist and the traditionalist positions.

This section includes the rabbis' positions on the following propositions: (a) three alternatives as to the nature of the Bible, including the view that it is "literally the word of God"; (b) indispensability to Judaism of belief in the actual occurrence of miracles; (c) whether or not the Biblical story of creation is a myth; (d) whether or not Judaism must be hostile to any science which is in contradition to the Bible; (e) "there are instances of human conduct which according to the Bible had divine sanction and which should now be considered immoral"; (f) Moses is the author of the Pentateuch.

(a) The view that the Bible is "literally the word of God," which is the supernaturalistic response, finds no support whatever in the Conservative and Reform wings, but in the Orthodox wing it has more support than either of the other two concepts. The issue among the Reform and Conservative rabbis is not whether the Bible is literally the word of God, but rather whether it is "the word of God in the sense that it reflects the human striving after wisdom and goodness" or is merely "a record of the moral and religious evolution of the Jews." The former view, which is a compromise between the traditional beliefs and the modern empirical attitude, is held by only a little more than half as many rabbis as affirm the latter out-and-out empirical view. In the Orthodox wing the issue is mainly whether the Bible is the word of God in a literal sense or in the figurative sense of reflecting the human striving after wisdom and goodness (11–II). The division is about equal, with a slight advantage for the literalist view.

(b) With virtual unanimity the Conservative and Reform rabbis likewise reject the supernaturalistic view of *belief in the actual occurrence of miracles as indispensable to Judaism*. The Orthodox wing, however, is divided on this issue, with almost one half of the group insisting on the indispensability of belief in the actual occurrence of miracles, slightly less than one third rejecting this belief, and about one fifth questioning the indispensability of it. It should be noted that a rabbi who holds that belief in miracles is indispensable to Judaism in all likelihood personally believes in miracles. He is a teacher of Judaism and presumably accepts its essential doctrines (2–I).

(c) Concerning the proposition that "the Biblical story of creation is a myth," large majorities in the Conservative and Reform wings, taking the naturalistic stand, affirmed the proposition. It is likely, however, that a considerable number of those who deny or question the statement do not view the Biblical version of creation as true history. They may reject the view that the version is a myth, yet hold that it is of the nature of a fable, a legend, or an allegory. In the Orthodox wing, only one of the thirty rabbis answering the questionnaire looks upon the story of creation as a myth, a preponderant majority reject this view, and five question it. Thus, apparently, Orthodoxy is divided on the question of whether the Biblical story of creation is true history. There is no way of determining precisely how they are divided on this question, for, as observed above, not all who deny the mythical nature mean to affirm the literal truth of it. However, this is certain: 135 of the 209 rabbis who responded do not accept the Biblical story of creation as literal truth (7–I).

(d) Few rabbis believe that *Judaism must be hostile to any teaching which is in contradiction to the Bible.* Such support as this view enjoys is limited almost exclusively to Orthodoxy, in which wing one out of every four rabbis would continue to fight the battles of religion against certain scientific doctrines. This view is rejected outright by virtually all Reform and Conservative rabbis, again taking the naturalistic approach (1–I).

(e) It is of interest to note that nearly three out of four rabbis in the group as a whole grant that "there are instances of human conduct which according to the Bible had divine sanction and which should now be considered immoral." However, this item is unrelated to the general issue of naturalism *vs.* supernaturalism. About seven per cent of the Reform and Conservative rabbis reject this proposition. The Orthodox wing is about equally divided among those who grant, who deny, and who question the immorality of certain acts which according to the Bible had divine sanction (9–I).

(*f*) Also of interest, although not pertinent to the larger issue of naturalism *vs.* supernaturalism, is the fact that more than two thirds of the entire group reject the traditional view which ascribes authorship of the Pentateuch to Moses. In the Reform group only two of the 105 individuals who indicated opinions on the question expressed the belief that Moses is the author of the Pentateuch. In the Orthodox group, however, this view is held by almost four out of every five individuals. In the Conservative group the traditional view is supported by about one out of seven individuals (3–I).

The Function of Prayer

On the subject of prayer, the inquiry was concerned with two points: (*a*) What do rabbis consider to be the principal function of prayer? (*b*)What in their opinion constitutes the highest type of prayer? On each of these points the rabbis were asked to check one of several choices.

(*a*) Taken as a whole, the entire group's concept of what makes prayers in the main worth while is remarkably free from supernaturalistic leanings, as less than 6 per cent of the 209 who registered their opinion on this question find the principal function of prayer to be that of actually bringing about divine aid. The remainder consider prayers to be worth while chiefly because they (*a*) *give the suppliant the feeling of divine support,* (*b*) *afford psychological release,* (*c*) *promote Jewish unity,* or (*d*) *raise the level of moral life.* None of these concepts is in contradiction to a naturalistic world orientation. More largely represented than any other views are those which consider prayers worth while principally because they raise the moral level of human life, or give the suppliant the feeling of divine aid.

It is interesting to note that only in the Orthodox wing is there a sizable group which sees the principal function of prayer as literally the bringing of divine aid to the suppliant. On the other hand, strong support for the view that prayers are worth while principally because of their contribution to Jewish unity is found only in the Conservative wing (1–II).

(*b*) Turning now to the rabbis' concept of what constitutes the highest type of prayer, it is to be noted that only one individual identifies it with prayer for the welfare of one's own person or one's associates. The group is divided between those stressing the theo-centric concepts represented by "prayer for the fulfillment of God's purpose" and prayer for "communion with God," and those emphasizing the socio-centric view as against the theo-centric concept. Of the three wings, the Orthodox gives the largest proportionate support to the theo-centric concept, which is the supernaturalistic view, and the smallest to the socio-centric view. The reverse holds true of the Conservative wing, with the Reform rabbinate occupying a middle ground (2–II).

Sin and Salvation

The traditional concept of sin is that of *disregard for the precepts which are prescribed in the Shulḥan 'Aruk.* None of the Reform or Conservative rabbis believe that this traditional concept calls for the greatest emphasis in this day and age. Precisely this concept is chosen for emphasis by the largest group of the Orthodox wing, thus representing the supernaturalistic point of view.

In the group as a whole, support for the traditional concept is small. The concept of sin as an act which emanates from one's base impulses receives support from only twenty-eight rabbis. A large majority of the group as a whole believes that the concept of sin which needs greatest emphasis in our age is to be expressed in social terms, either as: (*a*) *harm to neighbors, friends, and business associates;* (*b*) *harm to society;* (*c*) *support of or acquiescence to accepted institutions which are socially harmful.* The Orthodox group shows a somewhat greater predilection for small-group morality—identification of sin with (*a*)—than either of the two other wings. The Conservative wing shows a greater tendency to the "more modern" ideology. A greater proportion of this branch of the rabbinate than of either of the two other branches identifies the concept of sin which calls for greatest present-day emphasis with (*c*) above.

With respect to the concept of salvation which calls for present-day emphasis, no great differences can be noted among the respective groups. With the exception of two Orthodox rabbis, the group is unanimous in rejecting the view of salvation as happiness in the world to come. The group as a whole, as well as the several wings, is divided between acceptance of the concept of salvation as (a) *achievement of an integrated personality,* and (b) *participation in efforts for social progress* (3, 4–II).

Immortality

Of the group under investigation about the same number accept as reject the doctrine that the *immortality of the individual soul is essential to Judaism,* with about one out of every four in doubt. Those who affirm the primary place of faith in individual immortality in the body of Judaism are reasonably certain to accept it personally. It is characteristic of the supernaturalistic view of the Orthodox rabbis that in this wing a majority accept personal immortality, none rejecting it, with the rest either uncertain or noncommittal (6–I).

Happiness in the hereafter does not enter as a sanction for the practice of Jewish observances in the view of the majority of the group. The numbers in the several wings who have this conception are six Reform, eight Conservative, and twenty Orthodox rabbis, a total of thirty-four in the entire group of 207 rabbis who affirm the proposition that "in the hereafter observing Jews will be happier than non-observing Jews." It should be noted that consideration of the afterlife constitutes a sanction to the majority of the Orthodox wing, again showing a supernaturalistic bias (4–I).

Adequacy of the Torah as a Moral Guide

This topic, as well as the following one, was not considered germane to the general issue of naturalism *vs.* supernaturalism, as were the previous topics. Accordingly it was not included in Chart I of the Appendix as an index to positions on this general issue. However, differences among the wings may be noted. In the Orthodox ranks there is virtual concurrence that *the Torah— which includes the Bible, the Talmud, and the Codes—constitutes an adequate guide for the moral perplexities of today.* Not one of

the Orthodox rabbis denies this proposition, and only two question it. The Conservative and Reform wings, however, are divided
on this issue. Only a few in each of these wings have no opinion
on the subject. Among those Reform and Conservative rabbis
who have well-defined opinions, the view that the Torah constitutes an adequate guide has about the same number of adherents
as the diametrically opposed view that the Torah does not constitute an adequate guide (8–I).

Sabbath Observance

This topic, as already pointed out, is not pertinent to the
general issue of naturalism *vs.* supernaturalism. The preponderant
weight of sentiment of the rabbis' responses as a whole favors the
view that "Sabbath observance is a cardinal principle of Judaism."
On this question there is a unanimity of acceptance of the positive
view in the Conservative and Orthodox branches. Two out of
every three Reform rabbis concur in this view, with the remainder
about equally divided between rejection and uncertainty (5–I).

Naturalism vs. Supernaturalism

With the end in view of obtaining a composite picture of the
attitudes of the entire group of rabbis and of the separate wings,
the possible responses of the rabbis to twelve of the sixteen questionnaire items analyzed in this chapter were classified into those
which imply a naturalistic bias and those which imply an anti-
naturalistic bias, as indicated in the introduction to this chapter.*

Chart I of the Appendix gives the key to the classification of the
responses. Responses which can be accommodated within what is
usually considered the "scientific" framework were classified as
naturalistic. Those which could not be so accommodated were
classified as anti-naturalistic. The following postulates were employed in the construction of the chart as essential to the scientific
framework: (*a*) nature is regular; every natural phenomenon is
an exemplification of law; (*b*) nature is self-subsistent; any phenomenon must be explained in terms of other natural phenomena
and not in terms of the supernatural. On the basis of these two

---

* As noted above, items on the authorship of the Pentateuch, on Sabbath observance, on human conduct, and on the adequacy of the Torah (I, 3, 5, 9, 8) could not
be conveniently classified as indices of a naturalistic or supernaturalistic bias.

postulates it was possible to classify the responses to the twelve propositions chosen for the chart as either naturalistic or supernaturalistic.

It is by no means suggested that the responses to any or to all the twelve propositions are a positive criterion as to whether a rabbi is a naturalist or a supernaturalist. Not the rabbis but their responses are subject to classification. Naturalistic and supernaturalistic responses for each wing and for the entire group were derived from the tabulation sheets, with the following results:

Reform	Per Cent
Responses showing naturalistic bias	80
Responses showing supernaturalistic bias	12
Conservative	
Responses showing naturalistic bias	81
Responses showing supernaturalistic bias	11
Orthodox	
Responses showing naturalistic bias	39
Responses showing supernaturalistic bias	47
Total Group	
Responses showing naturalistic bias	74
Responses showing supernaturalistic bias	17

The percentages do not total 100 because three categories of responses are not accounted for: failure to indicate an opinion; expression of uncertainty, in the case of items expressed as true or false propositions; and responses other than those provided for in the questionnaire.

From the preceding analysis at least four deductions are evident:

1. In its approach to the questions of theology the majority of the group has little supernaturalistic bias; the responses showing a naturalistic bias are more than four times as numerous as those showing an anti-naturalistic or supernaturalistic bias.

2. The composition of response is identical for the Conservative and Reform groups, the ratio being about seven naturalistic responses to one supernaturalistic.

3. In contrast to the other wings, the dominant group of Orthodox rabbis incline to supernaturalism. Their supernaturalistic responses exceed in number the responses with a naturalistic bias.

4. We can distinguish between groups, but within groups there are marked variations.

SECTION II

PATTERNS OF BELIEFS IN MATTERS OF THEOLOGY

Section I concerned itself with an examination of the beliefs of rabbis on particular propositions and with comparing the extent of naturalistic and supernaturalistic biases implied in their responses. This section will examine the extent to which beliefs on propositions related to these biases go together in the minds of rabbis.

Six topics which enter into the composite on the general issue of naturalism *vs.* supernaturalism are discussed in the preceding section. These topics, numbered for convenience as follows, are: (1) nature of religion—is it changing or unchanging? (2) concept of God; (3) authorship and nature of the Bible; (4) the function of prayer; (5) sin and salvation; and (6) immortality. They will be related in various ways for discussion in the present section.

Interconnections between the beliefs of rabbis with respect to the Bible and to other doctrinal matters will include the static and dynamic in religion, the nature of God, and the function of prayer.

Various aspects of these topics will be interrelated in terms of interconnection of beliefs of rabbis with respect to the Bible, interconnections between the concept of salvation and beliefs on immortality, interconnection between belief in immortality and the God-concept.

Finally, interconnections of the beliefs of rabbis with respect to immortality will be discussed.

Interconnections Between the Beliefs of Rabbis with Respect to the Bible and to Other Doctrinal Matters*

Static and dynamic in religion.—The view that Judaism must be hostile to any science which contradicts the Bible (1–I) goes preponderantly in the rabbis' minds with another supernaturalistic view, namely that religion is a *divine institution whose funda-*

---

* It should be noted that occasional discrepancies in figures may be accounted for by the fact that one intertabulation may be using a different base from that used in another intertabulation.

mentals are not subject to change (6–II). On the other hand, those who reject the idea of essential and eternal hostility between Judaism and science preponderantly hold to the view that even fundamentals of religion are subject to change. The rejection of the belief in miracles as indispensable to Judaism voiced by 185 rabbis is with virtual agreement allied with the view that the fundamentals of religion are subject to reconstruction—both naturalistic views (2–I).

A commitment to one of the more or less naturalistic views that the Bible is the word of God in a figurative sense, or that it is a record of the moral evolution of the Jews (11–II), accompanies preponderantly, though not exclusively, the naturalistic viewpoint that even fundamental religious standards of conduct must be continually reconstructed (6–II). Of 191 rabbis who have a more or less naturalistic concept of the Bible, 169, or 88 per cent, believe religious fundamentals to be subject to change and deliberate human reconstruction.

The nature of God.—The division of the rabbinate on whether Judaism must or must not be hostile to any science which contradicts the Bible (1–I) roughly corresponds to the division among them as to the nature of God (5–II). In the small group of twelve who see Judaism in conflict with science only four hold one of the several naturalistic concepts of God, the others clinging to the creator idea. On the other hand, close to 88 per cent of the large group of 197 rabbis who deny that Judaism is in conflict with science which contradicts the Bible hold one of the naturalistic concepts of God.

It does not follow, however, that a rabbi who believes that God is the literal creator and ruler of the universe is likely to believe that Judaism is in conflict with science. In fact, only eight of the 31 rabbis who believe that the nature of God is best expressed in the idea of a literal creator see Judaism at odds with science. However, a naturalistic concept of God virtually rules out the view of conflict between Judaism and science.

As is to be expected, the rabbi's attitude toward the Biblically recorded miracles is another probable index of his God concept. Of the seventeen who assign to belief in miracles an essential place in Judaism (2–I) fourteen believe God to be the literal creator, one believes God to be the first cause, and only two have a naturalistic view of God (5–II). Among the large group of 186 respondents who deny the doctrine of miracles an essential place, only thirteen hold to the creator idea and the rest, with the exception of one, indicate a belief in one of the naturalistic concepts.

About half of those rabbis who believe that God is the creator of the universe assert and about half deny that Judaism makes it incumbent upon one to accept as fact the actual occurrence of Biblically recorded miracles. The likelihood that any rabbi who holds a naturalistic concept of God will assign an essential place in Judaism to the belief in miracles seems to be virtually excluded. Of the 181 who stress any of the naturalistic concepts of God listed in the questionnaire, only two adhere to the essentiality of the belief in miracles.

The function of prayer.—The view that the most important function of prayer is actually to bring divine aid to the suppliant of course rests on the assumption that miracles happen. The questionnaire returns indicate that rabbis who are committed to view the belief in Biblically recorded miracles as essential to Judaism (2–I) will identify the principal function of prayer with bringing divine aid to the suppliant (1–II) in greater proportion than will the rabbis who take the naturalistic view of denying the doctrine of miracles an essential place in Judaism.

It should be noted, however, that affirmation of the belief in Biblically recorded miracles does not necessarily indicate that a rabbi looks upon prayers as an instrument to bring divine aid. Nor does the denial of the doctrine of miracles exclude the view that prayers result in divine aid. Of the seventeen rabbis who believe in the truth of the Biblical version of miracles, eleven do not believe that the primary function of prayer is to bring divine aid. Among the 182 who deny that Judaism makes it incumbent to believe in Biblically recorded miracles, five nevertheless believe that prayers actually bring divine help.

Interconnections of the Beliefs of Rabbis
with Respect to the Bible

Three propositions will be interrelated here: (*a*) the Bible is literally the word of God and alternatives to this view; (*b*) Judaism should be hostile to any science which tends to undermine belief in the literal truth of the Bible; and (c) belief in the occurrence of Biblically recorded miracles is indispensable to Judaism. First the positive and then the negative view will be considered in each case. Proposition (b) will also be linked to a fourth question, namely, whether or not the Biblical story of creation is a myth.

"*The Bible is literally the word of God.*"—Of the 209 rabbis who replied to the questionnaire, only fourteen—all in the Orthodox wing—indicated that they believe the "Bible to be literally the word of God" (11–II). Their positions on other issues are as follows: (1) They are equally divided on the question of *whether Judaism should be hostile to any science which tends to undermine the belief that the Bible is the literal word of God* (1–I). (2) They are virtually unanimous in considering the belief in the actual occurrence of miracles an essential doctrine of Judaism (2–I). The latter linkage suggests an underlying supernaturalistic bias connecting both responses.

The large group of 196 rabbis who accept the Bible to be the word of God only in the sense that it reflects human striving after wisdom or goodness, or who view the Bible as a record of the moral and religious evolution of the Jews (11–II) reject with virtual unanimity both the view that Judaism must be hostile to science (1–I) and the view that belief in the occurrence of Biblically recorded miracles is an essential doctrine of Judaism (2–I), showing a linkage of the naturalistic responses.

"*Judaism must remain forever hostile to any science which tends to destroy faith in the literal truth of the teachings of the Bible.*"—Only twelve individuals take the supernaturalistic position that Judaism must be hostile to any science which undermines the literal truth of the Bible (1–I). Of these twelve individuals, the following expressions of opinion are given on different matters: (1) Eight rabbis accord belief in Biblically recorded miracles an essential place in Judaism (2–I). (2) Eight rabbis deny that the Biblical story of creation is a myth (7–I). (3) Seven rabbis believe the Bible to be literally the word of God (11–II).

In the large group of 199 who, taking the naturalistic view, deny the hostility between Judaism and any science which undermines faith in the literal truth of the Bible (1–I): (1) There is virtually

unanimous rejection of the view that belief in the occurrence of
Biblically recorded miracles is essential to Judaism (2–I). (2)
There are 131 rabbis who look upon the Biblical story of creation
as a myth (7–I). (No doubt there are others who consider the
creation story a fable, an allegory, or a legend, but certainly not
a true record of events.) (3) Only seven rabbis look upon the Bible
as "literally the word of God" (11–II). Again, there is a definite
alignment of naturalistic responses as well as supernaturalistic.

*"Belief in the actual occurrence of the miracles as recorded in
the Bible is indispensable to Judaism."*—Seventeen rabbis in the
group of 209 accept as an essential dogma the supernaturalistic
belief in the actual occurrence of miracles (2–1). In this group,
eight view Judaism as hostile to science which contradicts the
Bible (1–I); only two look upon the creation story as a myth, with
the large majority denying its mythical nature (7–I); eleven accept
the Bible as literally the word of God (11–II).

The large group of 189 rabbis who, taking the naturalistic view,
reject belief in Biblically recorded miracles as an essential dogma
(2–I) is virtually unanimous in rejecting the view of hostility
between Judaism and science (1–I). Actually, 195 rabbis believe
that the Bible is either the word of God in a figurative sense or
a record of Jewish religion and moral evolution (11–II). Of the
209 respondents, there are 195 who commit themselves on the issue
of the hostility of Judaism to any scientific teaching which runs
counter to the letter of the Bible (1–I). Apparent discrepancies
between figures given in Sections I and II are similarly to be accounted for by the fact that there are fewer responses to the particular pair of items than there are to either item individually.

*Interconnections Between the Concept of Salvation
and Beliefs on Immortality*

It would seem, on the basis of intertabulation of returns, that
belief in personal immortality does not imply the acceptance of
salvation as happiness in the afterlife. Only two out of the 76
rabbis who *affirm belief in personal immortality* (6–I) *assert that
their best concept of immortality is happiness in the afterlife* (4–II).
Rejection of the doctrine of immortality as indispensable to Judaism, or the questioning of its indispensability, rules out the possi-

bility of the concept of salvation as happiness in the hereafter. The former is the naturalistic view and the latter the supernaturalistic.

Conversely, more rabbis who hold that the concept of salvation that calls for most emphasis in this age is the achievement of an integrated personality believe in personal immortality than do rabbis whose concept of salvation is participation in the social movements which make for social progress. The incidence of belief in immortality among the 94 rabbis subscribing to the first concept of salvation is about 40, or 43 per cent, as compared with only 34, or about 32 per cent, in the group of 107 holding the latter view of salvation. The minority percentage in each instance may again be attributed to some extent to the fact that one member of each pair of propositions is naturalistic and the other supernaturalistic.

Interconnections Between God Concept and Belief in Immortality

The concept of God as the literal creator and active ruler of the Universe seems to be definitely associated with a second supernaturalistic view of belief in immortality. The large majority of the 30 rabbis who view God as a creator (5–II) affirm the belief in personal immortality (6–I) and none in this group denies it. Of these 30 there are, indeed, seven who place the doctrine of immortality in question, but it is not certain whether they question the belief itself or only the place of that belief in the scheme of Judaism.

The acceptance of the doctrine of personal immortality is by no means an indication that a rabbi accepts the creator concept of God. Of the 80 rabbis who affirm the essentiality of immortality in Judaism, 56, or 70 per cent, nevertheless hold a naturalistic conception of God. Yet belief in immortality indicates a greater likelihood than non-belief that a rabbi will hold to the creator concept. In the group of 80 that is committed to the belief in immortality, 23 conceive God as a creator; among the 71 who deny immortality, none holds the view of God as a literal creator. Rejection of the doctrine of immortality as essential to Judaism is apparently related to a rejection of the creator concept of God.

Interconnection of Beliefs of Rabbis
with Respect to Immortality

It may be assumed that assertion on the part of a rabbi that belief in personal immortality is an essential doctrine of Judaism is equivalent to his acceptance of the doctrine. Denial of this doctrine renders it probable but gives no certainty that the rabbi denies personal immortality. While he may not feel bound to accept personal immortality on Jewish grounds he may, nevertheless, feel constrained to accept this doctrine on philosophical grounds.

To what extent do those who accept this doctrine as essential to Judaism employ it as a sanction for Jewish observance? Belief that immortality is an essential doctrine of Judaism seems to be bound up with the belief in rewards and punishment in the hereafter only in the minds of a small proportion of rabbis. Among the 78 who believe "personal immortality to be an essential doctrine of Judaism" (6–I) there are 26 who deny and 22 who affirm that observing Jews will be happier in the hereafter than non-observing Jews (4–I). The remainder are either uncertain or noncommittal. It should be noted, however, that in the case of the Orthodox rabbis, belief in personal immortality tends to accompany belief in a preferential status for observing Jews, both being supernaturalistic views. None of the twenty rabbis who affirm the former proposition deny the latter, and five of them place the proposition of the preferential status of observing Jews in question.

There are two indications that a number of rabbis reject belief in immortality as an essential doctrine of Judaism and accept this belief on other grounds: (1) Of 60 individuals who reject the essentiality of the doctrine, six still believe that observing Jews will be happier in the hereafter; (2) of the 33 rabbis who maintain that Jews will be happier in the hereafter, eleven either deny or are uncertain about the truth of the statement that personal immortality is an essential doctrine of Judaism.

Of course these individuals may simply contradict themselves, as some of them no doubt do, but others probably mean to deny immortality as a Jewish doctrine but nevertheless believe in it as a fact.

CHAPTER VI

PHILOSOPHIES OF JEWISH LIFE

THIS CHAPTER is concerned with the beliefs of rabbis with reference to: the relation of Judaism to the Jewish people; the significance of national elements in the Jewish scheme of life; the nature of the bond which holds the Jews together as a people; the appraisal of some of the suggested methods of solution to the Jewish problem; the goals and methods of Zionism; general issues in the philosophy of Jewish life.

Again, as in Chapter V, the last topic, comprising general issues, is a composite of practically all the items in the previous topics. The general issues here are two in number: Jewish nationalism, and recognition of the connection of Jewish destiny with that of mankind in general, which will be termed simply "linkage." Thus it will be important, in summary, to determine the positions of the several wings as well as of the entire group on these two general issues. The organization followed in Chapter V will be observed in this chapter also: Section I will be devoted to an analysis of beliefs on particular items and Section II to an examination of patterns of beliefs.

SECTION I

THE BELIEFS OF RABBIS WITH RESPECT TO CERTAIN ISSUES OF JEWISH LIFE AND ADJUSTMENT

The Relation of Judaism to the Jewish People

It has been observed in Chapter I that early Reform dominantly took the anti-nationalistic position that Judaism is not a way of life unique with the Jewish people, but rather a religious outlook which, though developed by Jews, is nevertheless an independent entity. It has further been noted that the events of the years following World War I have resulted in a shift of Reform ideology toward a fuller acceptance of the organic unity of Judaism and the Jewish people.

The extent of the shift is indicated by the questionnaire returns. A majority of the Reform rabbis now reject outright the proposition that "Judaism is essentially a religious outlook upon life which can be preserved even if the Jews as a distinct group disappear." This is the nationalistic response relative to the first of the two general issues mentioned above. The remaining number of Reform rabbis are equally divided between those who affirm and those who question this proposition.

In spite of the post-war shift, the relation between Judaism and the Jews is thus still a controversial matter within the ranks of Reform. Within the Orthodox and Conservative wings it is not an issue, however. Less than one out of ten rabbis in these wings view Judaism as independent of the Jewish people, with an additional one out of every ten uncertain. The remainder conceive Judaism as inextricably bound up with the Jewish people.

The vote of the group as a whole on this issue is about as follows: that Judaism is bound up with the Jewish people, two out of every three; that Judaism is an independent entity, one out of every six; uncertainty on the issue, one out of six (10–I).

The Place of National Elements in the Pattern of Jewish Life

Through the ages, no matter what language the Jews happened to speak in their everyday intercourse, the basic language of Judaism was Hebrew. It was the literary and religious tongue of the Jewish people. Similarly, Palestine has remained during the centuries of Jewish dispersion an object of religious adoration for the Jews.

Denationalization of Judaism has been noted as one of the principal objectives of early Reform. In the light of these objectives, Reform leaders reiterated that the connection between Judaism, on the one hand, and Palestine and Hebrew, on the other, is a historic one but not at present an essential one. The role of Hebrew in the ritual was continuously diminished, and the traditional prayers voicing Jewish aspirations for a return to Palestine were eliminated.

That a shift[1] has occurred within Reform ranks with regard to this proposition is evidenced by the fact that more than half of the rabbis in this wing indicated assent to the statement: "The cultivation of the Hebrew language and literature and loyalty to the cause of rebuilding Palestine as a Jewish homeland are essential to the Jewish pattern of life." The proposition still remains an issue, however. One out of every five of the Reform rabbis still denies that cultivation of Hebrew and loyalty to Palestine are essential in the scheme of Judaism, and a similar proportion is uncertain.

The Conservative group is unanimous and the Orthodox group is in virtual agreement in favoring commitment to the cultivation of Hebrew and loyalty to Palestine.

Thus the total group of rabbis divides on this issue as follows: three out of every four are favorable to the inclusion of Hebrew and Palestine in the essential pattern of Jewish life, and the remainder either deny or are uncertain about the place of these elements. A few individuals distinguish between Hebrew, whose place in Judaism they recognize, and Palestine, which they reject (11–I).

Nature of the Bond Which Holds Jews Together

The idea of the relation of Judaism to the Jews and the place of aspirations which center in Palestine and the Hebrew language in the scheme of Jewish life lead to the more general question: What is the nature of the bond which holds the Jews together as a people? Is it principally a racial, a national, or a religious tie?

The concept of nationality as a historic force in Western civilization goes back no further than the eighteenth century. Even more recent is the emphasis on the concept of race. Nevertheless, Jewish tradition, if interpreted in modern terms, views the Jewish people as a race, a nation, and a religious community all in one. In fact, it is this synthesis which tradition considers the unique characteristic of the Jewish people.

The following tabulation shows the division of opinion in the entire group on the question of what the term "Jewish people" denotes:

[1] See Chapter I, pp. 20, 21, for position in the past.

	Per Cent
Race	6
Nationality	38
Religious community	41
Combinations of the above	7
Noncommittal	8

Thus the preponderant sentiment of the rabbinate is about evenly divided between the views that Jews constitute a religious community and that they constitute a nation.

As is to be expected, the Reform wing shows a greater inclination than the two other sections of the rabbinate to the view that Jews constitute a religious community. A majority of sixty-six rabbis express this belief, as against twenty-two who view the Jews as a national group. The Orthodox and Conservative wings, on the other hand, tend to view the Jews as a nationality. This view is held by a large majority of the former and a majority of the latter. Thirteen Conservative rabbis and eleven Orthodox rabbis view the Jews as a religious community. It will be remembered that the chief task of early Reform was the denationalization of Judaism. In pre-World War I Reform ideology, the Jewish people as a whole were conceived as living exclusively for their mission. To fulfill this mission they must eliminate the political, nationalistic, and separatistic elements which developed in the course of their earliest history. Apparently the Reform rabbinate in the main still clings to this view.

In spite of the differences between the various wings it should be noted that the question of what is the nature of the Jewish people is an issue before all of them. Moreover, it is an issue on which a large proportion of rabbis find it difficult to take a decided stand. This is evidenced by the comparatively large number of rabbis—eighteen in the entire group, of whom eleven were in the Reform wing—who completely failed to commit themselves. An additional fifteen of the entire group indicate their position by a combination of choices or by writing in a choice not listed in the questionnaire (12–II).

Solutions to Jewish Problems

This topic will be divided into four parts as follows: anti-Semitism in America; hope for Jewish adjustment in the emergence of a collectivist social order and greater world unity; participation of Jews in radical social movements; and suggested methods appraised as major, minor, or having no solution to the problems of Jewish adjustment.

Anti-Semitism in America.—During the nineteenth century and the pre-World War I years of the twentieth century, it was the fond conviction of Jewish as well as of Gentile liberals that anti-Semitism was a vestige of a cruder age which was bound to disappear in the course of human progress. This optimism was lucidly reflected in the ideology of pre-war Reform. Although unrelated to either of the general issues of this chapter, it is of interest to note that such a notion is no longer maintained, even among the Reform rabbinate. This becomes evident upon examination of the rabbis' reactions to the proposition, "Anti-Semitism cannot take deep root in America." Only one out of every eleven individuals in the group as a whole gives assent to this proposition. The Conservative and Reform wings are somewhat less optimistic in this regard than the Orthodox group. In the first two wings the majority find no reason for optimism, and about one out of every three is uncertain. In the Orthodox wing, the dominant group is uncertain about the proposition (12–I).

Hope for Jewish adjustment in the emergence of a collectivistic social order and greater world unity.—A majority of the rabbinate see the Jewish future organically bound up with the destiny of mankind in general, the second of the two general issues mentioned above. Almost two thirds of the rabbis in the entire group give assent to the proposition, "The chief hope for Jewish adjustment to the world lies in the emergence of a collectivist social order and greater world unity," with only one out of every five expressing uncertainty, and an additional one out of every seven dissenting.

The acceptance of a linkage between brighter prospects for the Jewish people and the rise of a new economic and international social order is strongest among the Conservative rabbis and weakest in the Orthodox wing. This conviction is shared by 77 per cent of the Conservative and 64 per cent of the Reform rabbis, as compared with only 41 per cent in the Orthodox wing. Out of about every three Orthodox rabbis, one indicates uncertainty with respect to this issue (13–I).

Participation of Jews in radical social movements.—The view that solution of the problems of Jewish adjustment is bound up with the emergence of a new social order implies, of course, that Jews must participate in building the new society. Frequently the opinion is voiced by prominent Jewish laymen that Jews for their own good must steer clear of radical movements and activities. Only 32 rabbis, or 15 per cent of the entire group, share this view. On the other hand, 146 rabbis dissent from the proposition, "It is in the best interests of the Jewish people that Jews discontinue participation in radical social movements." The remainder are undecided in their attitude on this issue.

The Conservative group shows the smallest and the Orthodox the largest proportion of objectors to Jewish participation in radical social movements. In the Conservative wing one out of every fifteen rabbis objects to such participation; in the Reform group about one out of every seven objects. The Orthodox wing is fairly evenly divided among those who believe that Jewish participation in radical social movements is injurious to their interests, those who reject this view, and those who are uncertain (14–I).

Suggested methods appraised as major, minor, or no solutions to the problems of Jewish adjustment.—The rabbis were asked to indicate whether in their opinion each of the following means, four of which are related to the two general issues of this chapter, constitutes a major, a minor, or no solution to the problems of Jewish adjustment: (*a*) self-removal of Jews from prominent places in business, politics, and intellectual endeavor; (*b*) good will conferences between Jewish and Gentile leaders; (*c*) Zionism, which is, of course, related to the first general issue of nationalism; (*d*) a militant fight against anti-Semitism; (*e*) a scheme of general education which aims at raising the intelligence level of the population (connected with the second general issue of "linkage"); (*f*) improved religious training; (*g*) a socialist economy; (*h*) emergence of an international spirit—the last two being related to the second general issue of "linkage."

In order to obtain a composite picture of how the group as a whole and the three wings separately appraise each of the above suggested methods, the following procedure of weighting the responses was employed. A value of 0 is assigned to "no solution";

1 to "major solution"; ½ to "minor solution." On this basis of weighting, group weights of close to 0, .50, and 1.00 obtained for suggested methods correspond respectively to the qualitative estimates of "no solution," "minor solution," and "major solution." The weighted estimates for the total group and the separate wings of the rabbinate are given in Table XV. From the tabular data

TABLE XV

WEIGHTED ESTIMATES OF SUGGESTED SOLUTIONS TO JEWISH PROBLEMS*

	ESTIMATES OF RABBIS			
Suggested Methods	*Reform*	*Conservative*	*Orthodox*	*Entire Group*
Self-removal of Jews from prominent places	.04	.03	.13	.05
Good will conference between Jews and Gentiles	.55	.51	.53	.53
Militant fight against Anti-Semitism	.59	.60	.48	.58
Socialist economy	.59	.80	.38	.63
Zionism	.54	.91	.82	.71
Religious education	.80	.82	.79	.81
General education	.88	.81	.69	.83
International spirit	.86	.92	.61	.84

* 1.00 denotes *major solution;* .50, *minor solution;* .0, *no solution.*

the positions of the entire rabbinate and of the Reform, Conservative, and Orthodox wings seem to be somewhat as follows:

1. The group as a whole reposes greatest hope in general education which aims at raising the intelligence level of the population, in improved religious education, and in the emergence of an international spirit. The rabbinate's appraisal of these methods comes closer to that of "major solution" than to "minor solution." Zionism is evaluated by the group as a whole as between a major and a minor solution. A socialist economy, a militant fight against anti-Semitism, and good will conferences between Jewish and non-Jewish leaders are viewed as minor solutions. Self-removal of Jews from positions of prominence as a method of solving Jewish problems is rejected, even as a minor solution.

2. The Reform wing places greatest confidence in general education and in internationalism, appraising these methods as close to major solutions. Its estimate of improved religious education

is only slightly lower. In the opinion of the Reform wing, good will conferences, Zionism, a militant fight against anti-Semitism, and a socialist economy do not rise above the level of minor solutions. Self-removal of Jews from positions of importance is viewed as "no solution."

3. The Conservative group looks upon both Zionism and internationalism as close to major solutions. Other methods which loom important in the outlook of the Conservative rabbinate are general education, religious education, and a socialist economy. Good will conferences and a militant fight against anti-Semitism are appraised as minor solutions. Self-removal is rejected.

4. The Orthodox wing ranks no method higher than midway between major and minor solutions. However, Zionism and religious education are viewed as holding out greatest promise as solutions to the problems of Jewish adjustment. General education comes next in order of promise. Internationalism, good will conferences, and a militant fight against anti-Semitism are rated minor solutions, and socialism is on a level considerably lower than minor solution. Self-removal is rejected, but with a smaller degree of consensus than in the Conservative and Reform wings.

It will be observed that the distinguishing characteristic of the Reform wing is the low estimate of Zionism and the higher estimate of general education. The outstanding fact about the Conservative group is the high estimate of socialism as a solution to the Jewish problem. Orthodoxy, on the other hand, places a very low estimate on socialism.

Omitting "self-removal," the average weighted estimate for all other factors made by the three wings respectively is Reform .69, Conservative .77, and Orthodox .62 (1–III).

Program of Jewish Work in Palestine (Zionism)

There is considerable controversy in Jewish life regarding the political ends which Jews should seek in Palestine and the means whereby these ends are to be realized. The differences among the three wings on the propositions in this area are of interest, although none of these items are used in determining the composite on either of the general issues in this chapter. Up to the end of

World War I the political aim of Zionism, generally speaking, was to establish a *purely Jewish state in Palestine*. Almost one third of the contemporary American rabbinate as a whole seems to identify itself with this goal. However, there is a marked difference in this regard between the Orthodox and the other two wings. Of the Orthodox rabbis, about four out of every five still cling to the ideal of making Palestine a Jewish national state, as compared with one out of every six Reform and one out of every three Conservative rabbis who look toward that goal. The majority in the two latter wings seek a *bi-national state in the control of which both Jews and Arabs will share*. The scheme of partition of Palestine into separate Jewish and Arab territories finds little support in any of the three groups (14–II).

With respect to methods to be employed in removing the obstacles which Jews encounter in their work in Palestine, the preponderant majority of the rabbinate as a whole is committed to a policy of "attempting to arrive at an understanding with the masses of the Arab people." This program is supported by 73 of the 77 Conservative rabbis, 94 of the 104 Reform rabbis, and 22 of the 31 Orthodox rabbis. Struggle with Arabs as a method is rejected by virtually all rabbis. The only substantial difference among the three wings of the rabbinate is with respect to employing a policy of "convincing England that her interest would best be served by supporting Jews rather than Arabs." Such policy is supported by only ten individuals—two Reform, two Conservative, and six Orthodox rabbis (13–II).

Rabbis' Positions on Two General Issues in the Philosophy of Jewish Life

The responses of the rabbis to some of the propositions dealt with in this chapter give an approximate idea of their position on the general question of Jewish nationalism, and of the interdependence of the destiny of the Jews with that of all mankind.

Chart II of the Appendix served as a key in classifying the responses of the rabbis into two groups—pro- and anti-nationalistic. In justification of the chart it may be pointed out that recognition of the organic unity of Jews and Judaism, the view that Hebrew and Palestine occupy an important place in the scheme

of Jewish life, commitment to the racial or national view of the
Jewish people, and appraisal of Zionism as a major solution of the
Jewish problem are characteristic contemporary national views.
The opposite views may with justice be classed as anti-nationalistic,
or at least non-nationalistic. The results obtained by the employ-
ment of this chart are:

Reform   *Per Cent*
    Responses showing pro-nationalistic leanings   40
    Responses showing non- or anti-nationalistic leanings   44
Conservative
    Responses showing pro-nationalistic leanings   81
    Responses showing non- or anti-nationalistic leanings   11
Orthodox
    Responses showing pro-nationalistic leanings   73
    Responses showing non- or anti-nationalistic leanings   17
Total Group
    Responses showing pro-nationalistic leanings   59
    Responses showing non- or anti-nationalistic leanings   28

Chart III of the Appendix served as a key for computation of
the percentages of responses which show and those which do not
show recognition of the connection of Jewish destiny with that of
mankind in general. A glance at the items will show why they
were included in this chart.* The results obtained are as follows:

Reform   *Per Cent*
    Responses which indicate recognition   66
    Responses which do not indicate recognition   25
Conservative
    Responses which indicate recognition   73
    Responses which do not indicate recognition   19
Orthodox
    Responses which indicate recognition   34
    Responses which do not indicate recognition   48
Total Group
    Responses which indicate recognition   63
    Responses which do not indicate recognition   27

* The responses do not add up to 100 per cent because those indicating noncommitment or lack of a definite stand have been left out.

The conclusions that seem to issue from the foregoing analysis
are that in its approach to the Jewish problem the rabbinate as a
whole shows a majority tendency to accept Jewish nationalism and

to place dependence for the solution of the Jewish problem upon social progress in general. With respect to nationalism, the pro- and anti- or un-nationalistic tendencies in the Reform wing are almost equally pronounced. The nationalistic tendency in the Conservative wing is expressed by a preponderant majority, and in the Orthodox wing by a large majority.

The tendency to see Jewish problems within the framework of general social problems and movements distinguishes a large majority sentiment of the Conservative and Reform rabbis. In the Orthodox wing recognition of the connections between Jewish and world problems is felt by only a sizable minority.

SECTION II

PATTERNS OF THOUGHT CONCERNING JEWISH LIFE

The first three topics in this section—the concept of Judaism as a factor in rabbis' orientation; the concept of the Jewish people as a factor in rabbis' beliefs; and the attitude toward Zionism as a factor in rabbis' beliefs—are related to the general issue of nationalism *vs.* anti-nationalism. The explanation of consistent patterns of belief on pairs of propositions under each topic may be found in the fact of a general underlying attitude on the above-mentioned issues.

On the last topic—interrelations between approaches to the solution of the Jewish problem—the general issue of "linkage" of Jewish destiny with that of mankind in general is tied to the question of nationalism.

Only propositions of Charts II and III of the Appendix, which thus entered into the composites on the two general issues of this chapter, will be paired in this section.

*The Concept of Judaism as a Factor
in the Rabbi's Orientation*

A rabbi's belief as to whether or not Judaism is indissolubly bound up with the Jewish people seems to figure in his concept of the content of Jewish life, his view on the nature of the bond which holds the Jews together, and his appraisal of Zionism as a method of Jewish adjustment. The tie connecting these issues is the general issue of nationalism *vs.* anti-nationalism. With minor exceptions, it apparently makes for consistency of pairs of responses in this area.

Among the rabbis who believe that *Judaism can have no existence without a Jewish people* (10–I) there is virtual agreement that "the cultivation of the Hebrew language and literature and loyalty to the cause of rebuilding Palestine are essential in the pattern of Jewish life" (11–I). Of 138 rabbis who see Judaism as indissolubly linked with the Jewish people, 126 recognize in Palestine and the Hebrew language elements basic in the scheme of Jewish life. Of 35 who conceive of Judaism as an ideal entity distinct from the Jewish people, as many deny as affirm the importance of the Hebrew language and the rebuilding of Palestine.

Rabbis who believe in the *organic unity of the Jewish people and Judaism* (10–I) are likely to see nationalism as the principal bond of the Jews as a group (12–II). Of 122 rabbis who reject the notion that Judaism is an entity separate and apart from the Jewish people, 69 regard nationality as the principal binding force. On the other hand, it is extremely unlikely that a rabbi who rejects the organic unity of Jews and Judaism will affirm nationalism as the prime characteristic of the Jewish group. In fact, among the 33 rabbis who conceive of Judaism as a separate entity only two are committed to the nationalistic view.

Belief in the *independence of Judaism and the Jews* (10–I) is associated largely with the appraisal of Zionism as no solution, or at best as a minor solution, to the problems of Jewish adjustment (1–III). Only eight of the 33 rabbis who hold this concept of Judaism see in Zionism a major solution. On the other hand 93 of the 141 who cannot conceive of Judaism apart from the Jewish people give this high estimate of Zionism.

The Concept of the Jewish People as a Factor in Rabbis' Beliefs

A rabbi's concept of the nature of the bond which makes the Jews a distinct group seems to be an important consideration in arriving at a conclusion concerning the nature of Judaism, the place of Hebrew and Palestine in the pattern of Jewish life, the degree of importance of Zionism as a solution to the problems of

Jewish adjustment, and the particular goal which Jews should set for work in Palestine. Again, it may be noted that the issue of nationalism *vs.* anti-nationalism runs through most of these propositions and thus largely explains the results presented below.

It has been noted in preceding paragraphs that the view that Judaism is a spiritual entity separate from the Jewish people is bound up with the concept of the Jewish people as a religious community, and that, on the other hand, the view of the organic connection between Jews and Judaism is bound up with the nationalistic concept of Jewish group unity. It may be observed now that of the 81 rabbis who hold the national concept of the Jewish group (12–II) only two are of the opinion that Jews and Judaism are two distinct entities (10–I). On the other hand, the religious concept of Jewish peoplehood in the group of 90 is associated with the notion of the dualism of Judaism and the Jews in 28 instances.

Rabbis who view the Jewish people either as a race or as a nation (12–II) are of a majority opinion in deeming Hebrew and Palestine as focal points in the Jewish scheme of life (11–I). Among these 87 respondents who adhere to the religious concept of Jewish peoplehood, 34 deny or question the importance of Hebrew and Palestine in the scheme of Jewish life.

The identification of the Jewish people as a race or a nation (12–II) is accompanied by the view that Zionism is a major solution to the Jewish problem (1–III). Sixty-three of 81 rabbis who hold the nationalist concept of the Jewish people, and three of the thirteen who hold the racial concept, place this high estimate upon Zionism as a solution. Only 24 of 88 who see the Jewish people as a religious community believe Zionism is a major solution.

Attitude Toward Zionism as a Factor
in Rabbis' Beliefs

How and to what extent do particular appraisals of Zionism as a solution to the Jewish problem figure in the rabbi's orientation to the questions of the nature of Judaism, the importance of Palestine and Hebrew, and the character of Jewish peoplehood?

The higher a rabbi's appraisal of Zionism as a solution to the Jewish problem (1–III), the less his adherence to the view that Judaism is apart from the Jewish people (10–I). Those who think that Judaism can be preserved, even if the Jews as a distinct people disappear, constitute 7 per cent of the 113 who deem Zionism a major problem, 22 per cent of the 74 who consider it a minor solution, and 38 per cent of those who think it no solution.

The conviction that Zionism is a major solution to the Jewish problem is almost a certain indication that a rabbi cherishes Hebrew and Palestine as primary elements in the pattern of Jewish life (11–I). Among the 114 rabbis who see in Zionism a major solution to the problem of Jewish adjustment, 111 consider Hebrew and Palestine as focal points to Jewish life. But among 22 rabbis who fail to see in Zionism any solution whatever, only six assign that role to Hebrew and Palestine; and among 71 rabbis who designate Zionism a minor solution, 46 recognize Hebrew and Palestine as important.

Rejection of Zionism as a solution (1–III) is almost completely associated with the denial of Jewish nationhood and the identification of the Jewish people with a religious community (12–II). On the other hand, to 63 out of the 95 rabbis who appraise Zionism as a major solution, the Jewish people connotes a nationality.

Interrelations Between Approaches to the Solution of the Jewish Problem

How do appraisals of different solutions to the Jewish problem accompany one another?

There is a tendency for high appraisal of Zionism (1–III) to accompany recognition of the supreme importance to Jews of the rise of a new world order (13–I). On the other hand, those who deny the bearing of internationalism and a socialist economy on the Jewish future also tend to be apathetic to the possibilities of Zionism as a solution to the Jewish problem. Of those 112 rabbis who see in Zionism a major solution to the Jewish question, 76 also look to a collectivist economy and an international world order as chief hopes of the Jewish people. Among 22 rabbis who reject Zionism outright as a solution, only nine are hopeful about the possibilities of a new world order. Also, the percentage of those who see in Zionism a major solution is slightly higher among those who look toward internationalism and collectivism than among those who do not do so or who are uncertain.

CHAPTER VII

THE SOCIAL FUNCTION OF RELIGION

THIS CHAPTER is concerned solely with the conceptions of the rabbis with regard to the social implications of religion in general and of Judaism in particular. How rabbis stand on specific social issues, regardless of what they conceive to be the dictates of religion, will be examined in subsequent chapters.

SECTION I

BELIEFS OF RABBIS WITH RESPECT TO THE SOCIAL IMPLICATIONS OF JUDAISM

The topics under consideration here are: (1) the moral philosophy of religion; (2) the function of religion in social reconstruction; (3) implications of Judaism for the goals of social reconstruction; (4) implications of Judaism for specific social issues.

These issues will be treated individually only, and not in relation to any broader issue discussed in this chapter. However, the greater "progressivism" of the Conservative and Reform wings—particularly the former—over the Orthodox may be noted generally throughout Section I. Under topic (4), on the connection of Judaism and the interests of labor, responses of the rabbis will figure in their general attitude toward labor, one of the general issues to be considered in the next chapter.

The Moral Philosophy of Religion

Though the questionnaire inquiry with reference to basic moral philosophy failed to mention either Judaism or religion, the results of the inquiry are nevertheless included in this chapter. A preponderant majority of the American rabbinate is committed to a utilitarian moral philosophy. Of the entire group of 212 rabbis, 186 believe that *the primary considerations in determining*

the morality of an act are its individual and social consequences.
Only one of every 20 rabbis sees the *criterion of morality to reside
in tradition,* and an additional one out of every 14 sees *such criterion to reside in the dictates of the individual conscience.*

The Conservative wing is virtually unanimous in its acceptance
of the utilitarian criterion. In this wing only one individual each
selects tradition and conscience as criteria. Three quarters of the
Orthodox group accept the criterion of utilitarianism (7–II).

The Function of Religion in Social Reconstruction

A preponderant majority of the group as a whole share in the
*conviction that religious motivation is essential to socially recon-
structive efforts.* The Orthodox group approaches unanimity on
the question and the Reform group shows the greatest proportion
of individuals who concede that the effort to build a new society
may be worth while even if it is not religiously motivated (15–I).

There is virtual unanimity of belief in the group as a whole
that *if Judaism is to remain a vital force in contemporary life it
must identify itself with the movements which aim to create a
better social order* (18–I).

Judged by its actual function in contemporary society, organized
religion falls short in the estimate of the rabbis of what it should
and might be. In the entire group, 144 rabbis believe that, generally speaking, "organized religion as it now functions is only
a slight factor in the improvement of human life, but that it can
be made into an important factor by changing the content of the
religious message and the function of the religious teacher." On
the other hand, only 60 rabbis believe that *organized religion today
is an important force in improving human life.* A negligible
proportion hold that it must necessarily remain a slight factor.

A majority in the Orthodox wing, but only one out of every
seven in the Conservative wing, believe that religion is now an
important force in improving human life. In contrast, about 80
per cent of the Conservative rabbis believe that at present organized religion is but a slight factor in the improvement of life but
that its role might be enlarged in the future. This view is also
held by 14 of the 33 Orthodox rabbis. The Reform wing occupies
a midway position between these viewpoints (8–II).

In connection with the difference among the wings of the rabbinate on the social function of religion, it may be well to recall some of the findings embodied in Chapter V:

1. Within the Conservative and Reform wings there is virtual unanimity that even religious fundamentals must be continually reconstructed, whereas Orthodoxy shows a majority opposed to changes of religious standards of conduct.

2. The proportion of rabbis who hold that the highest type of prayer is a petition for the establishment of social justice is decidedly greater in the Reform and Conservative wings than in the Orthodox wing.

3. The social concept of sin is emphasized by large majorities of rabbis in the Reform and Conservative groups but by only about one out of every three Orthodox rabbis.

4. There is greater emphasis on social progress in the concept of salvation in the Reform and Conservative groups than in the Orthodox.

Implications of Judaism for the Goals
of Social Reconstruction

That the spirit of Judaism demands either "support of our present economic institutions" or "neutrality on the question of economic reconstruction" is maintained by only one out of every twelve rabbis in the group as a whole. The issue before the rabbinate is whether *Judaism demands the fundamental abolition of the private profit and property system or only correction of certain evils of our industrial system within the framework of capitalism.* Between these two alternatives the latter view has greater support.

The trend toward economic radicalism is most pronounced among the Conservative rabbis and least among the Orthodox. The percentage of those in the three groups who see Judaism committed to basic social reconstruction along socialist lines are Conservative 56, Reform 33, Orthodox 18. The percentage who believe Judaism demands changes *within* the framework of capitalism are, Conservative 37, Reform 57, Orthodox 72 (9–II).

Though 79, or more than one third of the total group, believe that the spirit of Judaism demands the abolition of the profit system, only 12 rabbis deem the most important function of the

Jewish ministry to be the advocacy of "the replacement of our inherited institutions by a cooperative society." On the other hand, the proportion of those who would *dedicate the ministry to affording comfort and support to individuals but would keep it out of controversy on economic issues* is but 2 per cent. The preponderant majority maintain that it is the principal function of the rabbinate "to teach those moral ideals and religious insights which have a bearing on contemporary social problems" (10–II).

Implications of Judaism for Specific Social Issues

The succeeding paragraphs will be devoted to a discussion of what the rabbis regard as the implications of Judaism for questions of labor, education, sex morality, and peace.

Judaism and labor.—Majorities in all three groups—a large majority in the case of Conservatism and a bare majority in the case of Orthodoxy, with Reform in between—are committed to the proposition that "in the issues between labor and capital the spirit of Judaism should impel one, generally, to identify himself with labor" (17–I). About one in every eight rabbis in each wing rejects blanket identification of Judaism with the cause of labor. Some of the respondents elucidated their viewpoint by writing in the questionnaire that Judaism is neither for capital nor for labor, but for "justice." The Orthodox wing shows the largest proportion of uncertainty with respect to this proposition.

The rabbinate shows a much stronger sentiment in favor of support of collective bargaining than of unqualified identification with labor in its struggle with capital. There is virtual unanimity in the Reform and Conservative groups in favor of extending rabbinic support of "the right of labor to engage in collective bargaining through unions of their own choosing." Among the 33 Orthodox rabbis 23 favor support of the cause of collective bargaining by the rabbinate; three deny it is the duty of the rabbinate to support collective bargaining; seven are uncertain (27–I).

While the rabbinate theoretically recognizes support of collective bargaining as a duty of the pulpit, the rabbis individually are somewhat less certain about their own role in the case of a strike in their communities. Fifty-seven are in doubt about *the wisdom of expression of an opinion in the face of a strike situation in one's own community,* whereas the doubters on collective bargaining are only twelve in number (16–I).

Religion and education.—Only a negligible proportion of the rabbinate as a whole favors *imposition of religious restriction on the content of teaching by schools and colleges.* Religious censorship of school is favored by one in every three in the Orthodox group, with an additional one in every eight uncertain (48–I).

Sex and Judaism.—Majorities in the Reform and Conservative groups see no reason why "sex problems should not be discussed from the pulpit." The Orthodox group is equally divided among those who would include, those who would exclude, and 27 per cent who are uncertain about the inclusion of sex topics (77–I).

There is virtual unanimity in the Reform and Conservative groups that *the practice of birth control is not contrary to the spirit of Judaism.* Only about one fifth of the Orthodox group are opposed to this view, the rest being about equally divided between affirmation and uncertainty (73–I).

Religion and peace.—*Support of conscientious objectors in time of war* is favored by 195 of the entire group of 215 rabbis. In the Reform and Conservative wings the sentiment for support is virtually unanimous. Of the 33 in the Orthodox group, 10 refuse support or are uncertain; the remaining 23 favor support (61–I).

Summaries concerning the attitudes of the rabbis on the issues treated in this chapter are included in subsequent chapters.

SECTION II

PATTERNS OF SOCIO-RELIGIOUS THOUGHT

This section will attempt to relate responses on pairs of propositions in the area of the social function of religion. The first pair were treated in Section I separately, under the implications of Judaism for the goals of social reconstruction; the second, under the implications of Judaism for specific social issues.

(1) Interrelation between concept of goals of economic reconstruction and views on the function of the ministry.

(2) Interrelations between view of Judaism's implications for labor issues generally and belief concerning the rabbi's duty in regard to collective bargaining.

*Interrelations Between Concept of Goals of Economic
Reconstruction and Views on the Function of the Ministry*

The rabbis' beliefs that *the spirit of Judaism demands the
abolition of the inherited industrial system, the correction of
capitalism, the support of existing institutions, or neutrality on
economic questions* (9–II) are accompanied in virtual agreement
by the opinion that the chief responsibility of the ministry is
"teaching those moral ideals and religious insights which have a
bearing on contemporary social problems" (10–II). There is a
slight trend among those who see radical economic implications
in Judaism toward commitment of the ministry to advocacy of a
cooperative society. Among 78 individuals who believe that
Judaism demands the socialization of our economy, ten would
dedicate the ministry to the building of a cooperative society.
Among the 123 rabbis who see other economic implications in
Judaism, only two favor the advocacy of a cooperative society by
the Jewish ministry.

As is to be expected, a rabbi's conviction that the ministry
should dedicate itself to the advocacy of a cooperative society is
accompanied essentially by the belief that Judaism is in contradiction to the system of production for profit, and implies favoring a system of production for use. Of the twelve rabbis who believe it the duty of the ministry to oppose the old and to aid in the
establishment of a new order, ten believe Judaism to be at odds
with the economic system based on private ownership of the means
of production. Only 67 in the group of 184 who would limit the
ministry to the dissemination of ideas and insights which have a
bearing on contemporary problems believe that Judaism without
any definite collectivistic commitments demands the establishment
of social ownership of the means of production.

*Interrelation Between View of Judaism's Implications for Labor
Issues Generally and Belief Concerning the Rabbi's Duty
in Regard to Collective Bargaining*

One hundred forty-seven rabbis affirm the proposition that
"in the issues between labor and capital the spirit of Judaism
should impel one, generally, to identify himself with labor" (17–I).

Of this group, 94 per cent believe that "rabbis should support the right of labor to engage in collective bargaining through unions of its own choosing" (27–I). On the other hand, only 73 per cent of those who favor the latter stand also accept the former. This accords with expectation on the basis of the wider scope of the former proposition.

It is instructive to note that almost 99 per cent of the Reform group who accept the broader proposition also affirm the narrower one. The percentage in the Conservative wing is 93 and in the Orthodox wing only 76. In tracing the reverse relationship, the proportions in the separate wings, as pointed out above for the group as a whole, are smaller. Again the Orthodox group shows the lowest ratio; 62 per cent of this wing who are in favor of collective bargaining also feel that the spirit of Judaism would have one uphold the side of labor more generally. In the Conservative and Reform wings, the corresponding figures are 80 per cent and 70 per cent.

CHAPTER VIII

VIEWS OF THE RABBIS ON SOME ISSUES
OF ECONOMIC RECONSTRUCTION

IN THIS CHAPTER the attitudes of the rabbis toward existing social arrangements, goals, extent, and methods of economic reconstruction will be analyzed. The examination of positions will be organized around the following general issues: (1) economic reconstruction; (2) social responsibility for individual welfare; (3) attitudes toward labor; (4) composites of positions on each of these three general issues.

SECTION I

ANALYSIS OF POSITIONS ON ISSUES OF ECONOMIC RECONSTRUCTION

Evaluation of the existing capitalist social order.—There is widespread conviction among the rabbinate taken as a whole that the bulk of the wealth in this country is owned by a small portion of the population. Equally widespread, if not somewhat greater, is the belief that the existing system of distribution of wealth and income is far from equitable. Of the total group of rabbis, 161, or 74 per cent, believe that "radical agitators do not exaggerate when they assert that the bulk of the wealth in this country is owned by a very small portion of the population" (19–I). The remainder are divided between uncertainty and the belief that such a statement is an exaggeration. Of the entire group, 166 rabbis, or 77 per cent, deny that our economic system "distributes wealth and income among the various individuals in proportion to their ability, energy, and usefulness to society" (20–I). Of the remainder, more are doubtful than are certain of the equity of our system of distribution.

Comparing the three separate wings, it is to be noted that both with respect to the recognition of the facts of distribution and the adverse judgment on its equity, the Conservative group is more critical of our economy than the Reform wing, with the Orthodox group ranking last in this regard. The fact of concentration of wealth is recognized by 86 per cent of the Conservative, 72 per cent of the Reform, and 61 per cent of the Orthodox rabbis. The existing system of distribution is deemed inequitable by 88 per cent of the Conservative, 76 per cent of the Reform, and 53 per cent of the Orthodox rabbis.

Economic individualism is condemned by 133, or 61 per cent, of the total group, on the ground that it "has degraded human character and has appealed to the most selfish impulses of man" (33–I). Difference among the wings is maintained along the lines indicated previously. The Conservative group rejects economic individualism by a vote of 77 per cent, the Reform group by 59 per cent. In the Orthodox group 36 per cent find economic individualism morally objectionable; the majority are uncertain.

Only 32, or 15 per cent, of the group as a whole deem *the preservation of capitalism essential to human culture* (35–I). The remainder are divided between those who are uncertain about and those who deny the essential linkage between human culture and the capitalist economy. Obviously there is more widespread objection to economic individualism on grounds of its morally degrading effect than there is to capitalism on grounds of its effects on culture. What does this difference mean? In the light of the analyses to be presented in Section II of this chapter, it probably indicates that a large number of rabbis are opposed to "economic individualism" but that they nevertheless support the essential framework of capitalism. Only in the Conservative group does a majority deny categorically the indispensability of capitalism to culture. A majority of the Orthodox rabbis and 44 per cent of the Reform group indicate doubt as to whether or not the preservation of capitalism is essential to human culture.

About three out of every four rabbis in the total group believe that "it is more difficult for the poor than for the rich to get justice in our courts" (32–I).

About two out of every three imply that *prostitution would be materially lessened by the improvement of economic conditions of the masses* (34–I). About one out of two sees in the management of the radio, press, and cinema, with a view to profits, *a contributory cause of the perversion of taste and lowering of intelligence (31–I)*. The first two of these convictions are shared by relatively more Conservative rabbis than Reform or Orthodox. There is relatively greater opposition to the private control of the radio, press, and cinema among the Orthodox than among the Reform rabbis. This is one of the few instances where the Orthodox wing is further to the left than the Reform wing. A possible explanation of this exception is that some of the Orthodox rabbis may have meant to register objections to radio, cinema, and press content rather than to the profit motive.

Socialization of particular elements in our economy.—The rabbinate is overwhelmingly in favor of government ownership and operation of public utilities, railroads, and coal mines (38–I). Opposition to the socialization of these elements of our economy is voiced by only nine rabbis, with thirty-one expressing uncertainty. The percentages of those who are for public ownership and control of these vital elements in our economy in the Reform, Conservative, and Orthodox wings and the total group are respectively 75, 90, 81, and 81.

Just what proportion of the rabbinate approves of governmental ownership and control of the radio cannot be gathered from the returns. All that is known is that about one out of every two in the group as a whole, as already pointed out (31–I), finds the profit motive in the management of the radio industry detrimental to public taste and intelligence. Presumably many of these critics of individual ownership and control of the radio would sanction government ownership and some degree of control of this important instrument of public education.

Nor is it possible to determine what proportion of the rabbinate favors consumer cooperatives. Only one individual in the entire group believes that consumer cooperatives are detrimental to the country's prosperity, 175 rabbis failing to see any danger in them, the remainder being uncertain. Judging by the general temper of the group it may be presumed that the preponderance of those who are not opposed to cooperation actually favor it. Sentiment friendly to cooperation is most widespread among the Conservative rabbis and least among the Orthodox. The latter wing is about equally divided between those who fail to see a danger to prosperity in cooperatives and those who are uncertain (39–I).

Basic reorganization of society along socialistic lines.—Some light on the attitude of the entire group toward a basic reconstruction of our economy along socialistic lines is indicated by the following facts:

Of the entire group, 160 rabbis, or 77 per cent of the total, find *our industrial structure in contradiction with the democratic ideals of the American people* (30–I).

Of the entire group, 152 rabbis, or 71 per cent, deny that "public business enterprises are generally unsuccessful" (24–I).

Of the entire group, 150 rabbis, or 69 per cent, deny that "social control of industry will destroy personal initiative" (21–I).

Of the entire group, 130, or 60 per cent, deny that the abolition of private ownership in industry would result in an appreciable decline in the American standard of living (22–I).

It would thus seem that a majority of the rabbinate generally prefers a collectivist to an individualist economy. When the issue is reduced to socialism *vs.* capitalism, however, the collectivist sentiment of the rabbis begins to weaken. Only 95 rabbis of the total group are committed to the idea that "a socialist system would provide better opportunities for the average person to exercise worth-while personal initiative than the capitalist system" (36–I), with almost an equal number uncertain and the remainder implying a preference for capitalism. It should be noted that the pro-socialist bias is shared by 63 per cent of the Conservative wing as compared with 34 per cent in the Reform and 33 in the Orthodox wings who indicate a preference for socialism.

Perhaps a better indication of an individual's attitude toward capitalism would be his belief or denial that "economic planning for the good of our entire population is possible within the framework of capitalism (23–I). Judged by this criterion, only 43 rabbis in the group as a whole indicate an attitude of out-and-out rejection of capitalism. But 104 rabbis do not despair of the possibilities of capitalism. Complete rejection of capitalism on the ground of its inability to plan is favored by 16 per cent of the Reform rabbis, 27 per cent of the Conservative, and 16 per cent of the Orthodox.

An inquiry was made into what rabbis consider the degree of socialization which would constitute a sound policy for America (17–II). Only one of the 210 rabbis recommends "leaving our economic order much as it is," and only six fail to commit themselves to any definite economic policy but favor centralization of power to effect political changes in the hands of an honest, energetic, and intelligent leader. The large number who constitute the remainder are dissatisfied with the *status quo* and believe that changes must be stated in terms of program and not in terms of power concentration and leadership. Of the entire group, 73, or 35 per cent, recommend the policy of leaving individual ownership of the means of production intact but adding regulation of industry and provisions for social security; 85 rabbis, or 40 per cent, are committed to state ownership of basic industry and the banking system, and 45 rabbis, or 21 per cent, are content with nothing less than "the complete socialization of production and distribution."

On this question there are appreciable differences among the three wings. Considerably greater sentiment is expressed in favor of corrected capitalism[1] in the Reform and Orthodox wings than in the Conservative group. Fifty-five per cent of the Orthodox and 44 per cent of the Reform rabbis support this policy. But only 13 per cent of the Conservative rabbis are content with corrected capitalism. On the other hand, the sentiment sanctioning both partial and complete socialization is stronger in the Conservative group than in either of the two other wings. Complete or partial socialization of our economy is supported by 84 per cent of the Conservative, 53 per cent of the Reform, and 39 per cent of the Orthodox rabbis.

Some methods of economic reconstruction.—A farmer-labor party is held to be necessary in order to effect "needed changes in our political and social structure" by more than 50 per cent of the group as a whole (43–I). However, fewer than one in three Orthodox rabbis favor such a party.

There is less support for the employment of the class appeal than for the labor party (41–I). Only 43 per cent of the group

[1] See Item 17b, Section II, of questionnaire for what is meant by "corrected capitalism."

see no reason for rejecting methods calculated to set workers against the present order. The remainder are divided between those who do reject such methods and those who are uncertain, with the latter somewhat more numerous than the former. Hostility to the class approach is registered to the extent of 41 per cent in the Orthodox group and 18 per cent in the Conservative wing.

On the question of depriving the Supreme Court of its power to invalidate legislation enacted for the economic protection of the masses (42–I) in the group as a whole, the division is as follows: 38 per cent are in favor, 40 per cent are opposed, and 22 per cent are uncertain. Within the Reform and Orthodox wings more rabbis oppose than favor curtailing the power of the Supreme Court in the manner indicated. The reverse is true of the Conservative group.

The views of the rabbis on the function of education in social reconstruction will be discussed in Chapter IX.

Social Responsibility for Individual Welfare

Conservative rabbis are almost unanimous, and the members of the two other wings are preponderant, in their recognition that *the state is responsible for the maintenance of an adequate health level for the entire community* (37–I). Likewise, there is practical unanimity of opinion within all three wings that *insurance against sickness, accident, unemployment, death, and old age is a responsibility of the government* (15–II). Only one Reform rabbi, one Orthodox rabbi, and two Conservative rabbis feel that insurance against these contingencies should be "left to individuals interested." The issue was not whether insurance is a governmental responsibility but whether social insurance is a Federal or State responsibility. The preponderant sentiment of 182 rabbis favors the former.

While a majority of 133 members of the entire group favor *direct outlays for relief of the unemployed* (40–I), this majority is in no degree so great as the one which favors unemployment insurance. Only 63 per cent of the rabbinate favor increased outlays for unemployment relief as compared with the practical unanimity favoring unemployment insurance. Sentiment favoring added relief outlays is expressed to the extent of 73 per cent in the Conservative group and 52 per cent in the Orthodox.

The rabbinate rejects with virtual unanimity the view that "the provision for the helpless members of soicety should be the concern exclusively of private charities" (16–II). The point at issue is on the degree of responsibility of private charities and State institutions. The majority of the group as a whole favors provision primarily by the government, assisted by private charities. Those remaining are almost equally divided between supporters of the view that the responsibility is exclusively the government's and those who emphasize private institutions but provide for government participation.

Attitudes toward Labor

The sentiment in all the wings of the rabbinate is strongly pro-labor, most of all in the Conservative group and least of all in the Orthodox group. The preceding chapter pointed out the high proportion in favor of the proposition that the spirit of Judaism should generally impel one to identify himself with labor in its struggle against capital and disclosed an even greater rabbinic support of collective bargaining.

The Conservative and the Reform wings are virtually unanimous in denying that "trade unions do more harm than good to our industrial progress" (26–I). The Orthodox group rejects this view by a 78 per cent vote. The rejection of the notion that "most labor trouble is due to the work of radical agitators" is a little less overwhelming (25–I).

On the question of whether or not the use of injunctions should be barred from labor disputes there is, however, decidedly less agreement (28–I). A majority of the rabbinate favors elimination, but 38 rabbis are for the continued use of the injunction and an additional 58 suspend judgment. No appreciable difference with respect to this issue is to be noted between the Reform and the Conservative wings. But the Orthodox group is somewhat less pro-labor than either of the other two.

With respect to the sit-down strike[2] there is an even more pro-

---

[2] Decision of the Supreme Court was not known at the time the questionnaire was compiled.

nounced lack of agreement (29–I). The group as a whole is about equally divided among those who deem "the sit-down strike contrary to law and order," those who reject this view, and those who are uncertain, whereas the Orthodox, Reform, and Conservative wings show a 39, 38, and 22 per cent opposition respectively.

Composites of Positions on Each of the Three General Issues

The discussion so far has been integrated around the three general topics of economic reconstruction, social responsibility for individual welfare, and attitude toward labor. In order to determine how the various wings and the group as a whole divide on the large issue of each of these areas, composites of responses were made along the following lines: In connection with the first topic, Chart VI of the Appendix was used to evaluate responses as to whether they were critical of the capitalist economy and favorable toward the socialization of particular elements in that economy. This is termed a collectivistic attitude. Charts IV and V were used to classify responses under the issue of recognition *vs.* non-recognition of social responsibility for the welfare of the individual and the issue of pro-labor sympathies *vs.* anti-labor or no labor bias, respectively.

The percentages of responses in the various categories were as follows:

Recognition of social responsibility for the welfare of individuals:
Reform 81%, Conservative 89%,
Orthodox 77%, Total group 83%.

Non-recognition of social responsibility for individual welfare:
Reform 10%, Conservative 5%,
Orthodox 12%, Total group 9%.

Pro-labor sympathies:
Reform 69%, Conservative 75%,
Orthodox 55%, Total group 69%.

Anti-labor or no labor bias:
Reform 13%, Conservative 10%,
Orthodox 10%, Total group 12%.

Tendencies to economic collectivism:
Reform 58%, Conservative 71%,
Orthodox 43%, Total group 61%.

A number of conclusions seem to be warranted:

1. The rabbinate in all its wings is preponderantly in favor of social provisions for the welfare of individuals. Only a few are opposed to such provisions and a slightly larger number are uncertain about the wisdom of such measures.

2. The sentiment of the rabbinate is in the case of a large majority pro-labor. The extent is somewhat less than that favoring social provisions for individual welfare. With regard to the sit-down strike, however, those who oppose or those who question the use of this technique are as numerous as those who do not feel that the sit-down strike is contrary to law and order.[3]

3. The sentiment of the rabbinate is on the whole favorable to collectivism, though to a decidedly smaller extent than to labor and social welfare provisions. Were the analysis carried further, it might be shown that some rabbis make a distinction between mild collectivism and more radical forms of socialization. Opposition to collectivism and uncertainty with regard to it are most pronounced in the replies presented in the form of a choice between socialism and capitalism.

4. If a favorable attitude toward welfare provisions, the aspirations of labor, and collectivism be accepted as criteria of liberalism, the Conservative group would rank first in liberalism on all three counts, Reform second, and Orthodox last.

SECTION II

PATTERNS OF ATTITUDES CONCERNING ECONOMIC ISSUES

Of the three general issues in Section I, the two principal ones were concerned with economic reconstruction, by far the most important topic, and the related question of attitude toward labor. In Section II only items which entered into the composite stand on each of these two issues, as indicated in Charts V and VI of the Appendix, are interrelated under each issue separately.

Parallel to the treatment in Section I, under economic reconstruction of (a) evaluation of the existing capitalist order; (b) socialization of particular elements in our economy; (c) basic reorganization of society along socialistic lines; and (d) some methods

---

[3] The ruling of the Supreme Court makes this question purely academic.

of economic reconstruction; the first four topics of Section II, dealing with interrelation of responses directly related to the four of Section I just mentioned, will be: (1) evaluation of the capitalist order; (2) considerations in the choice of goals for economic reconstruction; (3) goals of economic reconstruction as related to public ownership of mines, railroads, and utilities; (4) methods of economic reconstruction.

The farmer-labor party was presented as one method of reconstruction and will be treated in a fifth topic (5), under differences between those who do and do not favor a farmer-labor party (one of the propositions entering into the composite on the first general issue of economic reconstruction); the final topic (6) will be concerned with interrelations among responses on the second general issue of attitude toward labor and among connections between views on various issues concerning labor.

Evaluation of the Capitalist Order

Differences concerning the merits of prevailing social arrangements rest on contrasting views concerning (*a*) the effects of economic individualism on human character, (*b*) capitalism's capacity to plan for the welfare of the masses, (*c*) the extent of opportunity afforded to the common man under capitalism and the connection between capitalism and culture, and (*d*) the effect of socialization on individual initiative. Section I presented the divisions of the rabbinate with respect to these topics of controversy. In this section an attempt will be made to study how a rabbi's attitude on one of the issues is likely to color his view about other issues.

Moral indictment of economic individualism.—The indictment of economic individualism on the ground that it degrades character and appeals to the most selfish instincts is an element in the rabbi's view with respect to capitalism's capacity to plan, the comparative merits of socialism and capitalism in affording opportunities to the average man, and the effects of socialization of industry on personal initiative.

Forty per cent of the 131 rabbis to whom the morality of our economy is unacceptable are nevertheless unwilling to believe that capitalism cannot be managed so as to result in general welfare. However, only one of the 28 rabbis who find nothing wrong with economic individualism rejects capitalism on the basis of its in-ability to plan for the general welfare.

A rabbi's attitude on the question of the morality of economic individualism is a fairly good indication of how he is likely to stand on the choice between capitalism and socialism. Of the 132 rabbis who find that economic individualism is morally degrading (33–I), 76 believe that socialism carries greater promise of opportunities for the average man than does capitalism (36–I). But only five of the 26 rabbis who fail to see any degrading effects in economic individualism show a preference for socialism. All in all, it would seem that a sizable proportion of the rabbinate would like to see capitalism purged of its individualistic excesses, but given the choice between capitalism as it is and socialism they would nevertheless prefer the former.

Irrespective of a rabbi's view concerning the moral effects of economic individualism, he is not likely to subscribe to the idea that social control of industry will destroy personal initiative. There is a greater likelihood, however, that this belief will be entertained by those who reject economic individualism. Of the 131 rabbis who find morally degrading effects in economic individualism (33–I), four hold that "social control of industry will destroy personal initiative" (21–I); such a view of the consequences of socialization of industry is shared by nine individuals among the 28 who dissent from the indictment of economic individualism.

Capitalism's planning capacity.—The belief that planning for the welfare of the entire population is impossible under capitalism is widely associated with the rejection of economic individualism for moral reasons and a preference for socialism on the ground that it would afford greater opportunities for the common man than capitalism.

Of the 43 rabbis who deny capitalism's ability to plan (23–I), 36 reject economic individualism (33–I). Hope in the possibilities of capitalism is no indication, however, of satisfaction with economic individualism. Of those 103 persons who feel that planning within the framework of capitalism is possible, 50 per cent nevertheless reject economic individualism.

Opportunities under capitalism and socialism.—A rabbi who prefers socialism (36–I) in the belief that this system would afford greater opportunities for initiative in the case of the common man, is extremely unlikely to view capitalism as essential to the interests of human culture (35–I). Only two of 95 individuals hold these views simultaneously. The absence of a preference for socialism on the grounds indicated, on the other hand, is associated by 14 out of 30 cases with a commitment to capitalism in the name of culture. Looking at the relation in the reverse order, the data show only two preferring socialism among 32 rabbis who find capitalism indispensable to culture, and 71 preferring socialism among the 99 respondents who deny an essential connection between culture and capitalism.

Effect of socialization of industry on personal initiative.—How important a factor consideration of the effect of socialization of industry on individual initiative is in the rabbi's view with respect to the moral effects of economic individualism and the connection between capitalism and culture will be realized from the following data:

(*a*) Of the 20 respondents who believe that "social control of industry will destroy personal initiative" (21–I), only four find economic individualism to have degrading effects upon character (33–I). Of the 150 religious leaders who deny the incompatibility of socialized industry with personal initiative, 106 reject economic individualism as morally degrading.

(*b*) Of the 20 rabbis who see socialization of industry as inimical to personal initiative (21–I), 11 believe that the decline of capitalism would endanger culture (35–I). None in this group denies the danger. Of the 149 who do not see any incompatibility between socialization of industry and personal initiative, 91 deny the essential connection between capitalism and culture and only 14 rabbis consider capitalism and culture as bound together.

Considerations in Choice of Goals for Economic Reconstruction

Results so far derived in this study have shown the extent to which varying arguments for and against capitalism go together in the minds of the rabbis. The next task is to consider how important these arguments are in the choice of a specific goal for economic reconstruction.

Convictions with respect to (*a*) the effect of economic individualism upon human character; (*b*) comparative opportunities for the common man under capitalism and socialism; and (*c*) the relation of capitalism to culture seem to be definitely connected with the rabbis' choices of goals for economic reconstruction.

(*a*) Commitment to a policy of partial or complete socialization of economic resources is several times as likely among those who ascribe morally degrading effects to economic individualism as in the group which denies the truth of this indictment. Close to 100 of the 132 rabbis who reject economic individualism (33–I) believe that either our essential industries and banking system should be socialized or that socialization should embrace the entire system of production and distribution (17–II). Such socialistic commitments are made by nine of 26 rabbis who do not find economic individualism degrading. The majority of the 17 who do not object to economic individualism on moral grounds are content with corrected capitalism in which provision is to be made for regulation of industry and social security. In contrast, only 28 individuals of those who reject economic individualism are content with corrected capitalism.

(*b*) A rabbi's concept of comparative opportunities for the individual under capitalism and socialism seems to be an even more important element than the moral appraisal of economic individualism in the rabbi's commitment to particular goals of economic reconstruction. Less than 10 per cent of those 93 rabbis who believe that socialism carries the possibilities of greater opportunities for initiative (36–I) are content with corrected capitalism (17–II). Virtually all others in this group set up either complete or partial socialization as a goal. Of the 30 individuals who deny the superiority of socialism, 21 are satisfied with regulated capitalism.

(*c*) Almost an equally important consideration in a rabbi's choice of a goal for economic reconstruction is the matter of the connection between capitalism and culture. Of the 31 rabbis who believe that the interests of human culture call for the preservation of capitalism (35–I), 24 favor corrected capitalism (17–II). Only 12 of the 99 who deny the necessary connection between capitalism and culture are committed to corrected capitalism, and virtually

all the others in this group favor either partial or complete socialization as a goal.

Goals of Economic Reconstruction as Related to Public Ownership
of Public Utilities, Railroads, and Mines (38–I)

A commitment to regulated capitalism is by no means an indication of opposition to public ownership. In fact, about 60 per
cent of those 73 individuals who are sympathetic toward corrected
capitalism support public ownership of utilities, mines, and railroads.

Methods of Economic Reconstruction

Nor is it surprising to find that there is considerable tendency
toward association of the left wing economic goals with radical
economic methods. The incidence of a favorable attitude toward
the employment of the class appeal and the utilization of a farmer-
labor party is more frequent among rabbis who are content with
partial socialization; it is also more usual among the latter than
among the advocates of corrected capitalism.

Few individuals among the 45 respondents who advocate complete socialization of production and distribution (17–II) object
to the *employment of the class appeal* (41–I). Only three rabbis
who are substantially committed to socialism believe that "methods
calculated to set workers against the present order should be rejected." But, fifteen of the 79 individuals who look toward
partial socialization as a goal, and almost half of the 73 rabbis
who are committed to the goal of corrected capitalism reject the
class appeal as a method of reconstruction. Why more than 50
per cent of those who wish to see capitalism preserved, though in
a corrected form, do not expressly object to the employment of
the class appeal can be explained either by the liberalism of the
rabbis, which makes them reluctant to take a definite stand on any
method, or on the assumption that they believe that the class
appeal should not be used to bring about drastic changes in the
economic order.

That a farmer-labor party is needed to bring about modifications
in the political and social structure (43–I) is maintained by 16
of the 71 individuals who are committed to corrected capitalism,

by 53 of the 83 who look toward a partially socialized economy, and by as many as 37 of the 45 who advocate no less than the complete socialization of production and distribution (17–II).

Differences Between Those Who Do and Do Not Favor a Farmer-Labor Party

The returns to the questionnaire make it possible to contrast the beliefs of the supporters and opponents of this political policy with respect to specific social issues and general outlook on the economic reorganization of society. The propositions on which opposing reactions toward a farmer-labor party will be compared fall under these categories: viewpoints on capitalism and socialism and attitudes toward the socialization of industry; attitude toward the employment of class appeal.

Viewpoints on capitalism and socialism.—There is widespread conviction among the supporters of the farmer-labor party that economic individualism has degraded human character. Among the 114 rabbis who favor a farmer-labor party (43–I), 88 find economic individualism morally objectionable (33–I), 4 do not find it so, and the remainder are uncertain. Among the 34 rabbis who reject the farmer-labor party, only 14 share in the indictment of economic individualism, 13 reject the indictment, and 7 are in doubt.

Though majorities of both the supporters and the opponents of the farmer-labor party either reject or question the view that the interest of human culture demands the preservation of capitalism, the majority is much the larger among the proponents. The view that the decline of capitalism would endanger human culture (35–I) is denied by 65, or 58 per cent, of the 113 proponents, and by 8, or 24 per cent, of the 33 opponents of the farmer-labor party (43–I). The interesting fact is that 48 individuals, or over 40 per cent of those who favor a farmer-labor party, are, nevertheless, either convinced or entertain the notion that capitalism may be necessary to the interests of culture.

That support of a farmer-labor party by no means indicates despair of the possibilities of capitalism is further illustrated by the fact that only 28 per cent of the 114 advocates of such a party (43–I) believe that planning for the general welfare is impossible under capitalism (23–I). Among the 33 rabbis who are hostile to a labor orientation in politics, only 12 per cent despair of capitalism's ability to plan.

While support of a farmer-labor party cannot be taken as a certain indication of socialist commitment, it can be regarded as a likely indication of such commitment. Of the 113 rabbis who support a farmer-labor party (43–I), 66 individuals, or 58 per cent, believe that socialism has more than capitalism has to offer the common man in terms of opportunities, and only 9 individuals deny the advantages of socialism (36–I). On the other hand, among the 34 who reject the idea, only 4 individuals prefer socialism.

Those who believe that socialization of industry would destroy personal initiative (21–I) constitute minorities among both proponents and opponents of a farmer-labor party (43–I). In the case of the proponents the bias against socialization is shared by 1 out of 20 individuals; among the opponents by 1 out of 4.

Out of every 10 individuals who support the farmer-labor party (43–I), 9 favor governmental ownership of utilities, railroads, and coal mines (38–I), as compared with 64 per cent who advocate governmental ownership and operation among those 33 persons who do not recognize the need for a farmer-labor party.

The proponents of a farmer-labor party differ considerably from the opponents with respect to goals of economic reconstruction. Among the 111 supporters (43–I), 16 individuals, or 14 per cent, favor regulated capitalism, 53 individuals, or 48 per cent, favor gradual socialization, and 37 individuals, or 33 per cent, favor complete socialization (17–II). Among the 32 persons who are not inclined toward a farmer-labor party, on the other hand, 22 individuals, or 69 per cent, favor regulated capitalism, 7 individuals, or 22 per cent, favor gradual and limited socialization, and only 2 individuals, or 6 per cent, favor complete socialization.

Attitude toward the employment of class appeal.—There is considerably less opposition to the use of class appeal for bringing about social change (41–I) among those who deem the farmer-labor party necessary than among those who do not (43–I). In the group of 110 who favor the farmer-labor party, 18 individuals, or 16 per cent, are in favor of "rejecting methods calculated to set workers against the present social order," 63 individuals, or 57 per cent, see nothing wrong with this method, and 29 individuals, or 26 per cent, question the wisdom of its employment. In the group of 33 rabbis who reject the farmer-labor party, 18 reject this method, and an additional 5 question its employment.

Interconnections Among Views on Various Issues
Concerning Labor

No matter how they may differ on other questions concerning labor, rabbis are agreed in their strong support of collective bargaining (27–I). Even thirteen respondents who affirm that "most labor trouble is due to the work of radical agitators" (25–I) are virtually agreed that rabbis should support the right to collective bargaining. Nor does a rabbi's view on whether the sit-down strike is contrary to law and order (29–I) seem to make a difference. To be noted also is the fact that both in the group of 115 rabbis who favor the elimination of injunctions in labor disputes (28–I) and in the group of 37 who are opposed to such change, the sentiment is predominantly in favor of the rabbi's support of collective bargaining.

Rabbinic support of collective bargaining is the only attitude which thus seems to be independent. A definite interconnection is to be noted with respect to the rabbi's attitude on other issues. Thus a rabbi who believed that most labor trouble is due to the work of radical agitators (25–I) is almost certain to view the sit-down strike as contrary to law and order (29–I). All thirteen individuals who see in labor unrest the work of agitators oppose the sit-down strike. But among those 177 religious leaders who reject this naïve view concerning the cause of labor unrest, only about one in every four definitely rejects the sit-down strike. Opposition to the elimination of injunctions in labor disputes (28–I) is greater proportionately among those who believe labor trouble to be due to the work of radical agitators than among those who do not.

The attitudes toward a sit-down strike (29–I) seem to be related in the minds of many rabbis to their attitudes on the issue of the elimination of the use of injunctions in labor disputes and vice versa (28–I). In the group of 68 opposed to the sit-down strike as contrary to law and order, the elimination of the use of injunctions has the support of only 24 individuals. But 45 of the 66 rabbis who do not view the sit-down strike as contrary to law and order favor the elimination of the injunction. Fully 51 per cent of those 37 respondents who are opposed to the elimination of the use of injunctions in labor disputes are also opposed to the employment of the sit-down strike, as compared with only one out of every five individuals who reject the sit-down strike in the group of 111 persons supporting the elimination of injunctions.

CHAPTER IX

RABBIS' VIEWS ON SOME ISSUES CONCERNING EDUCATION

THIS SECTION will present the division within the entire group and in the separate wings with regard to propositions related to each of four general issues in the field of education, and as a fifth topic will give composites of attitudes on each of the four issues. The issues in order of treatment are: social responsibility for education; control of teachers' opinions; employment of education in social reconstruction; provision for religious training in the public schools; composites of attitudes on each of these four issues.

Social Responsibility for Education

That at least secondary education should be made freely available to youth is virtually the unanimous opinion of the entire group of the rabbinate who are the subjects of this study. Only six Reform rabbis and one Orthodox rabbi believe society fully discharges its duty in offering elementary education to young people. No Conservative rabbi would limit social responsibility merely to the elementary school. Approximately 2 out of 3 of the Orthodox and Reform, and 4 out of 5 Conservative rabbis believe that society should freely provide for its youth facilities for obtaining a college education. The remainder of the respondents conceive the responsibility of society discharged with provision for free secondary education (19–II).

More than 90 per cent of the group as a whole believe* that society's responsibility is not limited to the education of children and youth but that it should also include the education of adults. Only one individual in the Conservative and three in the Reform wing reject the view that "It is the obligation of society to conduct a systematic program of adult education centering on the major economic and social problems of today" (50–I).

Sentiment favoring State equalization of educational opportunities in different communities is virtually unanimous. Of the 216 rabbis who responded to the questionnaire, only one dissents from and two are uncertain with regard to the proposition: "Where a community is incapable of providing adequate educational facilities for young people, the State should appropriate funds for that purpose" (51–I). Only slightly less conclusive is the sentiment of 198 rabbis favorable to the "apportionment of Federal funds for the improvement of education throughout the nation" (52–I).

In the group as a whole, 199 rabbis oppose economies in education, even in times of crises, except as a last resort. In the Conservative group the attitude against such economies is literally unanimous (56–I).

Control of Teachers' Opinions

Of the 216 rabbis in the group as a whole, 189 view "laws demanding special loyalty oaths from teachers as a threat to good teaching" (44–I). In the Conservative wing none dissents and only two individuals are in doubt. Aversion to special loyalty oaths within the Reform wing, though overwhelming, is somewhat less widespread than in the Conservative group. It is least evident in the Orthodox group, in which it is shared by 21 rabbis, or 64 per cent of the membership.

In the same spirit the total group is strongly opposed to the proposition: "Licenses to teach in the public school should be refused to socialists" (46–I). Although there is virtual unanimity in favor of rejection of this view in both the Conservative and the Reform groups, seven Orthodox rabbis either favor the barring of socialist teachers or are uncertain with regard to the matter.

Opposition to a policy of withholding teaching positions from known communists is, however, considerably less widespread than opposition to anti-socialist discrimination. In the group as a whole, 72 rabbis either favor the dismissal of communist teachers or are uncertain. There is little difference between the Reform and Conservative wings on this issue. In both groups about two out of every three rabbis are opposed to dismissal, about one out of every five is uncertain, and the remainder favor dismissal. In the Orthodox group, however, only 14 of the 32 rabbis object to the dismissal of communist teachers, with the remainder about equally divided between uncertainty and belief in the dismissal of communists (47–I).

Only 22 persons in the rabbinate as a whole are opposed to the organization of teachers along the line of labor unions; 176 definitely disclaim such opposition. Opposition to unionization of teachers is most pronounced among the Orthodox rabbinate, in which wing ten are opposed to or uncertain about unionization of teachers (45–I).

Employment of Education in Social Reconstruction

The rabbinate as a whole is virtually unanimous in favoring the employment of education as a means of developing social intelligence. Another indication of this is the virtually unanimous support of a program of systematic adult education centering on current social and economic problems, as noted previously.

The responses of the rabbis to the direct question as to what they believe to be the social objectives of education throw light on the rabbis' social philosophy of education. No Conservative rabbi, only one Reform, and three Orthodox believe that education should "remain neutral with respect to the problems of social reconstruction." The support in the rabbinate of the view that public education should help to "preserve our inherited institutions" is no stronger. Only six rabbis support the socially "left" view that public education should "lead students to identify themselves with social movements that aim at the creation of a collectivist commonwealth." Eschewing both extremes, 200 rabbis in the group as a whole believe that public education should aim at "stimulating students to think about the problems of social reconstruction." The proportions who share this view in the Conservative and Reform wings are almost identical, each bordering on unanimity. This attitude is shared, however, by only about three out of every four Orthodox rabbis (18–II).

That a sound educational policy demands the social encouragement of teachers "to fight against sub-standard conditions in the home" is a conviction shared by 89 per cent of the group as a whole (55–I).

The rabbinate as a whole is overwhelmingly opposed to compulsory military training in schools and colleges. In the entire group, 192 rabbis reject the view that compulsory military training is in the best interests of the country. Only one individual believes that it is. The chief differences among the wings are indicated by the ratios of those who are in doubt about the merits of compulsory military training: Reform, 9 out of 104; Conservative, 3 out of 76; Orthodox, 8 out of 33. With the few exceptions noted, the remainder of the rabbis in the three wings are opposed to compulsory military training (49–I).

Provision for Religious Training in the Public Schools

Of the group as a whole, 71 per cent view the designation of periods during school hours for religious instruction as contrary to the principles of non-sectarianism in the public schools. Opposition to such practice is registered to the extent of 75 per cent in the Reform wing, 70 per cent in the Conservative wing, and 64 per cent in the Orthodox wing (53–I).

Equally widespread is the opposition to the "inclusion of Bible reading in the public school curriculum" (54–I). With regard to this proposition, a number of interesting differences between the Reform wing and the two remaining wings can be noted. Only in the Reform group is the opposition to the inclusion of the Bible in the curriculum greater than that to the designation of special hours for religious instruction. In the Conservative wing an attitude of opposition to the inclusion of the Bible is maintained by a bare majority; in the Orthodox wing by somewhat less than a majority. In both the Orthodox and the Conservative wings opposition to the inclusion of the Bible in the curriculum is less marked than to the designation of special hours for religious instruction; the figures are 45 and 57 per cent for the first proposition and 64 and 70 per cent for the second proposition.

As has been pointed out in Chapter VI, the rabbinate as a whole, and especially the Conservative and Reform wings, is overwhelmingly opposed to *limiting instruction in such a way as to safeguard belief in the literal truths of the Bible* (48–I).

Composites of Attitudes on Each of the Four Issues

Charts VII, VIII, IX, and X of the Appendix were employed, respectively, in appraising the responses of the rabbis with respect to attitudes on the scope of social responsibility of education, control of teachers' opinions, employment of education for socially reconstructive ends, and provision for religious training within the framework of the public school.

With respect to the concept of social responsibility for education implied in the responses, the results obtained are given below.

Issue	Position	Reform	Conservative	Orthodox	All Rabbis
Concept of	*N. I.	8%	4%	5%	6%
Social Respon-	Broad	89	96	92	92
sibility	Narrow	3	0	3	2
Control of	N. I.	10	9	21	11
Teachers'	Unfavorable				
Opinions	attitude	82	87	64	81
	Favorable				
	attitude	8	4	15	8
Employment of	N. I.	7	5	10	7
Education in	Favorable				
Social Recon-	attitude	91	95	76	90
struction	Unfavorable				
	attitude	2	0	14	3
Provision for	N. I.	10	19	19	15
Religious	Unfavorable				
Education	attitude	83	71	54	74
	Favorable				
	attitude	7	10	27	11

* N. I. = No Indication.

On the basis of the findings above certain conclusions may be drawn:

1. Rabbis in all wings with virtual unanimity favor the broadening of social responsibility and governmental support of education.

2. Equally overwhelming in the rabbinate is the opinion that the aim of education is to develop social intelligence to the end of social reconstruction. Majorities in the Reform and Conservative wings on this view are much greater than in the Orthodox wing.

3. There is somewhat greater disagreement among the rabbis regarding control of teachers' opinions. Even in this respect the sentiment is preponderantly opposed to control of teachers' opin-

ions and to discrimination against teachers who hold certain
unpopular views. Conservative and Reform rabbis are almost
unanimous in their opposition, while the Orthodox simply show
a large majority opposed to control.

4. Rabbis are divided most on the questions concerning provisions for religious training within the framework of public education. Nevertheless, the tendency in the rabbinate as a whole is
in a large majority of cases against such provision. The sentiment
opposed to religion in public education is strongest in the Reform
and weakest in the Orthodox wing. The proportion in the Conservative wing is closer to that in the Reform than to the ratio in
the Orthodox wing.

SECTION II

PATTERNS OF THOUGHT CONCERNING EDUCATION

The issues in Section I on which there were relatively large differences among the wings were control of teachers' opinions; employment of education in social reconstruction; provision for
religious training in the public school. In the present section interrelations of propositions connected with each of the above general
issues, either as possible explanatory factors or as direct contributors to the composite stands on the issues, will be taken up. The
three issues will be treated in the order outlined above.

Interrelation of Attitudes on Some of the Propositions
Concerning Control of Teachers' Opinions

It is interesting to note the relation of the rabbis' attitudes to
loyalty oaths and their attitudes on the issues of expulsion of
communist teachers. The preponderant majority views loyalty
oaths as a threat to good teaching. Further, as might be expected
from Chart VIII, it appears that opponents of anti-communist discrimination are somewhat more likely to be opposed to special
loyalty oaths than are proponents of anti-communist discrimination. Of the rabbis favoring dismissal of communist teachers
(47–I), 17, or about 71 per cent, nevertheless view the loyalty oath
as a threat to good teaching (44–I). The special oath for teachers
is viewed as a threat to good teaching by 94 per cent of the large

group of 141 who are opposed to anti-communist discrimination.

Again, in relating opinion on loyalty oaths (44–I) to that on organization of teachers in labor unions (45–I), attitudes opposed to control of teachers' opinions seem to go together. One hundred eighty-nine rabbis object to loyalty oaths for teachers. Of this group, 87 per cent would permit teachers to organize in labor unions. Conversely, of the 176 rabbis who take the latter view, 93 per cent believe that loyalty oaths are a threat to good teaching.

Relations Between Rabbis' Concepts of the Aim of Education and Their Views on the Goals of Social Reconstruction

No matter with what goal for social reconstruction the rabbi identifies himself, whether it be corrected capitalism, limited socialization, or complete socialization of production and distribution, he very strongly tends to see the aim of education as the development of social intelligence, as distinguished from propaganda either to the "right" or to the "left." However, the rabbis' commitment to certain of the concepts of educational aims seems to be a good indication of their social commitments. Eight rabbis who uphold educational neutrality or support of existing institutions as goals of education (18–II) are unanimous in their pro-capitalist bias (17–II). Among the 196 who uphold social intelligence as an educational aim, 83 are committed to limited socialization and 42 support the idea of thoroughgoing socialization of the present economy.

The returns fail to indicate any relation between the rabbis' concepts of the goals of education and their position on the question of whether the preservation of capitalism is necessary in the interest of human culture. All four rabbis who favor educational neutrality (18–II) either question or deny the *organic connection between capitalism and human culture* (35–I). All three who would make the preservation of inherited institutions the task of education are unconvinced of the need for the preservation of capitalism in the interests of human culture. On the other hand, among the 198 individuals who would employ education to the end of developing social intelligence, 16 per cent are convinced that capitalism is necessary to human culture, and 37 per cent are uncertain.

Interconnections of Attitudes Toward Religious Instruction
Within the Framework of the Public School and Stands
on Related Issues

Only fifteen of 213 rabbis who replied to the questionnaire are against such teaching in the public schools as might *shake the student's faith in the literal truth of the Bible* (48–I). What distinguishes this group from the large majority who are opposed to the placing of religious restrictions upon teaching as contradicting the principle of non-sectarianism of the public school (53–I)?

Among those who favor the imposition of religious restriction upon teaching material which might result in the student's doubting or questioning the Bible as containing the word of God there is a greater tendency to reject the opinion that the Biblical version of creation is a myth (7–I); view the actual occurrence of the miracles recorded in the Bible as essential to Judaism (2–I); view the Torah as an adequate guide for the moral perplexities of today (8–I).

CHAPTER X

RABBIS' VIEWS ON SOME OF THE ISSUES CONCERNING CIVIL LIBERTIES

SECTION I

CONCEPTS, OPINIONS, AND ATTITUDES

THIS SECTION will present the rabbinate's concept of the scope of civil liberties; opinion on the exclusion from the United States of communist and fascist agitators; attitude toward criticism of the Constitution; views on censorship; and their composite liberal *vs.* anti-liberal attitude on the general issue of civil liberties.

Scope of Civil Liberties

From what groups and under what conditions would the rabbis withhold freedom of speech? The questionnaire centered the inquiry on communists, fascists, advocates of violent seizure of governmental powers, advocates of disobedience among the armed forces of the nation, strike agitators, advocates of disobedience of mobilization orders, and critics of fundamental institutions. The rabbis were asked under what conditions they would deny members of each group freedom of speech—always, never, during periods of social and economic crises, during war times (2–III).

Table XVI shows the percentages of the three wings and the entire rabbinate who are opposed to withholding freedom of speech from the groups mentioned under any and all circumstances. In Table XVII are given the percentages of those who would deny freedom of speech under all circumstances. Table XVIII indicates the percentages of those who favor withholding freedom of speech in times of war; Table XIX, in times of social and economic crisis. Table XX shows percentages of those who favor withholding freedom of speech either always or in the special instance of war or social and economic crises.

Certain conclusions seem to be warranted on the basis of the tabular data.

TABLE XVI

PERCENTAGE IN RABBINIC WINGS AND THE ENTIRE RABBINATE OF THOSE WHO ARE
UNCONDITIONALLY OPPOSED TO WITHHOLDING FREEDOM OF
SPEECH FROM PARTICULAR GROUPS

| | PERCENTAGE IN RABBINIC WING | | | |
Group	Reform	Conservative	Orthodox	Entire Rabbinate
Critics of Constitution	89.8%	85.7%	75.8%	86.2%
Critics of fundamental institutions	88.0	89.6	66.7	85.3
Communists	75.9	76.6	33.3	69.7
Strike agitators	75.9	76.6	27.3	68.8
Fascists	68.5	64.9	30.3	61.4
Advocates of general strike	66.7	63.6	30.3	60.1
Advocates of disobedience of mobilization orders ..	62.0	58.4	15.1	53.6
Advocates of disobedience among armed forces	68.3	50.3	9.1	53.0
Advocates of violent seizure of governmental power ..	37.0	35.1	6.1	31.7

1. Devotion to the principle of freedom is widespread in Reform and Conservative wings. If the results for the different advocates are combined, about two out of every three Conservative and

TABLE XVII

PERCENTAGE IN RABBINIC WINGS AND THE ENTIRE RABBINATE OF THOSE WHO FAVOR
ABSOLUTE DENIAL OF FREEDOM OF SPEECH TO PARTICULAR GROUPS

| | PERCENTAGE IN RABBINIC WINGS | | | |
Group	Reform	Conservative	Orthodox	Entire Rabbinate
Advocates of violent seizure of governmental power .	40.7%	35.1%	54.5%	40.8%
Advocates of disobedience among armed forces	24.1	24.7	54.5	28.9
Fascists	8.3	10.4	15.1	10.1
Advocates of disobedience of mobilization orders ..	6.5	6.5	18.2	8.3
Advocates of general strike	11.1	2.6	9.1	7.8
Communists	2.8		6.0	2.3
Strike agitators	2.8	1.3	3.0	2.3
Critics of the Constitution	.9			.4
Critics of fundamental institutions				

Reform rabbis favor unqualified freedom of speech for the average unpopular advocacy listed in the questionnaire, about one out of four favors either unqualified denial of freedom of speech or denial of freedom under the special circumstances of war or crises, and only one out of ten favors unqualified denial of freedom of

TABLE XVIII

PERCENTAGE IN RABBINIC WINGS AND THE ENTIRE RABBINATE OF THOSE WHO FAVOR
WITHHOLDING FREEDOM OF SPEECH FROM PARTICULAR GROUPS
IN TIME OF WAR ONLY

Group	PERCENTAGE IN RABBINIC WINGS			
	Reform	Conservative	Orthodox	Entire Rabbinate
Advocates of disobedience of mobilization orders ..	17.6%	18.2%	42.4%	21.6%
Advocates of disobedience among armed forces	14.8	23.4	15.1	17.9
Advocates of general strike	7.4	14.2	24.2	12.3
Strike agitators	6.5	7.8	24.2	9.6
Communists	7.4	6.5	15.1	8.2
Fascists	5.6	7.8	15.1	7.8
Critics of the Constitution	3.7	5.2	15.1	6.0
Critics of fundamental institutions	2.8	2.6	12.1	4.1
Advocates of violent seizure of governmental power .	.9	3.9	9.1	3.2

TABLE XIX

PERCENTAGE IN RABBINIC WINGS AND THE ENTIRE RABBINATE OF THOSE WHO FAVOR
WITHHOLDING FREEDOM OF SPEECH FROM PARTICULAR GROUPS DURING
PERIODS OF SOCIAL AND ECONOMIC CRISES ONLY

Group	PERCENTAGE IN RABBINIC WINGS			
	Reform	Conservative	Orthodox	Entire Rabbinate
Advocates of violent seizure of governmental powers .	13.0%	18.2%	18.2%	15.6%
Strike agitators	9.3	5.2	39.4	12.4
Fascists	10.2	9.1	27.3	12.4
Advocates of general strike	6.5	10.4	30.3	11.5
Communists	7.4	9.1	27.3	11.0
Advocates of disobedience of mobilization orders ..	4.6	6.5	15.1	6.9
Advocates of disobedience among armed forces	4.6	1.3	12.1	4.6
Critics of fundamental institutions	1.8	1.3	15.1	3.6
Critics of the Constitution	.9	3.6	3.0	2.2

speech to the average advocacy. Among the Orthodox rabbis the sentiment favoring freedom of speech is, however, considerably less widespread. In this wing about one in six favors unqualified withholding of freedom of speech to the average advocacy, about

TABLE XX

PERCENTAGE IN RABBINIC WINGS AND THE ENTIRE RABBINATE OF THOSE WHO FAVOR
WITHHOLDING FREEDOM OF SPEECH FROM PARTICULAR GROUPS EITHER
ABSOLUTELY OR IN TIME OF WAR OR DURING PERIODS
OF SOCIAL AND ECONOMIC CRISES*

	PERCENTAGE IN RABBINIC WINGS			
Group	*Reform*	*Conservative*	*Orthodox*	*Entire Rabbinate*
Advocates of violent seizure of governmental power .	54.6%	57.2%	81.8%	59.6%
Advocates of disobedience among armed forces	43.5	49.4	81.7	51.4
Advocates of disobedience of mobilization orders ..	28.7	31.2	75.7	36.8
Advocates of general strike	25.0	27.2	63.6	31.7
Fascists	24.1	27.3	57.5	30.3
Strike agitators	18.6	14.3	66.6	24.3
Communists	17.6	15.6	48.4	22.0
Critics of the Constitution	5.5	8.8	18.1	8.7
Critics of fundamental institutions	4.6	3.9	27.2	7.8

* The percentages in this table were obtained by adding the percentages in Tables XVII, XVIII, and XIX.

three in five favor either withholding freedom of speech under all circumstances or during war or economic crisis, and only one out of three is unqualifiedly opposed to withholding freedom of speech.

2. The order in which advocates of various programs could expect support from the rabbis is practically the same for all wings of the rabbinate. First in order of support of their right of free speech are the critics of the Constitution and of fundamental American institutions. Close to six out of every seven rabbis in the group as a whole would under no condition deny freedom of speech to such critics, and practically no rabbis favor always withholding freedom of speech from them. The right of communists and of strike agitators to freedom of speech also finds strong support in the rabbinate in general, though by

no means as strong as the support accorded to critics of the Constitution and fundamental institutions. Somewhat less sympathy is shown to fascists than to communists, and to advocates of a general strike than to strike agitators in general. Even in the case of fascists, those absolutely opposed to denying them free speech are six times as numerous as those who would always deny them freedom of speech; those committed to freedom of speech for advocates of a general strike are about eight times as numerous as those who would always withhold that right from them. The right to freedom of speech for advocates of violent seizure of power finds less support than that of any other group. The rabbis who would always deny freedom of speech to this group exceed those who would always uphold this right. Comparatively little support is given by rabbis to advocates of disobedience of mobilization orders and of disobedience among the armed forces of the nation.

3. The exigencies of war as a reason for withholding freedom of speech are recognized by sizable groups of rabbis only with respect to advocates of disobedience among the armed forces and of disobedience of mobilization orders. Next in order in times of war are advocates of a general strike and strike agitators. These groups are followed by the communists and fascists. Only a negligible proportion of the rabbis see in war a particular reason for depriving critics of the Constitution or of fundamental institutions of the right of freedom of speech. There are even fewer rabbis who believe that war is a reason for refusing free speech to advocates of violent seizure of governmental power. Though surprising at first, this becomes intelligible in view of the fact that a large proportion of the rabbinate would forbid freedom of speech to advocates of violent seizure of power, as a general principle and under all circumstances.

4. Social and economic crisis as a reason for withholding freedom of speech from advocates of violent seizure of governmental power is given by a larger group of rabbis than from advocates of any other program. Comparatively large groups of rabbis also favor the denial of freedom of speech during periods of crisis to strike agitators, fascists, advocates of a general strike, and communists. Emergencies of social and economic crises are recog-

nized as a reason for refusing freedom of speech to advocates of disobedience of mobilization orders or disobedience among the armed forces of the nation by only small numbers of rabbis. The number of rabbis who would withhold freedom of speech in times of crisis from critics of the Constitution or of fundamental institutions is even smaller (2–III).

Exclusion from the United States of Advocates of Communism and Fascism

Of the 213 in the entire group who indicated their opinions on the issue of exclusion from the United States of advocates of communism, 144 are opposed, and the remainder are about equally divided between those who favor such action and those who are uncertain. Opposition to the exclusion of advocates of communism is strongest in the Conservative and weakest in the Orthodox wing (58–I).

Sentiment favoring exclusion of advocates of fascism is stronger in all the wings of the rabbinate than that favoring exclusion of advocates of communism (59–I). Yet 111 rabbis in the group as a whole are against the exclusion of those who wish to establish a fascist government. Tolerance toward the advocates of fascism is somewhat weaker among the Reform and Orthodox rabbis than among the Conservative rabbis, among whom slightly more than one in every two is opposed to the exclusion of fascist agitators.

Patriotism and the Constitution

Reform and Conservative rabbis reject with virtual unanimity the view that criticism of the Constitution is an unpatriotic act (57–I). This liberal attitude is shared by 26 of the 32 Orthodox rabbis.

Censorship of the Cinema, Art, and Literature

Of the 216 rabbis in the group as a whole who express an opinion on the issue, 139 deny that the interests of public morality demand censorship of the cinema, art, and literature (60–I). The remainder are equally divided between those who favor censorship and those who are uncertain. Opposition to censorship is decidedly greater in the ranks of Conservative and Reform rabbis than among the Orthodox rabbis. About 70 per cent of the first two wings and only 30 per cent in the last wing are in outright opposition to censorship. The dominant view in Orthodoxy with respect to the imposition of restrictions on the cinema, art, and literature is uncertainty.

*Composite Attitude on the General Issue
of Civil Liberties*

The responses of rabbis to the particular propositions concerning civil liberties were re-examined with a view to determining the degree of liberalism revealed in them by the various wings and by the group as a whole. Chart XI of the Appendix was employed as a basis for classification of responses. The following choices on the several items were taken as being the liberal responses, namely, unqualified opposition to denying freedom of speech to advocates of any "ism," opposition to exclusion from the United States of believers in unpopular forms of social organization, rejection of the view that criticism of the Constitution is unpatriotic, and opposition to censorship. Expression of the opposite views was taken as indicating an anti-liberal attitude toward civil liberties. This classification seems to be justified on the basis of the traditional meaning of liberalism. Replies indicating a willingness to defend the right of free speech of the upholders of various advocates only under certain conditions were not taken into account in this comparison.

Issue	Position	Reform	Conservative	Orthodox	Total
Civil Liberties	Liberal	68%	69%	38%	64%
	Non-liberal ...	13	11	18	13
	Uncertain	19	20	44	23

It thus appears that a sizable proportion of the rabbinate shows a noncommittal, uncertain, or qualified attitude on the issues of civil liberties. These attitudes are shared when all issues are considered by about one in every five Reform and Conservative rabbis and by almost one in every two Orthodox rabbis. It also seems that among those who have definite and unqualified attitudes the liberal sentiment is considerably stronger than the anti-liberal. Among the Conservative rabbinate the liberal sentiment is about six times as strong as the anti-liberal; among the

Reform rabbis it is five times as strong; and among the Orthodox rabbis twice as strong.

SECTION II

PATTERNS OF THOUGHT WITH RESPECT TO SOME ISSUES
ON CIVIL LIBERTIES

*Interconnections Between the Positions of Rabbis on Several
of the Propositions Concerning Civil Liberties*

How do the groups of rabbis who respectively favor and oppose the exclusion of communists from the United States compare with regard to their positions on the issues of exclusion of fascists from the United States and the denial of freedom of speech to communists?

It appears that in their approach to the question of exclusion of certain groups from the United States the rabbis take into consideration not only the abstract principle of civil liberties but also the ideas for which the group in question stands. Thus many rabbis make a distinction between the advocates of communism and the advocates of fascism. The distinction is almost exclusively in favor of the former. Among the 142 who oppose the exclusion from the United States of the advocates of communism (58–I), 20 favor the exclusion of advocates of fascism (59–I) and 12 are uncertain. In contrast, of the 111 rabbis who oppose the exclusion of advocates of fascism, only one favors the exclusion of advocates of communism and the remainder are opposed. Further, among the 37 rabbis who favor the exclusion of communists, one is opposed to and one is uncertain about the exclusion of fascists. Of the 62 rabbis who favor the exclusion of fascists, 20 are opposed to and 7 are uncertain about the exclusion of communists.

The figures indicate a definite relation between the position of rabbis on the question of exclusion of communists from the United States (58–I) and their position with regard to the denial, non-denial, and conditions of denial of freedom of speech to communists (2–III). Among the 35 rabbis who would exclude from the United States those who seek to establish a communist order, 5 would always deny them freedom of speech and 14 others would deny them freedom of speech during social or economic crises or in time of war. Thus more than 50 per cent of those who favor the exclusion of communists from the United States would deny them freedom of speech either under all or under certain conditions. Among the 132 rabbis who are opposed to the exclusion of the individuals who seek to establish a communist order in the United States, however, there are none who favor complete denial of freedom of speech to communists and only 14 per cent who favor denial of freedom of speech under conditions of war or of social and economic crisis.

On the other hand, all five individuals who are for complete denial of freedom of speech to communists favor exclusion of communist advocates from the United States. But only 11 per cent of the 150 individuals who are opposed to the denial of freedom of speech to communists under any circumstances favor the exclusion of advocates of communism.

CHAPTER XI

RABBIS' POSITIONS ON THE ISSUES OF PEACE AND INTERNATIONALISM

BECAUSE of the fateful events which have occurred since 1937, when the rabbis indicated the views which are presented and analyzed in this study, it is perhaps necessary to state briefly the general attitudes on war and peace, international relations and America's relation to the world, and related matters which then prevailed among large sections of the American population.

In 1937 the prevailing mood of the American people was still predominantly isolationist. This, despite the rising tide of authoritarian powers and the aggressive policy of Germany, Italy, and Japan. The view that Germany and the Allies were equally culpable in bringing about World War I was widespread. America's entry into the war was attributed by many people to British propaganda and the machinations of financial groups with vested interests in a British victory. *Road to War* (America 1914–1917) by Millis, documenting the propaganda which preceded America's entry into the war, was a best seller. During the middle 'thirties, the revelations of senatorial committees concerning the munitions industries and the involvement of financial groups in international matters had become headlines.

A Gallup poll conducted in April, 1937, on the question, "Do you think it was a mistake for the U. S. to enter the World War?" showed a 71 per cent vote in the affirmative. A Gallup poll conducted two years earlier had revealed that the proposed Lundeen Amendment placing the right to declare war directly in the hands of the electorate had the support of 75 per cent of those polled. Though its provisions were criticized in some circles as tending to benefit the Franco side in Spain, and Japan in its aggression against China, the Neutrality Act of 1935 enjoyed wide support. Large sections of college youth were participating in peace strikes

149

and subscribing to the Oxford Oath "not to support any war."

In 1937 the recognition by the liberals of the menace of fascism had not yet crystallized into the conviction that its power must be broken by the united military might of the democracies. The main front in the defense of America against fascism was in America, not in Europe or Asia. Many liberals feared that war even if invoked in the name of democracy would result in democracy's destruction.

The clergy, Christian and Jewish, helped to fashion these popular opinions. Some of the views of the clergy on questions relating to war and peace can be gathered from a result of a poll conducted by Protestant and Jewish religious leaders in 1936. About 100,000 Protestant clergymen of various denominations and Jewish rabbis were polled, and 12,854 responses were tabulated. Reproduced below is the distribution of opinions with regard to the questions raised, for the group as a whole, for a few Protestant denominations, for the seminary students, and for the rabbis.

SUMMARY OF REPLIES FROM 12,854 CLERGYMEN
ON QUESTIONS OF WAR AND PEACE

1. In seeking to protect the lives of its citizens in foreign lands and on the high seas, should the United States Government refrain under all circumstances from resort to war and always restrict itself to pacific methods?

	Total	*Percentage Answering*	
		Yes	*No*
Total of all responding	12,854	69	19
Presbyterian, U.S.A. (North)	1,465	64	22
Methodist Episcopal (North)	1,411	77	11
Lutheran	1,302	57	31
Protestant Episcopal	878	56	30
Seminary students	540	82	10
Jewish	158	80	11

2. Do you favor armed action on the part of the members of the League of Nations against a nation which the Assembly of the League pronounces guilty of armed invasion of another country, if public opinion, diplomatic pressure, and economic embargo prove inadequate as deterrents?

	Total	*Percentage Answering*	
		Yes	*No*
Total of all responding	12,854	36	46
Presbyterian, U.S.A. (North)	1,465	39	42
Methodist Episcopal (North)	1,411	34	46
Lutheran	1,302	36	44
Protestant Episcopal	878	48	36
Seminary students	540	21	57
Jewish	158	40	47

3. If all obligation to participate in the use of armed sanctions against an aggressor nation were removed from the Covenant, would you favor membership in the League of Nations by the United States?

	Total	Percentage Answering Yes	No
Total of all responding	12,854	65	22
Presbyterian, U.S.A. (North)	1,465	66	21
Methodist Episcopal (North)	1,411	74	14
Lutheran	1,302	35	50
Protestant Episcopal	878	71	16
Seminary students	540	79	10
Jewish	158	77	13

4. Do you favor participation by the United States in a world economic conference for the purpose of formulating a procedure by which the superior economic advantages now enjoyed by certain nations may be shared more equitably with less fortunate peoples?

	Total	Percentage Answering Yes	No
Total of all responding	12,854	89	5
Presbyterian, U.S.A. (North)	1,465	88	5
Methodist Episcopal (North)	1,411	94	3
Lutheran	1,302	78	12
Protestant Episcopal	878	92	4
Seminary students	540	94	3
Jewish	158	92	2

5. Are you personally prepared to state that it is your present purpose not to sanction any future war or participate as an armed combatant?

	Total	Percentage Answering Yes	No
Total of all responding	12,854	56	31
Presbyterian, U.S.A. (North)	1,465	46	38
Methodist Episcopal (North)	1,411	68	21
Lutheran	1,302	35	52
Protestant Episcopal	878	39	48
Seminary students	540	74	15
Jewish	158	59	28

6. Do you favor a nation-wide series of religious services in which individuals who have reached a mature decision not to sanction or participate in any future war may simultaneously proclaim this deep conviction?

	Total	Percentage Answering Yes	No
Total of all responding	12,854	64	19
Presbyterian, U.S.A. (North)	1,465	58	22
Methodist Episcopal (North)	1,411	75	11
Lutheran	1,302	40	41
Protestant Episcopal	878	47	31
Seminary students	540	80	9
Jewish	158	75	11

In general, the opinions of the rabbis on questions of war and peace seem to be divided along lines similar to those of the Protestant clergy.

SECTION I

ANALYSIS OF POSITIONS

This section will present the views of the rabbinate on the causes of war; support of, nonsupport of, and opposition to war; defense of American business interests abroad; methods of attaining peace; and intercession by the United States government in behalf of Jews and other minorities in Europe.

Causes of War

Human pugnacity, capitalist institutions, imperialist competition for markets, fascist militarism, missionary zeal of the communists, private manufacture and sale of munitions, and loans of foreign powers are commonly considered among the main causes of war. The rabbis were asked to indicate which of these they consider major factors in bringing about war, which minor, and which as no factors at all (4–III).

In order to compare the relative importance assigned by the group as a whole and the three separate wings to the various causes, a system of weighting was devised in which a value of 1 was assigned to the appraisal "major factor," $\frac{1}{2}$ to "minor factor," and 0 to "no factor." To obtain the group estimate, the sum of individual weights was divided by number of responses.

It is obvious that the group score of about .50 for a particular factor indicates that on the average this factor is estimated as a minor one, that as the group score approaches 1.00 the average estimate for the factor approaches "major" importance, and that as the group score approaches 0 the average estimate approaches the estimate of the "no factor." The results are tabulated in Table XXI. From this table it appears that, in the main, the order of importance attributed to the several factors is the same for the three wings and the entire rabbinate; that there is agreement among the three wings of the rabbinate in placing competition for markets as the most important factor making for war, fascist militarism as the next important factor, and the instinct of pugnacity and communist zeal as the least important; that the Orthodox wing attaches somewhat greater importance to the instinct of pugnacity and communist zeal as causes of war and somewhat

lesser importance to capitalist institutions than either the Reform
or the Conservative group.

TABLE XXI

RABBIS' WEIGHTED ESTIMATE OF THE IMPORTANCE OF SEVERAL
FACTORS IN BRINGING ABOUT WAR*

	RABBIS' ESTIMATE			
Factor	*Reform*	*Conservative*	*Orthodox*	*Total*
Competition for markets	.96	.97	.97	.96
Fascist militarism	.93	.95	.92	.94
Capitalist institutions	.84	.92	.76	.86
Foreign loans	.85	.82	.78	.83
Private manufacture and sale of munitions	.80	.82	.82	.81
Pugnacity	.47	.45	.57	.48
Communist zeal	.38	.35	.41	.37

* 1.00 signifies major importance; .50, minor importance; 0, no importance.

Support of, Refusal to Support, and Opposition to War

A fairly large majority of the rabbinate as a whole refuses to
be categorical in its commitments with respect to the issue of
supporting the government in war (3a–III). About two out of
every three rabbis in the group would support the government
under certain conditions and deny support under others. It should
be noted, however, that 41 rabbis would never support and only
18 would always support the government in war.

These figures are for the group as a whole. In the case of the
Orthodox wing the number who would unconditionally support
the government is 6; the number who would unconditionally
deny support is 2.

As to the special circumstances which would induce the rabbis
to support the government, it would appear that no rabbi would
support a war against communism as such, but seven would support
a war against fascism as such. About 60 per cent of the rabbis
in each wing would support a war in case of enemy invasion.
Enemy invasion seems to be in the view of the rabbis the only
justification for conducting a war.

Two further questions were asked: under what circumstances
would they refuse to support the government in war? (3b–III);

under what conditions would they oppose the government in conducting war? (3c–III). It is significant that approximately 40 per cent of the rabbis choose to be noncommittal on either question. This is by far a higher percentage of noncommitment than was encountered with respect to any of the other issues. From the distribution of responses it appears that:

1. A number of those who would refuse to support war would refrain from actively opposing it. Thus, 47 rabbis in the group as a whole state that they would always refuse to support the government, but only 31 say that they would oppose the government.

2. Many among those who would support the government only under certain conditions would, once war is declared, give unconditional support or at any rate withhold opposition to war policy. Thus, of the 196 rabbis who are willing to commit themselves on the question of whether they would support the government in war, only 18 assert that they would always support the government. But of the 124 who commit themselves on the issue of refusal of support, 56 say that they would never refuse support; and out of the 129 who commit themselves on the issue of active opposition to the government in war, 84 rabbis state that they would never actively oppose the government.

3. No rabbis would refuse to support the government or actively oppose the government in the pursuit of war for the special reason that the war is against a fascist power. But nine rabbis in the group would refuse to support the government and eight would oppose the government in a war against a communist power.

Defense of United States Business Interests Abroad

The United States rabbinate as a whole is overwhelmingly against the view that: "It is the duty of the United States government to protect United States business abroad even to the extent of making use of our armed forces" (65–I). This proposition is rejected by 186 members of the total rabbinate and by 93, 72, and 21 rabbis of the Reform, Conservative, and Orthodox wings respectively. Even more decisive is the rabbis' rejection of the view that the United States should defend the right of its citizens to carry on foreign trade even if such defense might embroil the country in war (64–I).

Methods of Attaining Peace

Military preparedness is not viewed by the rabbis in the *United States as a way of keeping America out of war* (63–I). Only one in every 10 in the group as a whole wishes to see America armed as a way of maintaining peace. But 133 rabbis of a total of 215 reject this view, and the remainder are uncertain. Sentiment favoring outright rejection of the policy of peace through armament is strongest in the Conservative wing, where it is supported by 70 per cent of the membership; it is weakest in the Orthodox wing, where it is shared by 42 per cent of the 33 individuals composing the wing.

There is virtual unanimity in all three wings in favor of the nationalization of the arms industry (62–I).

Of the 215 rabbis in the group as a whole, 173 are in favor of a governmental prohibition on loans to nations at war, 21 are opposed to such prohibition, and 21 others are uncertain; the remaining 3 failed to indicate their opinions (66–I). The majorities in favor of such prohibition are 87 per cent in the Conservative, 81 per cent in the Reform, and 64 per cent in the Orthodox wing.

Opinion in the rabbinate is heavily weighted against American isolationism (67–I); for American initiative directed toward international disarmament (68–I); and for participation in the League of Nations (20–II) and the World Court (30–I).

In the total group of 215 rabbis, 149 reject outright a policy of United States aloofness in dealing with European problems, and only 17 rabbis favor such a policy. In fact, 172 rabbis favor American initiative in bringing about international disarmament, and 194 deny that American participation in the World Court is in contradiction to the principle of national sovereignty.

With respect to the League of Nations, the issue before the rabbinate is not whether America should or should not join that body, but rather when America should affiliate with the League. The view that America should never join the League but rather keep aloof from it has no supporters in the rabbinate. Less than 10 per cent of the rabbis in the group as a whole are opposed to joining but favor American assistance to the League as a non-member. Of the total rabbinate, 27 per cent favor immediate joining and 63 per cent favor deferring actual joining until such time as the League proves itself a force for peace, but in the meantime they favor extending assistance to the League.

Sentiment favoring American isolation is weakest in the Conservative wing and strongest in the Orthodox wing, while sentiment sanctioning American participation in world affairs is quite the reverse.

Intercession of the United States Government in Behalf of Jews and Other Minorities in Europe

The preponderant sentiment favors American intercession in behalf of Jews and other minority groups in Europe (69–I). Out of the 211 rabbis in the group as a whole, 182 support intercession. Doubt of the wisdom of intercession and outright opposition to it are decidedly more marked in the Reform wing than in the other two wings, though even in the Reform wing opposition to intercession is maintained by only a small number.

SECTION II

PATTERNS OF BELIEFS CONCERNING ISSUES ON PEACE

Certain issues of Section I which are presumably highly related are here paired to determine patterns of responses in the area of peace and internationalism. The topics to be covered are the interrelation of attitudes on the League of Nations and positions with regard to other indices of pro- and anti-isolationist sentiment; the interrelation of attitudes on the question of American defense of business interests abroad and on the issue of prohibition of loans to nations at war; the interrelation of attitudes of rabbis on the issue of American isolation and on the issue of American intercession in behalf of Jews and other minorities.

Interrelation Between Attitudes on League of Nations and Positions with Regard to Other Indices of Pro- and Anti-Isolationist Sentiment

A rabbi's position on the issue of America joining the League of Nations may be assumed to be a fairly good indication of his attitude on the question of American isolation. Thus it appears that among the 57 rabbis who favor America's immediate entry into the League (20–II) there is only one who gives assent to the proposition: "America should keep strictly aloof from dealing with European problems" (67–I), and 46 rabbis, or over 80 per cent, are in outright opposition to isolation. Aloofness is opposed by 96, or 73 per cent, of those 132 rabbis who favor America's entry into the League when it proves itself to be a force for world peace. But only five of the 20 who are totally opposed to America's entry into the League oppose an isolationist policy.

Irrespective of their attitudes on the question of America's entry into the League (20–II), rabbis in virtual agreement reject the notion that America's participation in the World Court is in contradiction to her national sovereignty (70–I). While, however, none among the 57 rabbis who favor America's immediate entry into the League oppose America's participation in the World Court, and only one of them is in doubt about it, participation in the World Court is rejected by one and doubted by seven of the 20 who believe that America should never enter the League.

Interrelation of Attitudes on the Question of American Defense of Business Interests Abroad and on the Issue of Prohibition of Loans to Nations at War

Section I of this chapter called attention to the overwhelming sentiment in the rabbinate favorable to governmental prohibition of loans by business, industry, and finance to nations engaged in war. This sentiment seems to be contradictory to the position rabbis take on the question of American defense of our business interests abroad. In fact, all of the six rabbis who believe that America, even at the risk of war, should defend the right of Americans to trade abroad (64–I) nevertheless favor prohibition of loans to governments engaged in war (66–I).

Interrelation of Attitudes of Rabbis on the Issue of American Isolation and on the Issue of American Intercession on Behalf of Jews and Other Minorities

It appears that the rabbis' attitudes on the question of intercession is independent of their attitude on the question of America's aloofness from dealing with European problems. No matter how rabbis stand on the question of American isolation from Europe (67–I), the likelihood is great that they will favor intercession on the part of America in behalf of Jews and other minorities in European countries (69–I). Of the 146 rabbis who oppose aloofness, 125, or 86 per cent, favor American intercession; of the 49 who are uncertain on the issue of aloofness, 43, or 88 per cent, favor intercession; and of the 16 who favor aloofness, 14 rabbis, or 88 per cent, nevertheless favor intercession.

CHAPTER XII

VIEWS OF RABBIS CONCERNING SEX AND RACE RELATIONS

THIS CHAPTER is divided into two separate units. Part A is composed of the usual two sections found in previous chapters. Section I deals with positions on the particular and general issues concerned and Section II with interrelations of various propositions presented in Section I. Part B, however, contains only one section, that treating positions on the questions raised. No attempt is made to relate responses on various propositions to one another.

PART A: RELATION BETWEEN SEXES

Section I: Position of the Rabbinate on Specific Issues

The views of the rabbinate in the area of sex relations will be discussed under the headings: ethics of sex relations; sex equality; divorce laws; liberal *vs.* anti-liberal attitude of rabbis with respect to relations between the sexes. The last-named topic is the general issue of this section, being a composite of responses to various pertinent items covered in the first three topics.

Ethics of sex relations.—The attitude of the rabbis on the question of the appropriateness of discussion of sex problems from the pulpit, and their positions with respect to birth control and the causes of prostitution were previously discussed.[1] Because of their relevancy to this chapter the findings are briefly reviewed below. Also reviewed are the opinions of the rabbis on the double standard of sex morality together with their beliefs concerning extra-marital sex relations.

(*a*) Almost two out of three Reform and Conservative rabbis believe that sex problems are proper themes for discussion from

[1] See Chapters VII and VIII.

the pulpit. The 33 Orthodox rabbis are, however, fairly evenly divided among those who hold such themes to be appropriate, those who deny the propriety, and those who are in doubt. Reform and Conservative rabbis reject with virtual unanimity the view that birth control is contrary to the spirit of Judaism; within the Orthodox wing, six are opposed to birth control because of this consideration, while the remainder are equally divided between those who disavow opposition and those who are doubtful. Majorities in all of the wings of the rabbinate reject the view that prostitution is in the main due to character deficiencies. These majorities imply the belief that prostitution is due chiefly to the economic conditions of the masses. Such an explanation of prostitution finds strongest support (80 per cent) among the Conservative rabbis and weakest support within the Orthodox ranks (58 per cent).

(*b*) Only 27 in the total group of rabbis declare themselves to be in favor of a double standard of sex morality by assenting to the proposition that "In the interests of the race it is justifiable to demand a higher standard of sex morality from women than from men" (71–I). With respect to this question a difference among the wings is to be noted. The double standard is definitely rejected by 80 per cent of the Reform rabbinate, by 73 per cent of the Conservative rabbinate, and by 42 per cent of the Orthodox rabbinate.

(*c*) It is surprising to note that 47 rabbis in the group as a whole believe that "extra-marital sex relations between mature individuals is the legitimate concern of society only if such relations are likely to result in offspring" (72–I). This view, which runs counter to traditional sex morality, is supported by 23 of the 105 Reform rabbis, by 21 of the 75 Conservative rabbis, and by 3 of the 32 Orthodox rabbis. It is difficult to account for the fact that almost one out of four rabbis in the Reform and Conservative groups upholds a view which is in contradiction to the commonly accepted standards of sex morality and the Jewish ideal of sexual purity. Perhaps the explanation lies in the possibility that the reaction of these 47 rabbis is to be viewed as a statement of policy rather than as a moral pronouncement. Most of these 47 rabbis probably did not mean to say that extra-marital relations not resulting in offspring are morally neutral acts. They meant, rather, to say that decisions in such matters ought to be left to the religious conscience of the individuals concerned and that social institutions, the state included, had no right to interfere.

Sex equality.—A striking difference is to be noted between the positions of the Reform and Conservative wings on the one hand, and that of the Orthodox, on the other, with respect to the issues of economic equality for women. Large majorities in the Reform and Conservative wings favor equality of women, while only a relatively small minority in the Orthodox group holds this view. The opinion that "the best interests of society would be served if women could dedicate themselves solely to the care of families" (74–I) is maintained by about 1 out of every 3 Orthodox rabbis, about 1 out of every 11 Conservative rabbis, and about 1 out of every 26 Reform rabbis, totaling 21 rabbis in the entire group. The Conservative and Reform wings oppose the economic limiting of women implied in the above propositions by majorities of about 70 per cent, but only 9 Orthodox rabbis are in outright opposition to the placing of economic limitations upon women, while 14 are uncertain.

A similar difference is to be observed with respect to the issue of facilitating women's entry into the professions. More than 6 out of 10 Reform rabbis and more than 7 out of 10 Conservative rabbis affirm the proposition: "It is in the interest of moral advance to facilitate women's efforts to enter professions" (76–I) as compared with only 7 out of a total of 32 Orthodox rabbis who affirm this proposition. Less than 1 out of 5 Orthodox rabbis reject outright this statement, the majority opinion among them being that of uncertainty. The division of the group as a whole is 128 favorable to women's entry, 16 opposed, 67 uncertain, and 7 noncommittal.

Divorce laws.—Large majorities in all three groups favor the liberalization of divorce laws (75–I). The percentage is largest in the case of the Conservative wing and smallest in the Orthodox. Few Conservative and Reform rabbis are uncertain about their position with respect to this issue, as compared with almost 25 per cent of uncertainty in the responses of the Orthodox wing.

Liberal vs. anti-liberal attitude of rabbis with respect to relations between the sexes.—Chart XII of the Appendix was employed as a key in the classification responses on the basis of liberal bias or anti-liberal bias with reference to the issues concerning the relations between the sexes. In the construction of the chart, liberalism with respect to sex was taken to mean the commitment to equality of treatment of the sexes and a tolerant attitude toward deviations from traditional standards of sex morality.

The percentages in different categories of responses to the eight propositions in the entire group and the three separate wings are:

TYPE OF RESPONSES		PERCENTAGE IN EACH TYPE			
Issue	*Position*	*Reform*	*Conservative*	*Orthodox*	*All Rabbis*
Sex	Liberal	71%	72%	45%	68%
	Anti-liberal	10	11	22	12
	Uncertain	19	17	33	20

It thus appears that a little more than two out of three Reform and Conservative rabbis, on the average, are committed to a liberal view on the issues of relations between the sexes. The remainder are about equally divided between those who object to liberal views and those who are uncertain or noncommittal. It further seems that the Orthodox group is split among those who hold liberal views, those who oppose such views, and those who are uncertain or noncommittal.

Section II—Patterns of Belief with Respect to Relations Between the Sexes

Interrelations between attitudes on the question of the double standard and attitudes on other propositions.—It is of interest to analyze the interrelations of certain propositions entering into the general question of liberal *vs.* anti-liberal attitude on relations between the sexes treated in the last topic above. In the following paragraphs, views on the double standard of sex morality will be linked to those on extra-marital sex relations and to positions on the limiting of women's sphere of influence. The results will then be summarized in terms of liberal and anti-liberal viewpoints.

The view that extra-marital relations which are not likely to result in offspring are outside the field of society's legitimate concern (72–I) is rejected by majorities of those who favor as well as of those who reject the double standard of sex morality (71–I).

Nevertheless, it appears that the view of opposition to extra-marital relations as being outside the realm of society's concern is much stronger in the group which accepts the double standard than in the one which rejects it. The exact percentages of opposition to society's concern about extra-marital relations are 73 per cent among the 26 rabbis who favor the double standard and 60 per cent among the 150 who reject it.

Also, those who are committed to the double standard are some-what more likely to accept the view that the limitation of women's sphere of influence to the home is socially desirable than are those who reject the double standard. Of the 27 respondents committed to the double standard, 44 per cent deny the social desirability of restricting women's sphere of activity (74–I). This view is rejected by 74 per cent of the 152 who oppose the double standard of sex morality.

Thus for the 153 who take the more liberal viewpoint of rejecting the double standard as against the 27 who accept it, the findings with respect to liberalism on the other two propositions indicate that a smaller percentage of the former group than of the latter take the view that extra-marital relations are outside the sphere of social control. On the other hand, a larger percentage of the former group than of the latter, in characteristic liberal fashion, reject the limiting of women's sphere of influence to the home.

PART B: RACE RELATIONS

Section I—Positions on Specific Issues

There is greater agreement among the individuals in the group as a whole and among the wings on the issues concerning race equality than with respect to any other set of controversial social problems. The main part of the American rabbinate is committed to the principle of race equality. Because of the small size of the groups who take an anti-egalitarian stand no attempt will be made to analyze the interconnections between the views of rabbis on the several issues concerning relations among races.

Three topics will be treated here, the doctrine of superiority of the white race; political, economic, and social equality; and attitudes on the general issue of race equality. The third-named topic is a composite of items under the previous ones, the issue being that of egalitarian *vs.* non- or anti-egalitarian attitude.

Doctrine of superiority of the white race.—Only 5 rabbis of the 215 responding hold the view of the superiority of the white race as scientifically sound (83–I). That *there are valid grounds for the belief in the superiority of the white race* is rejected by 90 per cent of the Reform rabbis, by 86 per cent of the Conservative rabbis, but by only 53 per cent of the Orthodox rabbis. Of the Orthodox rabbis, 13 are uncertain about the question. More than 4 out of every 5 rabbis, totaling 178 in the group as a whole, reject the idea of white superiority. In principle, therefore, the preponderant majority of the rabbinate is in favor of race equality.

Political, economic, and social equality.—They are not so liberal, however, on some of the specific issues of political, economic, and social equality. The proposition that "It is in the interest of good government to maintain special qualifications for Negro suffrage in the South until such time when their cultural level will rise appreciably" (82–I) is negated by only about 66 and 62 per cent of the Reform and Conservative groups and 38 per cent of the Orthodox group. While only 8 Reform rabbis, 8 Conservative rabbis, and 7 Orthodox rabbis favor special qualifications, there are 27 Reform, 21 Conservative, and 13 Orthodox rabbis who are uncertain about the matter of special voting qualifications for Negroes.

The number of rabbis who are for complete disenfranchisement of certain groups on racial grounds is negligible. Only 9 of the 213 rabbis responding reject the proposition: "Orientals should be admitted to American citizenship" (81–I). About 5 out of 6 Reform and Conservative rabbis and 3 out of 4 Orthodox rabbis give support to the enfranchisement of Orientals.

There is a somewhat stronger tendency among the rabbis toward favoring economic egalitarianism than political egalitarianism. There are few rabbis among the Conservative and Reform groups who believe that "In view of the different standards of living, salary scales for Negro and white teachers in the South are justified" (80–I). Among Reform rabbis, 3 out of 4, and among Conservative rabbis about 5 out of 6 reject economic inequality the country over, at least for teachers. In the Orthodox group the principle of economic equality attracts considerably less support. Fifty per cent of the 32 Orthodox rabbis reject economic inequality; the remainder of that wing is split between those who justify economic equality in the South and those who are uncertain. In the group as a whole, 162 rabbis reject as unjustifiable a double standard of compensation in the South.

The American rabbinate preponderantly opposes *the Jim Crow system as being in contradiction to the principle of the brotherhood of man* (79–I). Only five Reform and two Conservative rabbis fail to find inconsistency between the practice of the Jim Crow system and the principle of the brotherhood of man. The Orthodox group differs from the other two groups in that 16 per cent within that wing are uncertain about the Jim Crow system as compared with negligible proportions of uncertainty among the Conservative and Reform rabbis.

Even greater agreement within and among the groups of the American rabbinate is to be noted on the issue of the enactment of a Federal anti-lynching law. There is practical unanimity in all three wings in favor of the proposition that "a Federal anti-lynching law should be enacted" (78–I).

Attitudes on the general issue of race equality.—Chart XIII of the Appendix was employed in classifying the responses into those that show a pro-egalitarian bias and those showing a non- or anti-egalitarian attitude with respect to racial issues.

The following is an analysis of the responses of the group as a whole and of the three wings on all the issues presented in the preceding paragraphs:

TYPE OF RESPONSE		PERCENTAGE IN EACH TYPE			
Issue	*Position*	*Reform*	*Conservative*	*Orthodox*	*All Rabbis*
Race	Egalitarian	83%	85%	64%	81%
	Non- or Anti-egalitarian ...	4	4	10	5
	Uncertain	13	11	26	14

From the distribution three deductions are possible: Rabbinic sentiment is predominantly weighted in the direction of race equality. The sentiment favoring race equality is decidedly stronger in the Conservative and Reform wings than in the

Orthodox wing. (For every response indicating a non- or anti-egalitarian bias there are in the Reform group about 18 responses, in the Conservative 23 responses, and in the Orthodox 7 responses favoring race egalitarianism.) The relatively small percentages of uncertainty and noncommitment indicate a greater definiteness of view with regard to questions on race than in regard to issues in other areas.

CHAPTER XIII

COHERENCE, NON-COHERENCE, AND APPARENT INCONSISTENCIES IN RABBIS' RESPONSES

EMPHASIS in the sections devoted to pattern analysis in the preceding chapters has been placed on what the rabbis' position on one topic was likely to mean in terms of a view on one or more other problems. Analysis in terms of the strict logical coherence of the several views was not the primary concern.

The present chapter, employing the intertabulation results, will analyze the paired responses with the end in view of discovering how the various wings compare with respect to the degree of coherence shown in the responses made by their members, and in what areas there is a greater and in what areas a smaller degree of coherence of responses.

METHODOLOGICAL EXPLANATION

In classifying the responses to pairs of propositions these categories were employed: non-indicative, coherent, non-coherent, apparently inconsistent. It is manifestly impossible within the confines of a brief space to explain in the case of each pair of propositions the reason for placing the responses in one or the other of the above categories, but a few sentences will suffice to indicate the criteria employed in the classification.

Failure of a rabbi to react to one or both of the members of a pair is classified as a *non-indicative* response with regard to logical connectedness of his responses to the pair.

The response of a rabbi to a pair of propositions in which his response to one can be reasonably taken as implying the other or as contributing a ground for his response to the other is classified as *coherent*.

The response of a rabbi to a pair of propositions being such that his response to one, while not contradicting his response to the

167

other, does not reasonably imply his acceptance of it nor afford ground for assuming acceptance, is classified as *non-coherent*.

The response of a rabbi to a pair of propositions being such that the response to one is in seeming contradiction to his reaction to the other is classified as *apparently inconsistent*.

The following pair of propositions will serve as an illustration of this point:

I. Judaism must forever be hostile to any science which tends to destroy faith in the literal truth of the teachings of the Bible.

II. Belief in the actual occurrence of miracles as recorded in the Bible is indispensable to Judaism.

With respect to either statement the responses may be non-committal (*No* response), Yes (+), No (−), and uncertainty (?).

If a rabbi is noncommittal with respect to either or both of the propositions, nothing is known about his reaction to the pair. Such response is classified as *non-indicative*.

Responses +I+II, −I−II, −I?II, and ?I?II are classed as *coherent* responses. Affirmation of hostility to any science which tends to destroy faith in the literal truth of the teachings of the Bible can be taken to imply belief in the actual occurrence of miracles; affirmation of the belief in miracles can be taken as a reason for hostility to science which contradicts the Bible. The same holds true when a rabbi rejects or questions both propositions. The response −I?II is classed as a *coherent* response to the pair because uncertainty about the occurrence of miracles is an adequate reason for denying the hostility between Judaism and science which tends to destroy faith in the literal truth of the teachings of the Bible.

Combinations −I+II and ?I+II are classed as *non-coherent* responses. One may question or even deny the hostility between Judaism and science, and without being guilty of logical contradiction may still maintain that the miracles as recorded in the Bible have actually occurred. For in rejecting or questioning proposition I, the rabbi may reject or question only the necessary hostility between Judaism and science but not the literal truth of the Bible. Nevertheless, his rejecting or questioning of proposition I cannot be said to imply or constitute the reason for his affirmation of proposition II. Hence these combinations are classed as *non-coherent*.

Combinations +I—II, +I?II, and ?I—II are classed as *apparently inconsistent*. To assert that Judaism must be hostile to science which tends to destroy faith in the literal truth of the Bible and at the same time to deny or question the truth of the Biblical record of miracles is to be guilty of self-contradiction. One who denies the literal truth of the Biblical record of miracles has no logical basis for affirming or even entertaining the possibility that Judaism must be hostile to science which contradicts the Bible.

The adjective "apparently" is employed advisedly and might in fact be added in characterizing the *coherent* and *non-coherent* responses. The nature of the propositions employed in the questionnaire excludes the possibility of asserting with apodictic certainty that a certain combination of responses to a pair is absolutely coherent, non-coherent, or contradictory. The terms employed in the proposition lack that precise meaning which alone can be the basis for an accurate appraisal of coherence, non-coherence, and inconsistency. Moreover, what may seem to be contradictory if a pair of propositions is taken in isolation may be perfectly consistent in terms of a third proposition or an embracing point of view of which no mention is made in the questionnaire. Thus in the illustration cited a rabbi may consistently maintain both that Judaism must be hostile to science which contradicts the Bible and that the Biblical story of creation is a myth if he believes in a third proposition, not listed in the questionnaire, namely, that Judaism should be rejected. It is highly improbable but nevertheless possible that a rabbi will entertain the last view. Thus the classifications obtained by the method reveal at best what may reasonably and probably be taken as cases of coherence, non-coherence, and self-contradiction. These classifications do not, however, afford ground for certainty that a paired response is either coherent, non-coherent, or contradictory.

In view of the above considerations the limitations of the method employed in this chapter are clearly recognized. They are: subjectivity in applying the criteria above formulated in classifying combinations of responses, and basing conclusions on responses to pairs of propositions which are taken in isolation.

Nevertheless, the writer feels that the method is justified for several reasons which include the following: An attempt has been made to apply the criteria rigorously; once the classification of responses was arrived at, it was applied objectively to all the wings of the rabbinate; the results show that the relative positions of the three wings are maintained from issue to issue, the Conservative being highest in the general over-all consistency, the Reform next, and the Orthodox last; while the study is based on isolated pairs, it is reasonable to assume that a high degree of coherence with respect to pairs indicates the probability of an integrated philosophy, and a high degree of non-coherence or inconsistency with respect to pairs probably indicates the absence of an integrated philosophy.

The responses of rabbis to 92 pairs of the most meaningful propositions were analyzed, in the hope that an adequate basis would be secured for conclusions with respect to the coherency, non-coherency, and inconsistency of the responses of the group. The questionnaire includes 130 propositions. Mathematically, combinations of thousands of pairs are possible. The number of pairs to be considered was limited, due to the fact that they had to conform to the certain criteria: They must be in the same issue; they must be so related that at least one combination of + +, + —, + ?, — ?, etc., will be of such a nature that the first necessarily contradicts the second of the pair.

LOGICAL CONNECTEDNESS OF THE THINKING OF THE RABBIS

Charts XIV to XX list the combinations of responses to pairs of propositions which through the application of the criteria stated previously fall within the categories of coherent, non-coherent, and apparently inconsistent responses. To avoid repetitiousness the non-indicative combinations were omitted from the charts, non-indicative combinations being noncommittal with respect to either or both members of a pair of propositions. Each chart is a key for the appraisal of the responses within a particular area of thought; namely, theology, philosophy of Jewish life, economic reconstruction, education, civil liberties, peace and internationalism, and relations between the sexes.

Tables XXII to XXVIII give the percentages of responses falling within each category. Each table gives the results for a particular area. Percentages were computed with total possible responses as a basis of calculation—Reform 108, Conservative 77, and Orthodox 33.

Judging from Tables XXII to XXVIII, it is obvious that there is a variation in the degree of coherence, non-coherence, and ap-

TABLE XXII

PERCENTAGES OF NON-INDICATIVE, COHERENT, NON-COHERENT, AND APPARENTLY INCONSISTENT RESPONSES TO PAIRS OF PROPOSITIONS WITHIN THE AREA OF THEOLOGY

	REFORM				CONSERVATIVE				ORTHODOX			
	Non-Ind.	Co.	Non-Co.	Inc.	Non-Ind.	Co.	Non-Co.	Inc.	Non-Ind.	Co.	Non-Co.	Inc.
a. Paired with 1–I												
2–I	2	95	..	3	3	95	1	1	3	73	24	..
7–I	5	73	20	2	4	68	27	1	9	27	64	..
8–I	4	34	60	2	3	40	57	..	3	24	73	..
9–I	3	87	6	4	5	85	9	1	6	79	12	3
5–II	4	85	7	4	1	90	8	1	3	67	27	3
6–II	4	89	5	2	1	90	8	1	9	46	45	..
11–II	7	89	..	4	1	98	..	1	6	64	21	9
b. Paired with 2–I												
7–I	5	73	21	1	4	68	27	1	9	46	33	12
1–II	5	90	5	..	5	91	4	..	9	46	45	..
5–II	4	88	1	7	1	93	1	5	6	64	12	18
6–II	4	90	6	..	1	89	9	1	12	52	36	..
11–II	7	92	..	1	1	97	1	1	9	55	21	15
c. Paired with 5–I												
11–II	7	54	39	..	1	36	63	..	..	42	3	55
d. Paired with 6–I												
4–I	6	33	57	4	8	43	35	14	12	55	21	12
4–II	6	62	32	..	3	67	30	..	18	30	52	..
e. Paired with 8–I												
9–I	4	38	58	..	5	42	53	..	6	33	61	..
3–II	7	62	31	..	1	57	42	..	6	39	55	..
4–II	6	56	38	..	3	56	41	..	9	12	79	..
f. Paired with 9–I												
7–I	5	81	14	..	5	62	29	4	9	42	49	..
g. Paired with 5–II												
6–I	6	62	32	..	1	72	27	..	12	61	27	..
h. Paired with 11–II												
5–II	7	86	1	6	1	91	..	8	9	76	3	12
6–II	8	85	..	7	1	92	..	7	15	58	..	27

Note: Items 1-I(a), 2-I(b), 5-I(c), 6-I(d), etc., are paired with the items listed directly under them.

parent inconsistency within and among the various areas. Table
XXIX compares the average percentage of coherent, non-coherent,
and apparently contradictory responses in the various areas. The
category of "apparently inconsistent" was found inapplicable to
a large number of pairs of propositions. Therefore, in finding
the average for this category the number of "apparently inconsistent" replies in a certain area was divided only by the number of

TABLE XXIII

PERCENTAGES OF NON-INDICATIVE, COHERENT, NON-COHERENT, AND APPARENTLY
INCONSISTENT RESPONSES TO PAIRS OF PROPOSITIONS WITHIN
THE AREA OF PHILOSOPHY OF JEWISH LIFE

	REFORM				CONSERVATIVE				ORTHODOX			
	Non-Ind.	Co.	Non-Co.	Inc.	Non-Ind.	Co.	Non-Co.	Inc.	Non-Ind.	Co.	Non-Co.	Inc.
a. Paired with 10–I												
11–I	5	77	18	..	4	87	9	..	6	88	6	..
12–I	14	44	42	..	18	64	18	..	15	61	24	..
b. Paired with 11–I												
12–II ...	17	48	34	1	6	69	25	..	12	55	30	3
c. Paired with 13–I												
1c–III ..	5	54	41	..	3	30	67	..	9	39	52	..

pairs to which this category was found applicable. This is one
reason why the figures for each wing fail to add to 100 per cent.
A second reason is the fact that pairs which included a non-indicative response did not enter into the final tabulation of Table
XXIX.

The data summarized in Table XXIX seem to point to a number of conclusions:

1. The answers of the Conservative and Reform rabbis are no-
tably free from inconsistency. The average rabbi in these wings
responds in an apparently inconsistent manner to about one in
every twenty pairs of propositions to which inconsistent responses
are at all possible.

2. In the Orthodox group of rabbis, it is to be observed that
on those pairs of propositions which permit of inconsistent responses, almost one in every seven responses is apparently inconsistent.

TABLE XXIV

PERCENTAGES OF NON-INDICATIVE, COHERENT, NON-COHERENT, AND APPARENTLY INCONSISTENT RESPONSES TO PAIRS OF PROPOSITIONS WITHIN THE AREA OF ECONOMIC RECONSTRUCTION

	REFORM				CONSERVATIVE				ORTHODOX			
	Non-Ind.	*Co.*	*Non-Co.*	*Inc.*	*Non-Ind.*	*Co.*	*Non-Co.*	*Inc.*	*Non-Ind.*	*Co.*	*Non-Co.*	*Inc.*
a. Paired with 14-I												
17-I	4	61	35	..	..	58	42	..	9	33	58	..
35-I	5	48	47	..	3	61	36	..	3	45	52	..
41-I	5	43	52	..	5	51	44	..	6	64	30	..
42-I	5	42	53	..	..	43	57	..	6	36	58	..
43-I	4	55	37	4	1	62	34	3	9	43	36	12
b. Paired with 21-I												
33-I	3	59	38	..	..	73	27	..	..	42	58	..
38-I	3	67	14	16	..	78	8	14	3	39	..	58
43-I	3	64	33	..	1	61	38	..	6	61	33	..
c. Paired with 23-I												
33-I	3	36	38	23	..	43	30	27	6	33	43	18
36-I	3	41	54	2	1	35	64	..	6	30	61	3
43-I	3	50	47	..	1	55	44	..	6	45	49	..
17-II ...	4	35	52	9	3	35	54	8	12	30	49	9
d. Paired with 25-I												
27-I	3	80	17	..	..	83	17	..	..	58	42	..
28-I	4	55	40	1	4	54	39	3	..	39	55	6
41-I	4	46	47	3	5	61	34	..	3	42	52	3
17-II ...	4	55	41	..	4	78	18	..	6	45	49	..
e. Paired with 27-I												
17-I	4	67	28	1	..	74	21	5	6	55	27	12
43-I	4	56	40	..	1	56	43	..	6	55	39	..
f. Paired with 28-I												
27-I	5	54	41	..	4	54	42	..	..	..	55	45
17-I	5	58	37	..	4	53	43	..	6	49	45	..
43-I	4	49	47	..	4	51	45	..	6	67	27	..
g. Paired with 29-I												
25-I	6	63	31	..	1	77	22	..	..	67	33	..
27-I	7	61	32	..	1	74	25	..	..	55	45	..
28-I	6	44	29	21	5	38	38	19	..	18	49	33
41-I	7	63	30	..	5	66	29	..	3	58	39	..
h. Paired with 33-I												
34-I	4	72	24	..	1	86	13	..	6	67	27	..
36-I	3	46	51	..	1	74	25	..	..	70	30	..
43-I	4	52	44	..	1	60	39	..	6	45	49	..
17-II ...	5	57	38	..	3	74	20	3	6	73	21	..
i. Paired with 35-I												
21-I	4	57	39	..	1	66	33	..	..	55	45	..
36-I	4	57	39	..	1	70	28	1	..	61	36	3
43-I	5	67	28	..	3	66	31	..	6	58	36	..
17-II ...	5	42	51	2	4	65	26	5	6	42	49	3

TABLE XXIV (*Continued*)

PERCENTAGES OF NON-INDICATIVE, COHERENT, NON-COHERENT, AND APPARENTLY
INCONSISTENT RESPONSES TO PAIRS OF PROPOSITIONS WITHIN
THE AREA OF ECONOMIC RECONSTRUCTION

	REFORM				CONSERVATIVE				ORTHODOX			
	Non-Ind.	*Non-Co.*	*Co.*	*Inc.*	*Non-Ind.*	*Non-Co.*	*Co.*	*Inc.*	*Non-Ind.*	*Non-Co.*	*Co.*	*Inc.*
j Paired with 36–I												
43–I	4	52	44	..	3	56	41	..	6	70	24	..
17–II	5	42	45	8	4	62	29	5	6	36	46	12
k. Paired with 38–I												
43–I	4	57	39	..	1	62	37	..	9	39	52	..
17–II	5	56	18	21	3	79	5	13	9	33	18	40
l. Paired with 41–I												
35–I	6	50	44	..	5	61	34	..	3	55	42	..
43–I	5	53	34	8	6	56	33	5	6	40	39	15
17–II	6	45	49	..	6	51	43	..	9	42	49	..
m. Paired with 43–I												
27–I	4	56	40	..	1	57	42	..	6	55	39	..
17–II	5	55	31	9	4	56	37	3	12	30	46	12

TABLE XXV

PERCENTAGES OF NON-INDICATIVE, COHERENT, NON-COHERENT, AND APPARENTLY
INCONSISTENT RESPONSES TO PAIRS OF PROPOSITIONS WITHIN
THE AREA OF EDUCATION

	REFORM				CONSERVATIVE				ORTHODOX			
	Non-Ind.	*Non-Co.*	*Co.*	*Inc.*	*Non-Ind.*	*Non-Co.*	*Co.*	*Inc.*	*Non-Ind.*	*Non-Co.*	*Co.*	*Inc.*
a. Paired with 44–I												
47–I	3	66	31	..	1	69	30	..	3	49	48	..
48–I	3	80	17	..	1	87	12	..	3	49	48	..
b. Paired with 45–I												
27–I	3	82	7	8	1	75	17	7	..	64	30	6
c. Paired with 48–I												
1–I	4	87	5	4	3	87	7	3	3	55	15	27
2–I	4	87	7	2	1	90	6	3	3	46	39	12
7–I	6	72	17	5	4	66	25	5	9	30	55	6
8–I	5	36	59	..	3	45	52		6	33	61	..
9–I	4	76	13	7	5	70	16	9	6	46	30	18
d. Paired with 51–I												
21–I	2	71	27	..	..	83	17	..	..	30	70	..
e. Paired with 18–II												
17–II	4	53	43	..	5	82	13	..	6	55	36	3

TABLE XXVI

PERCENTAGES OF NON-INDICATIVE, COHERENT, NON-COHERENT, AND APPARENTLY
INCONSISTENT RESPONSES TO PAIRS OF PROPOSITIONS WITHIN
THE AREA OF CIVIL LIBERTIES

	REFORM				CONSERVATIVE				ORTHODOX			
	Non-Ind.	*Co.*	*Non-Co.*	*Inc.*	*Non-Ind.*	*Co.*	*Non-Co.*	*Inc.*	*Non-Ind.*	*Co.*	*Non-Co.*	*Inc.*
Paired with 58–I												
14–I	4	61	35	..	..	68	32	..	12	52	36	..
44–I	3	67	30	..	..	77	23	..	6	58	36	..
17–II	5	66	29	..	3	66	31	..	12	39	49	..
2a–II	8	58	25	9	8	63	21	8	27	24	49	..

TABLE XXVII

PERCENTAGES OF NON-INDICATIVE, COHERENT, NON-COHERENT, AND APPARENTLY
INCONSISTENT RESPONSES TO PAIRS OF PROPOSITIONS WITHIN
THE AREA OF PEACE AND INTERNATIONALISM

	REFORM				CONSERVATIVE				ORTHODOX			
	Non-Ind.	*Co.*	*Non-Co.*	*Inc.*	*Non-Ind.*	*Co.*	*Non-Co.*	*Inc.*	*Non-Ind.*	*Co.*	*Non-Co.*	*Inc.*
a. Paired with 61–I												
63–I	2	66	32	..	3	66	31	..	..	45	55	..
66–I	2	75	23	..	3	84	13	..	..	58	42	..
b. Paired with 64–I												
66–I	3	74	14	9	1	86	4	9	..	58	15	27
c. Paired with 67–I												
69–I	3	56	17	24	4	71	5	20	3	45	3	49
d. Paired with 70–I												
20–II	5	82	7	6	1	91	3	5	6	58	6	30
e. Paired with 20–II												
67–I	5	68	7	20	3	74	6	17	6	36	21	37

TABLE XXVIII

PERCENTAGES OF NON-INDICATIVE, COHERENT, NON-COHERENT, AND APPARENTLY
INCONSISTENT RESPONSES TO PAIRS OF PROPOSITIONS WITHIN
THE AREA OF RELATIONS BETWEEN SEXES

	REFORM				CONSERVATIVE				ORTHODOX			
	Non-Ind.	*Co.*	*Non-Co.*	*Inc.*	*Non-Ind.*	*Co.*	*Non-Co.*	*Inc.*	*Non-Ind.*	*Co.*	*Non-Co.*	*Inc.*
a. Paired with 71–I												
34–I	4	60	36	..	4	56	40	..	6	30	64	..
72–I	4	28	65	3	5	34	60	1	3	39	55	3
74–I	3	88	9	..	4	82	14	..	..	45	55	..

TABLE XXIX

AVERAGE PERCENTAGES OF COHERENT, NON-COHERENT, AND APPARENTLY
INCONSISTENT RESPONSES IN THE SEVERAL AREAS[1]

	REFORM			CONSERVATIVE			ORTHODOX		
	C	NC	AI	C	NC	AI	C	NC	AI
Theology	73	20	3	74	22	3	49	35	10
(22–17)									
Philosophy	56	34	1	62	30	..	61	28	3
. (4–1)									
Economic	54	39	7	61	34	6	47	41	16
(42–18)									
Education	71	23	4	75	20	4	46	43	12
(10–6)									
Civil Lib.	63	30	9	69	27	8	43	42	..
(4–1)									
Peace	70	17	15	79	10	13	50	24	36
(6–4)									
Sex	59	37	3	57	38	1	38	58	3
(3–1)									
All Areas	62	30	6	67	27	5	48	39	14
(91–48)									

[1] Key: C = Coherent responses; NC = Non-coherent responses; AI = Apparently inconsistent. Percentages do not total 100% because of omission of non-indicative responses, etc.
First numbers in parentheses refer to number of pairs of propositions employed; second numbers,
the number of pairs in which inconsistency is possible.

3. If the percentage of coherent replies is an index, the thinking of the Conservative and Reform groups shows a high degree
of integration. In more than two out of every three cases the
response of the Conservative rabbis to one proposition of a pair
supplies a reason for his response to the second member; in the
Reform wing the proportion is somewhat less than two out of three,
and in the Orthodox group somewhat less than one out of two.

4. Only in the area of philosophy of Jewish life does the Reform wing (56%) show a lower degree of integration of thinking
than the Orthodox (61%). This is probably due to the recent
reorientation of Reform thinking on Jewish life and problems.

5. In all three wings the thinking on theological matters seems
to be better integrated than that on the issues of economic reconstruction. On account of the relatively few pairs used on the other
issues, and because of the diversity in the numbers of pairs of
propositions employed in the different areas of thought, no other
comparisons between areas were made.

CHAPTER XIV

PREACHING EMPHASES * OF THE RABBINATE
AND FREEDOM OF THE PULPIT

PREVIOUS CHAPTERS (V–XII) concerned themselves with what rabbis who answered the questionnaire say they believe. The present chapter will be devoted first, in Section I, to an examination of their preaching emphases.

The respondents were requested to indicate whether or not they preach the belief they hold, and if so, whether frequently or occasionally. The instructions made it clear that "preaching" was not to be understood in a limited sense, but was to include writings, personal contacts, teaching adult groups, lectures, etc.

The rabbis were asked to appraise the importance of a number of factors which are listed in the questionnaire as bars to freedom in preaching. This appraisal is analyzed in Section II of this chapter. A number of rabbis supplemented the appraisal of the factors listed in the questionnaire with their own comments.

SECTION I

PREACHING EMPHASES OF THE RABBINATE

This section will attempt to answer the question: How do the various areas of thought, such as theology, philosophy of Jewish life, economic reconstruction, compare with respect to the preaching emphasis they receive? Comparisons were made for the group as a whole as well as for the separate wings.

In order to study the preaching emphases placed on certain areas of thought, the responses of the rabbis were weighted. The word "frequently" as referred to in the questionnaire received the weight of 1; "occasionally," the weight of 1/2. A rabbi's failure

* The term "preaching emphases" as used here refers to frequency of preaching of the particular item or issue. Frequency and importance are not identical. (Note: See also questionnaire instructions.)

to indicate how frequently he preached on a topic was weighted as $\frac{1}{4}$, on the assumption that surely he did not preach about this issue frequently and that the chances are about even that he never preached on it or that he preached on it occasionally. The response of a rabbi that he never preached on a certain issue received the value of 0.*

Weights were computed for (*a*) each proposition as a whole irrespective of the position the rabbi took with respect to it, and (*b*) for each separate position (+, — and ?) in the case of a proposition stated in false or true form and each alternative choice in the case of the multiple choice propositions. A value of 1.00, according to this method of weighting, indicates an emphasis of "frequently." A value of .50 indicates "occasionally." A zero, 0, indicates "never." An average of more than .50 indicates a trend toward "frequently"; less than .50 a trend toward "never."

Comparative Preaching Emphases on Areas of Thought

Averages of the weighted preaching emphases for all the propositions falling within the different areas were obtained, although there is no way of telling what "occasionally" and "frequently" actually mean. It may be assumed that they have different connotations for different rabbis and even for the same rabbi when applied to different areas and issues. With this reservation the following results are indicated by the data presented in Table XXX.

TABLE XXX

PREACHING EMPHASES OF RABBIS IN DIFFERENT AREAS[1]

	PREACHING EMPHASIS			
Area	*Reform*	*Conservative*	*Orthodox*	*Total*
Philosophy of Jewish life	.61	.66	.62	.63
Theology	.57	.57	.59	.57
Social function of religions	.58	.56	.49	.56
Peace and internationalism	.55	.53	.49	.53
Civil liberties	.47	.44	.36	.44
Education	.45	.45	.40	.44
Economic reconstruction	.39	.40	.35	.39
Race	.37	.33	.37	.36
Sex	.32	.31	.35	.32

[1] 1.00 signifies frequently; .50, occasionally; .25, no indication; 0, never.

* Too much emphasis should not be placed on numerical values, for the scale used is a very rough measure.

1. The order of topics is almost exactly the same for the three wings, with the exception of small reversals between areas rated very nearly the same.

2. The Orthodox group shows more than an "occasional" emphasis only on the philosophy of Jewish life and theology.

SECTION II

FACTORS MILITATING AGAINST FREEDOM
OF THE PULPIT

Estimate of Various Factors

The rabbis were asked to indicate whether each of the following factors constituted in their opinion no obstacle, a major obstacle, or a minor obstacle to freedom in preaching: (*a*) the level of intelligence of the congregation, (*b*) local biases, (*c*) conservatism on economic issues, (*d*) pressure groups such as the American Legion and the Daughters of the American Revolution, (*e*) the press, (*f*) vested interests of some of the members of the congregation, and (*g*) consideration of the feelings of Gentiles. The responses are tabulated in Table XXXI.

All responses were weighted according to the following scheme: no factor (0), minor factor (½), major factor (1). Those who failed to report were eliminated from the computation. Table XXXII gives the average weighted estimates of these listed factors as obstacles in the way of freedom in preaching. From this table it seems that:

1. The level of intelligence of the members of the congregation and local biases are, in the minds of the members of all three wings of the rabbinate, relatively serious factors militating against freedom of the pulpit.

2. There is also agreement among the three wings that, of the obstacles named in the questionnaire, pressure groups and the press constitute the least important obstacles to freedom in preaching.

3. All three wings are agreed in considering economic conservatism, vested interests, and consideration of the feelings of Gentiles as fairly important obstacles.

TABLE XXXI

RABBIS' ESTIMATE OF THE IMPORTANCE OF CERTAIN FACTORS AS OBSTACLES
TO FREEDOM OF THE PULPIT

Factor	RABBIS' ESTIMATES			
	Reform	Conservative	Orthodox	Entire Group
Level of intelligence				
Number not reporting	12	2	3	17
Number reporting "no factor"	19	10	4	33
Number reporting "minor factor"	33	25	10	68
Number reporting "major factor"	44	40	16	100
Local biases				
Number not reporting	11	2	4	17
Number reporting "no factor"	14	13	5	32
Number reporting "minor factor"	43	29	10	82
Number reporting "major factor"	40	33	14	87
Economic conservatism				
Number not reporting	11	5	3	19
Number reporting "no factor"	20	14	8	42
Number reporting "minor factor"	37	29	15	81
Number reporting "major factor"	40	29	7	76
Pressure groups				
Number not reporting	10	4	4	18
Number reporting "no factor"	53	35	15	103
Number reporting "minor factor"	30	28	11	69
Number reporting "major factor"	15	10	3	28
Press				
Number not reporting	10	5	3	18
Number reporting "no factor"	56	36	15	107
Number reporting "minor factor"	26	26	8	60
Number reporting "major factor"	16	10	7	33
Vested interests				
Number not reporting	11	2	3	16
Number reporting "no factor"	22	14	9	45
Number reporting "minor factor"	39	29	11	79
Number reporting "major factor"	36	32	10	78

TABLE XXXI (*Continued*)

RABBIS' ESTIMATE OF THE IMPORTANCE OF CERTAIN FACTORS AS OBSTACLES
TO FREEDOM OF THE PULPIT

Factor	RABBIS' ESTIMATES			
	Reform	Conservative	Orthodox	Entire Group
Feelings of Gentiles				
Number not reporting	10	2	3	15
Number reporting "no factor"	13	16	12	41
Number reporting "minor factor"	54	40	10	104
Number reporting "major factor"	31	19	8	58

TABLE XXXII

WEIGHTED ESTIMATES OF CERTAIN FACTORS AS OBSTACLES TO FREEDOM
OF THE PULPIT[1]

Factor	WEIGHTED ESTIMATES			
	Reform	Conservative	Orthodox	Entire Group
Level of intelligence	.63	.70	.70	.67
Local biases	.63	.63	.66	.63
Economic conservatism	.60	.60	.48	.58
Vested interests	.57	.62	.52	.58
Feelings of Gentiles	.59	.52	.43	.54
The press	.30	.32	.37	.32
Pressure groups	.31	.33	.29	.31

[1] 1.00 signifies major factor; .50, minor factor; 0, no factor.

Voluntary Comments

In addition to estimating the factors listed in the questionnaire, 57 of the total of 218 rabbis responding volunteered comments on the conditions that stood in the way of freedom of the pulpit, and made suggestions toward increasing the scope of preaching freedom.

Seven rabbis denied that there are any serious impediments in the way of rabbinic teaching. A typical statement follows: "I have not, in my own experience, suffered any limitation of pulpit freedom." Another rabbi, however, wrote: "I have always preached what I believed, regardless of consequences, hence I am out of a pulpit." A preponderant number of the statements indicate that rabbis feel seriously hampered in delivering the message they believe they have for their congregations.

Many believe that the chief hindrances to freedom of the pulpit arise from their personal traits and methods. Some also score against the training of the rabbis and criticize rabbinic associations. Five rabbis are convinced that what is needed is greater rabbinic courage. An equal number feel that the resistance of congregations is not so much resistance to what rabbis say as to their manner of saying it. If rabbis learned to express their messages tactfully and with due consideration for the feelings of the congregation, they would encounter no serious obstacles. In the mind of one individual inadequate preparation constitutes a serious limitation upon the effectiveness of the sermon. Two junior rabbis find their senior colleagues to be serious obstacles to freedom of preaching. Criticism is leveled against the methods of teaching and preaching employed by the rabbis. One rabbi finds fault with preaching in general as a method. "I find that the pew lacks freedom to answer back. We cannot have freedom of the pulpit if we do not have freedom of the pew." Inadequate training given to the community by his predecessor is said by one individual to be the principal reason for his inability to give full expression to his ideas in the pulpit.

A few believe that the fault lies in the rabbinical training schools and the rabbinical bodies. The training schools graduate too many rabbis, and the resulting over-supply renders present incumbents of the pulpit insecure in their jobs and, therefore, fearful of expressing ideas that might antagonize their congregations. A few rabbis believe that the organized rabbinical bodies are failing to take the steps necessary to secure freedom of the pulpit. "The limitations to freedom of speech in the pulpit are largely due to the fact that the rabbis do not attack problems in an organized, concerted manner. Thus if one is attacked for his utterances it should mean facing the American rabbis generally who have kindred views. Temples which dismiss a rabbi for his utterances should be nationally boycotted and ostracized." Another rabbi writes: "A definite, positive, unequivocal statement addressed at different intervals to the congregations by the various rabbinical assemblies would facilitate the maintenance of free pulpits."

While there are thus a number of rabbis who believe that the attempt to secure greater freedom of the pulpit should be directed to the rabbis themselves, individually and collectively, a larger number of rabbis see the great obstacles to freedom in preaching in the mentality of the congregations and in the economic status of the rabbi. Ten rabbis complain of the low level of intelligence, defective education, and lack of worth-while interests on the part of the members of their congregations. Typical of this class of indictments are:

"The general level of intelligence of the congregation precludes the possibility of discussing any social problem deeply."

"The lack of contact of the congregations with contemporary Jewish and non-Jewish issues . . ."

"Lack of interest in, or knowledge of social and religious problems of today . . ."

"The preacher is hampered in his freedom by the uninformed minds of his congregation on Jewish and current problems."

"Not more intelligence but more knowledge and cultural background are needed."

In addition to these wholesale indictments of the congregational members, a few rabbis go into detail. Some suggest that members are ready to listen only to those ideas which conform to their prejudices. A few others suggest that people attend services not for the purpose of being enlightened about Jewish and general conditions and problems but to be entertained. "Since a good many of my worshipers regard the synagogue as a social outlet rather than an institution of religion, inspiration, or study, preaching is of a common type and the effectiveness of the rabbis is therefore limited." Prejudices of the members of the congregation on Jewish matters seem to discourage not a few of the rabbis from speaking their mind. A number of them call attention to the conviction on the part of some of their members that Jews and Judaism are above criticism. Others point to sectional prejudices among Jews who hail from different parts of Europe and to narrow concepts of the nature of Judaism, acquired by their congregants in the past. In addition, a few write about the conservatism of their members on economic issues. One rabbi sees the crux of the matter in "the enthronement by the capitalist system of intellectual and spiritual midgets in the seat of the mighty—boards of trustees, executive directors, etc."

By far the largest number of rabbis point to insecurity of their jobs as the great hindrance to free preaching and teaching, as exemplified by the following quotations:

"Dependence of rabbis financially upon those who are large contributors to the temple budget . . ."

"The fact that the rabbi derives his salary from dues paid by members, the majority of whom are because of their economic interest opposed to social change . . ."

"Insecurity of tenure of office of the rabbi . . ."

"Limitation of tenure is the predominant factor in my opinion."

Three rabbis find fault with the nature of the rabbi's relation to the synagogue, pointing out that the rabbi is the servant of individual members rather than of the community. To correct this situation, one suggests that an effort be made to change the status of the rabbi from that of an employee of the synagogue to that of an employee of the community. In addition, three rabbis find powerful members of their congregation an inhibitive factor. One of these writes: "The sole important factor is the personal opinion of an individual who wishes to exercise power in the congregation. He does not believe the rabbi's view important either way, but he wants the thrill of exercising his power."

A number of rabbis point to certain characteristics of the community generally as the important conditions which militate against freedom of expression from the pulpit. Two complain of the conservatism of the churches and the lack of interest in social issues. One rabbi comments on the sad state of civil liberties in this country. He writes: "Violation of civil liberties is a regular practice due to certain political officials. Local Christian ministers are taking no interest in current social problems." Another writes of his city: "The city at large has little or no social consciousness and is very conservative. This is why I did not indicate the frequency of preaching in the questionnaire."

The relations between Jews and non-Jews often result in the rabbi's moderating his message. Five rabbis write about the minority status of the Jews and their fear of anti-Semitism. One of them points out that "the interests of the Jewish community call for circumspection and responsible utterances," but he does not recognize this as a limitation of freedom. Another writes that there is a feeling "that radical views will hurt the Jewish group." He also writes of the congregational fear of anti-Semitism.

In spite of these factors, many rabbis indicate that they make a brave effort to overcome these obstacles. As one expressed it: "While these conditions prevail I do not surrender my freedom of speech."

CHAPTER XV

PRINCIPAL FINDINGS AND CONCLUSIONS

THE PRIMARY PURPOSE of this investigation has been to discover what American rabbis believe and preach concerning important issues in theology, Jewish adjustment, and social organization, and how the three wings of the rabbinate differ on these issues.

I. BELIEFS OF RABBIS

Theological Views

1. With regard to the theological issues on which the rabbis were canvassed there appear to be no beliefs which are universally affirmed by the entire group. Nor are there any theological propositions on which there is unanimity of agreement in any of the three wings.

2. Within the Reform and Conservative wings there is a preponderant tendency to place theological beliefs within the framework of a naturalistic world view.

3. On the issue of naturalism as opposed to supernaturalism, the Orthodox wing differs significantly from the other two, the latter being definitely inclined toward the naturalistic view.

4. The views of a rabbi on different issues in theology seem to fall consistently into either a naturalistic or a supernaturalistic pattern. A rabbi who holds a naturalistic view with respect to one issue tends to hold a naturalistic view with regard to other issues. Conversely, a supernaturalistic attitude with respect to one issue is accompanied by a supernaturalistic bias toward other issues.

Philosophy of Jewish Life

1. The Orthodox and Conservative groups are preponderantly nationalistic in their approach to Jewish life and problems; the Reform group is about equally divided in this respect.

187

2. The responses of the Conservative and Reform rabbis give evidence of widespread recognition of the linkage of Jewish destiny with that of human society in general.

3. The beliefs that Judaism is indissolubly bound up with the Jewish people, that the Jews are a national entity, that Zionism constitutes an important solution to the problem of Jewish adjustment, that devotion to the cause of the rebuilding of Palestine and to the Hebrew language and literature is essential in Judaism tend to be related to one another. A rabbi who holds any single one of these opinions generally adheres to the others.

4. Zionism, on the one hand, and socialization and internationalism, on the other, are viewed by the rabbis as mutually complementary rather than mutually exclusive solutions to the Jewish problem. A hopeful outlook with respect to one of these methods tends to be accompanied by acceptance of the other.

5. The two fundamental issues in the philosophy of Jewish life covered in the present investigation are Nationalism *vs.* anti-Nationalism (universalism), and the question of whether the Jewish destiny is linked with or independent of the destiny of mankind as a whole. With regard to these issues the gulf between the Reform wing and the other wings has considerably narrowed since the inception of the Reform movement. Many contemporary Reform rabbis are nationalistic in their approach to Judaism. They recognize the unique Jewish culture and the Hebrew language and the Jewish aspirations in Palestine as indispensable aspects of Judaism. On the other hand, many Orthodox rabbis seem to have substituted the orientation, the Jews *in* the world, for the earlier orientation, the Jews *and* the world, and to have recognized that Jewish destiny is linked with that of mankind. The differences that remain are sharpest between the Orthodox and Reform wings. The Conservative group equals the Orthodox in its support of the nationalistic view of Judaism and the Reform in its view of the linkage of the Jewish destiny with that of mankind.

The Social Function of Religion

1. The preponderant majority of the American rabbinate is committed to a utilitarian moral philosophy.

2. The rabbinate is well-nigh unanimous in its conviction that religion, to be a vital force, must identify itself with reconstructive social movements. The majority is, however, convinced that religion as it now functions is only a slight factor in the improvement of life but that the role of religion in social progress is capable of growth.

3. A large proportion of the rabbinate see socially reconstructive implications in the spirit of Judaism. This is especially marked in the case of the Conservative wing, a majority among whom believe that the spirit of Judaism demands the abolition of the private ownership and profit basis of present-day economy. That Judaism is compatible with acceptance of an economic *status quo* or with neutrality on basic economic issues is rejected by well-nigh the entire rabbinate.

4. Majorities in all wings see pro-labor implications in Judaism.

Economic Reconstruction

1. The rabbinate in all its wings is preponderantly in favor of increasing social responsibility for the welfare and security of the individual.

2. The sentiment of the rabbinate is decidedly pro-labor.

3. On the issue of collectivism the rabbinate as a whole adopts a middle-of-the-road policy, the Reform wing following this most closely, the Conservative tending to veer away in favor of collectivism, and the Orthodox in the opposite direction.

4. In respect to (1), (2), and (3) the Conservative wing is the most liberal.

5. In the choice of an economic policy for America among the following alternatives—(a) leaving the economic order as it is, (b) leaving capitalism intact but with the addition of provisions for government regulation of industry and social security, (c) limited and gradual socialization of economic resources, and (d) complete socialization of production and consumption—the rabbis seem to be largely influenced by a number of considerations. These considerations include: (1) the rabbi's estimate of the effects of economic individualism upon human character—whether or not they are morally degrading; (2) his view as to comparative merits of socialism and capitalism in affording opportunities to

the common man; (3) his conjecture as to whether or not socialization of industry would impair individual initiative; (4) his view
on the question of whether or not economic planning for common welfare is possible under capitalism; and (5) his conviction
as to whether or not the maintenance of human culture demands
the retention of capitalism.

6. Those among the rabbis who favor a farmer-labor party are
considerably more favorable toward organized labor, collectiviza-
tion of economy, and the employment of the class appeal in social
reconstruction than are those opposed to the farmer-labor party.

Education

1. The rabbinate in all its wings is virtually unanimous in
favoring the extension of the scope of social responsibility for
education beyond the prevailing level.

2. The rabbinate is preponderantly opposed to outside control
of teachers' opinions.

3. There is virtual agreement in favor of the employment of
education to the end of developing social intelligence.

Civil Liberties

1. Only a small percentage of the rabbinate favors the absolute
denial of freedom to advocates of unpopular views; a sizable majority of the rabbinate is opposed to the denial of freedom of
speech to any group under any circumstances; the remainder favor
withholding freedom of speech from specific groups only under
specified conditions such as war and social crises.

2. The rabbinate is opposed to censorship of motion picture
plays and of art.

3. In both the above respects the Conservative and Reform
wings stand on about the same level of liberalism.[1]

Peace and Internationalism

1. In the view of the rabbinate, competition for markets, fascist
militarism, capitalist institutions and private manufacture and
sale of arms and munitions are, in the order named, the most important causes of war.

[1] The liberal sentiment in this regard among Orthodox rabbis is less marked.

2. Few rabbis would either support or oppose war unconditionally. The preponderant majority reserve the right to arrive
at a decision in the light of particular circumstances.

3. The rabbinate is opposed to such defense of American business interests as might lead to war.

4. The rabbinate favors the nationalization of the arms and
munitions industry.

Treatment of Women and Minority Racial Groups

1. There is decided opposition in the Reform and Conservative
wings to the double standard of sex morality.[2]

2. There is a strong sentiment in favor of economic egalitarianism of the sexes in the Reform and Conservative wings.[3]

3. The rabbinate in all its wings strongly favors the enactment
of more liberal divorce laws.

4. The rabbinate in all its wings is strongly in favor of race
equality.

Coherence of Thought

1. The thinking of the rabbis as a group on the issues on which
they indicated their positions is fairly free from inconsistencies.

2. On the whole, a fairly large majority of the Conservative
and Reform groups show evidence of integrated, coherent thinking.

3. In all three wings, the thinking on theological matters seems
to be better integrated than that on the issues of economic reconstruction.

II. PREACHING EMPHASES OF RABBIS AND THEIR BELIEFS
CONCERNING OBSTACLES TO FREEDOM IN PREACHING

Preaching Emphasis

1. Issues falling within the areas of the philosophy of Jewish
life, theology, and the social function of religion receive considerable preaching emphasis. Comparatively little preaching
emphasis is placed on the issues of economic reconstruction.

---

[2] The Orthodox group is about equally divided on this issue.
[3] Egalitarian sentiment is decidedly weaker in the Orthodox wing.

Rabbis' Beliefs Concerning Obstacles to Freedom in Preaching

1. In the opinion of the rabbis, the level of intelligence, local biases, and economic conservatism of the members of congregations closely approach being outstanding obstacles to the freedom of the pulpit.

2. Many rabbis see in their economic insecurity, and in the general conservative climate of opinion in their communities, conditions which militate against their effective teaching and preaching.

III. TENDENCIES IN THE BELIEFS OF THE AMERICAN RABBINATE

The preceding findings represent the state of mind of several hundred rabbis at about the close of 1937, a period of economic breakdown and political crisis the world over, of the retreat of the values of rationality, liberalism, democracy, and humanism before the forces of obscurantism, totalitarianism, dictatorship, and exclusive nationalism and racism, of intensification of anti-Semitism in Europe as well as in America, and of unrest in Palestine so serious as to shake the hope of possibility of rebuilding that country as the national homeland of the Jewish people. In the years that have elapsed since this study was undertaken the crisis has come to a head. The principal issue at stake in the present conflict is whether or not there will be an opportunity to reconstruct the world on the basis of democratic justice. To avail itself of this opportunity mankind will need the realistic, clear-thinking leadership of teachers and preachers, among others. Do the patterns of beliefs and preaching revealed in the course of this investigation represent merely a "snapshot" of the state of mind of rabbis at a particular period? Or can these findings be taken as representative of an abiding tendency? Assuming there is such an abiding tendency, what does it spell for the approach to the problems of world reconstruction when hostilities come to an end?

The data brought to light in this investigation probably represent more than a passing state of mind. Analysis of the questionnaire data was preceded by an historical study of the ideological developments of the principal wings of contemporary Judaism and of the orientation and attitudes of rabbis to socio-economic problems. The responses of the rabbis to the issues raised in the questionnaire correspond in a considerable degree to the recent phases of rabbinic thought as revealed in the corporate declarations of the different wings of the rabbinate and in the writings of prominent spokesmen of these wings. As pointed out previously, the pronouncements of the several wings indicate only approximately the views of their membership. However, in the absence of other evidence, past tendencies as revealed in the official pronouncements were linked to the present results. The questionnaire data when read against the background of historic development thus probably indicate a few more or less abiding tendencies in the thinking of the rabbis. These tendencies are:

1. A respect for scientific facts, methods, and world-orientation. The attempt to systematize religion and science into a unitary and organic philosophy of life is evident in the thinking of many rabbis.[4]

2. Related to the aforementioned is the view that Judaism is not a closed system of beliefs, practices, ideals, ideas, and values, but a developing process of life and belief. This view, least prominent among Orthodox rabbis, is most pronounced among Reform rabbis, and the major part of the American rabbinate can be said to be imbued with this orientation.

3. Intensification of the spirit of Jewish nationalism and appreciation of national elements in Jewish life and religion. Traditional Judaism by implication has always been nationalistic; now Orthodox and Conservative Judaism are explicitly nationalistic. Reform Judaism, which began partly as a negation of Jewish nationalism, has within the last few decades covered quite a distance on the way back to nationalism. There is a keener realization in the ranks of Reform than ever before of the Jewish peoplehood, of the common problems confronting the Jews, and of the need for a cooperative search for methods of resolving these problems.

4. A keen appreciation that the destiny of the Jewish people is bound up with that of mankind in general.

5. A growing interest in the economic, political, and social prob-

---

[4] A sizable section of the Orthodox rabbis are content with merely tolerating science without letting it influence the content of religion.

lems of mankind coupled with an increasing realistic and liberal approach to these problems, as evidenced by:

    a. Strong pro-labor sympathy.

    b. A tendency to favor more or less socialization of means of production.

    c. Conviction that society is responsible for securing the individual against old age, sickness, and unemployment.

    d. Favorable attitude toward extension of civil liberties to dissenters.

    e. A sentiment in favor of American participation in international movements calculated to secure peace, of sacrificing business "rights" where they may involve America in war, and of opposition to participation in war.

    f. A sentiment favorable to egalitarian treatment of women and minority races.

    6. A widespread conviction that Judaism is vitally concerned with social reconstruction, and that the spirit of Judaism demands anything from correction of certain abuses of capitalism to a complete refashioning of the pattern of life along collectivistic lines.

It was noted in the body of the report that a number of these trends originated in or were heightened by post-World War I experience, particularly during the years of political and economic crisis in the United States and abroad which culminated in World War II. It seems fair to assume that rabbis' beliefs and teachings will continue to be influenced by economic, political, and social developments and by the way these developments affect the position of Jewry in the community as a whole. Whatever aspects of the present beliefs of the rabbis are due to the world crisis are likely to be further deepened and crystallized in the process of future events which will call for some of the most crucial decisions that have faced mankind in the course of its entire history.

Some indication of what the approach of the American rabbinate is likely to be can be gathered from the various pronouncements on social justice and world reconstruction issued by the Reform Central Conference and the Conservative Rabbinical Assembly during the war years, the statement of the American Institute on *Judaism and a Just and Enduring Peace,* issued in 1942, and the

Pattern for Peace, a Catholic, Jewish, and Protestant Declaration on World Peace which appeared in 1943.

The idea of the fatherhood of God and its corollaries, the sanctity of the individual and the brotherhood of the human race, constitute the unitary ground for the principles offered, in all these statements, as a basis for post-war reconstruction. The statements are thoroughly pervaded with the conviction that only a just peace can be an enduring peace. They differ in respect to the degree with which they draw the specific implications from the concepts of the fatherhood of God, the sacredness of the individual, and the brotherhood of man. The most important implications that can be gleaned from the statements taken together are:

1. Moral principles constitute the ultimate basis of validity of any political, economic, and social arrangements.

2. Democracy is the only pattern of social relations which constitutes a design for human living.

3. The scope of democracy must be broadened so as to include the entire human race, and deepened so as to refashion the present economic system and to enrich life in all its aspects.

4. The close links of interdependence between human beings residing in different parts of the globe, created by science and technology, necessitate the establishment of a world parliament and the creation of a world police force.

5. Imperialism abroad and oppression and inequalities at home which are based on racial differences are contradictory to the concepts of religion.

6. No individual or group has a preemptive claim to any part of the world's riches. Society is the source of all wealth, and its function is the improvement of the quality of life of all mankind. Individuals and groups can claim only temporary stewardship. Organized society is entitled to devise means for better distribution of socially created wealth.

7. All peoples are entitled to access to natural riches no matter where located.

What distinguishes the Conservative from the Reform statements is greater detail in criticism of contemporary society and greater specificity of suggestion for social reconstruction. Whereas the statements of the Central Conference content themselves with the formulation of general principles, the statements of the Rabbinical Assembly come out vigorously against class and race domination and in support of collective ownership of natural resources and some wealth-producing instrumentalities and greater access to the riches of human culture for all members of society. Another distinction is the emphasis in the Conservative statements on minority cultural rights for Jews and the place of a Jewish Palestine in the scheme of reconstruction of Jewish life.

IV. HOW REPRESENTATIVE ARE THE ABOVE TRENDS AND FINDINGS?

The investigation has limited itself to the Reform and Conservative wings largely, taking in only a specific section of the Orthodox rabbinate. One third of the total membership of these bodies has responded to the questionnaire.

The large body of Orthodox rabbis omitted entirely from the study are in all probability of foreign birth, were educated abroad, and serve in congregations whose members have arrived somewhat more recently in this country. The specific Orthodox section included in the present study, as well as the total Reform and Conservative wings, represent principally native-born, American-trained rabbis serving in congregations whose membership is also largely native born. In view of the virtual cessation of immigration to America, it is fair to assume that the rabbis who were the subjects of this study represent a type that will become ever more dominant in American Jewry.

V. THE SOCIAL SIGNIFICANCE OF THE BELIEFS AND TEACHINGS OF THE "DISCIPLES OF THE WISE"

In appraising the social influence of the rabbis it is important to note that their audience consists largely of middle-class individuals. The incomes of members of the congregation are much higher than those of the American population in general and the Jewish population in particular. Occupationally the rabbis' audience is overweighted with individuals who derive their subsistence from ownership of property or through commercial, managerial, and professional activities, and it is underrepresented so far as industrial workers are concerned.

The rabbis thus exercise most of their influence on the Jewish section of the American middle class. To this group they convey the message of religious traditions, as they see them, the worthwhileness of the Jewish pattern of life in general, the need for an effort to solve the problem of Jewish adjustment along the lines of general social reconstruction and Jewish nationalist effort, and finally the need for social reconstruction away from strict economic individualism and toward a mild form of socialization. To the task of conveying this message they bring a combination of Jewish training, general education, and interest in social issues. To what extent they actually succeed in refashioning opinion cannot even be conjectured. What they are likely to accomplish in the future will depend considerably on the degree of effectiveness they develop, and on the role which the middle class will be called upon to assume in the reconstruction of American society. Should the rabbinate succeed in attracting to the synagogue the Jewish working population, its sphere of influence would be considerably increased. For the present its task seems to be limited to an effort to influence the Jewish middle class toward acceptance of a point of view that may be characterized as socialized, pro-labor, and generally liberal.

BIBLIOGRAPHY

American Jewish Year Book, 5698, Vol. 39. Jewish Publication Society of America, Philadelphia, 1937.

AMES, EDWARD SCRIBNER. *The Psychology of Religious Experience.* Houghton Mifflin Company, Boston, 1925.

BARON, SALO W. *A Social and Religious History of the Jews.* 3 Vols. Columbia University Press, New York, 1937.

BERNFELD, SIMON. *Juden und Judentum im Neunzehten Jahrhundert.* Cronbach, Berlin, 1898.

BERNFELD, SIMON. *Toledot ha-Reformazion ha-Datit be-Yisrael,* Achiasaf, Warsaw. Crakow, 1900.

BETTS, GEORGE HERBERT. *The Beliefs of 700 Ministers and Their Meaning for Religious Education.* Abingdon Religious Education Monographs. Abingdon Press, New York, 1929.

CASE, ADELAIDE T. *Liberal Christianity and Religious Education.* The Macmillan Company, New York, 1924.

CENTRAL CONFERENCE OF AMERICAN RABBIS. *Year Book.* 47 Vols. Cincinnati, 1891–1937.

COE, GEORGE ALBERT. *Psychology of Religion.* University of Chicago Press, Chicago, 1916.

DEWEY, JOHN. *A Common Faith.* Terry Lectures. Yale University Press, New Haven, 1934.

DININ, SAMUEL. *Judaism in a Changing Civilization.* Bureau of Publications, Teachers College, Columbia University, 1933.

EDDY, GEORGE SHERWOOD. *Religion and Social Justice.* George H. Doran Company, New York, 1927.

EISENBERG, F. *Staat und Religion mit besonderer Rücksicht auf die Stellung der Israeliten in dem sogenannten christlich-germanischen Staaten.* Leipzig, 1844.

FINKELSTEIN, ROSS, BROWN. *The Religions of Democracy.* Devin-Adair Company, New York, 1941.

FINKELSTEIN, LOUIS. *Role of Dogma in Judaism.* Reprint from *The Thomist,* Jan. 1943. *The Maritain Volume.*

FOSDICK, HARRY EMERSON. *As I See Religion.* Harper & Brothers, New York, 1932.

FOSDICK, HARRY EMERSON. *Christianity and Progress.* Cole Lectures. Fleming H. Revell Company, New York, 1922.

FRANZBLAU, ABRAHAM NORMAN. *Religious Belief and Character Among Jewish Adolescents.* Teachers College, Columbia University, 1934.

GAMORAN, EMANUEL. *Changing Conceptions in Jewish Education.* The Macmillan Company, New York, 1924.

GEIGER, ABRAHAM. *Judaism and Its History.* Translated by Maurice Mayer. New York, 1866.

GINZBERG, LOUIS. *Students, Scholars, Saints.* Jewish Publishing Company, Philadelphia, 1928.

GRAETZ, HEINRICH. *History of the Jews.* 6 Vols. Jewish Publication Society of America, Philadelphia, 1891–1898.

HARPER, M. H. *Social Beliefs and Attitudes of American Educators.* Bureau of Publications, Teachers College, Columbia University, 1927.

HARTSHORNE, HUGH and MAY, MARK A. *Studies in Deceit.* The Macmillan Company, New York, 1928.

HIRSCH, EMIL G. *My Religion.* The Macmillan Company, New York, 1925.

HUSIK, ISAAC. *A History of Medieval Jewish Philosophy.* The Macmillan Company, New York, 1916.

Jewish Encyclopedia. 12 Vols. Funk & Wagnalls Company, New York, 1906.

Jewish Library. Edited by Leo Jung. First Series, The Macmillan Company, New York, 1928. Second Series, Bloch Publishing Company, New York, 1930. Third Series, Jewish Library Publication Company, New York, 1934.

JOHNSON, FREDERICK ERNEST. (In collaboration with a group of consultants.) *Economics and the Good Life.* Association Press, New York, 1934.

JOSEPH, MORRIS. *Judaism as Life and Creed.* The Macmillan Company, London, 1903.

KAPLAN, MORDECAI M. *Judaism as a Civilization.* The Macmillan Company, New York, 1934.

KAPLAN, MORDECAI M. *The Meaning of God in Modern Jewish Religion.* Behrman's Jewish Book House, New York, 1937.

KARPF, MAURICE J. "Jewish Community Organization in the United States." *American Jewish Year Book,* Vol. 39, pp. 47–148. Jewish Publication Society of America, Philadelphia, 1937.

KINZLER, ESTHER. *Some Aspects of Occupational Declaration of Jews in New York City.* Graduate School for Jewish Social Work, New York, 1935.

KOHLER, KAUFMANN. *Jewish Theology.* The Macmillan Company, New York, 1918.

LEVEN, MAURICE, MOULTON, HAROLD G., AND WARBURTON, CLARK. *America's Capacity to Consume.* Brookings Institution, Washington, 1934.

LEVY, BERYL HAROLD. *Reform Judaism in America.* A Study in Religious Adaptation. Thesis published by Columbia University Press, 1933.

LINFIELD, HARRY S. *Jews in the United States (1927).* A Study of Their Number and Distribution. American Jewish Committee, Statistical Department, New York, 1929.

LOWELL, EDWARD J. *The Eve of the French Revolution.* Houghton Mifflin Company, Boston, 1893.

MACMURRAY, JOHN. *Creative Society.* A Study of the Relation of Christianity to Communism. Association Press, New York, 1936.

MALLER, JULIUS B. *Testing the Knowledge of Jewish History.* Union of American Hebrew Congregations, Department of Synagogue and School Extension. Cincinnati, 1932.

MILLIS, WALTER. *Road to War; America 1914–1917.* Houghton Mifflin Company, Boston and New York, 1935.

MARGOLIS, MAX L., AND MARX, ALEXANDER. *History of the Jewish People.* Jewish Publication Society, Philadelphia, 1927.

MONTEFIORE, CLAUDE G. "A Justification of Judaism." Reprinted from the *Unitarian Review,* Boston, August and September, 1885; and from the *Jewish Chronicle,* London, September 11–October 9, 1885.

NATHAN, MARVIN. *The Attitude of the Jewish Student in the Colleges and Universities Toward His Religion.* Bloch Publishing Co., New York, 1932.

NATIONAL CONFERENCE OF JEWISH SOCIAL SERVICE. *Proceedings—Annual Session, Boston, 1930.* New York, 1934.

Orthodox Union, The. Published monthly by The Union of Orthodox Jewish Congregations of America, Yeshiva College, New York.

PHILIPSON, DAVID. *The Reform Movement in Judaism.* The Macmillan Company, New York, 1907, 1931.

Pronouncement of Social Justice. Rabbinical Assembly of America, New York, 1935.

RABBINICAL ASSEMBLY OF THE JEWISH THEOLOGICAL SEMINARY OF AMERICA. *Proceedings:* Vol. 1, 27th Annual Conference at Asbury Park, N. J., July, 1927. Vol. 2, 28th Annual Conference at Wilkes-Barre, Pa., 1928. Vol. 3, 29th Annual Conference at Long Branch, N. J., July, 1929. Vol. 4, 30th Annual Convention at Tannersville, N. Y., July, 1930; 31st Annual Convention at Long Branch, N. J., July, 1931; 32nd Annual Convention at New York City, May, 1932.

RAISIN, JACOB S. "Reform Judaism Prior to Abraham Geiger." Central Conference of American Rabbis, *Year Book,* Vol. XX, pp. 197–245. Charlevoix, 1910.

RAISIN, MAX. *Israel in America.* Selected Essays. Achiever Publishing House, Jerusalem, 1928.

RUPPIN, ARTHUR. *Sozialogia der Juden.* 2 Vols. Berlin, 1930–1931.

SCHECHTER, SOLOMON. *Seminary Addresses and Other Papers.* Cincinnati, 1915.

SCHECHTER, SOLOMON. *Some Aspects of Rabbinic Theology.* The Macmillan Company, New York, 1923.

SCHECHTER, SOLOMON. *Studies in Judaism.* Edited by Marx, Alexander and Schechter, Frank I. 3 Vols. Jewish Publication Society, Philadelphia, 1924.

SELIGMANN, CAESAR. *Geschichte der Jüdischen Reformbewegung von Mendelssohn bis zur Gegenwart.* Frankfurt a.M., 1922.

Talmud Babli, Shabbat. New York, 1919.

Talmud Yerushalmi, Peah. Chapter II. Krotoschin-Berlin, 1920.

THURSTONE, L. L., AND CHAVE, E. J. *The Measurement of Attitude.* Chicago University Press, Chicago, 1929.

12,854 Clergymen on War and Peace. (Pamphlet.) Published by Bishop James C. Baker and 28 Associates. The World Tomorrow, May, 1931 and May 10, 1934.

Union of American Hebrew Congregations. Reports 62 and 63. Cincinnati, 1936, 1937.

WATSON, GOODMAN BARBOUR. *Experimentation and Measurement in Religious Education.* Association Press, New York, 1927.

WIENER, MAX. *Jüdische Religion im Zeitalter der Emanzipation.* Berlin, 1933.

WIERNICK, PETER. *History of the Jews in America.* Second revised and enlarged edition. Jewish History Publishing Company, New York, 1931.

Zohar. 3 Vols. Vilna, 1924.

APPENDIX A

QUESTIONNAIRE ON RELIGIOUS AND SOCIAL ATTITUDES
OF AMERICAN RABBIS

SECTION I

PLEASE READ THE DIRECTIONS BEFORE YOU BEGIN TO
FILL IN THE QUESTIONNAIRE

DIRECTIONS:—(1) In the left hand margin (Attitude) are symbols + ? —. If you agree with the statement more than you disagree draw a circle around the +, thus ⊕, if you disagree more than you agree draw a circle around the —, thus ⊖, if you are doubtful draw a circle around the ?. If you feel very strongly about your answer underline it, thus ⊕ or ⊖.

(2) In the right hand margin (Frequency of Preaching or Teaching) are the letters F, O, N. If in your sermons, writings, personal contacts, teaching adult groups, etc., you frequently advocate the position indicated by your answer in the left margin encircle F, if you advocate this position only occasionally encircle O, if never encircle N.

VIEWS ON RELIGION, MORALS, JUDAISM, AND JEWISH PROBLEMS

ATTITUDE

FREQUENCY OF PREACHING OR TEACHING

1. + ? — Judaism must remain forever hostile to any science which F O N tends to destroy faith in the literal truth of the teachings of the Bible.

2. + ? — Belief in the actual occurrence of the miracles as recorded F O N in the Bible is indispensable to Judaism.

3. + ? — Moses wrote the Pentateuch. F O N

4. + ? — Observing Jews will be happier than non-observing Jews in F O N the hereafter.

5. + ? — Sabbath observance is a cardinal principle of Judaism F O N

6. + ? — Personal immortality is an essential doctrine of Judaism. F O N

7. + ? — The Biblical story of creation is a myth. F O N

8. + ? — The Torah (Bible, Talmud, Codes, etc.) constitutes an ade- F O N quate guide to the moral perplexities of the present.

9. + ? — There are instances of human conduct which according to F O N the Bible had divine sanction that should now be consid- ered immoral.

10. + ? — Judaism is essentially a religious outlook upon life which F O N can be preserved even if the Jews as a distinct group dis- appear.

203

ATTITUDE

11. + ? — The cultivation of the Hebrew language and literature　F　O　N
and loyalty to the cause of rebuilding Palestine as a Jewish
homeland are essential to the Jewish pattern of life.

12. + ? — Anti-Semitism cannot take deep root in America.　　　　F　O　N

13. + ? — The chief hope for Jewish adjustment to the World lies in　F　O　N
the emergence of a collectivist social order and greater
world unity.

14. + ? — It is in the best interests of the Jewish people that Jews　F　O　N
discontinue participation in radical social movements.

15. + ? — To be worth while, efforts to build a better social order　F　O　N
must be religiously motivated.

16. + ? — To preserve his usefulness to the community a rabbi　F　O　N
should not express pro-labor sympathy in the face of a
strike in his own community.

17. + ? — In the issues between labor and capital the spirit of Juda-　F　O　N
ism should impel one, generally, to identify himself with
labor.

18. + ? — In order to be a vital force in contemporary life Judaism　F　O　N
must identify itself with those movements which aim to
create a better social order.

VIEWS ON ECONOMICS AND ECONOMIC RECONSTRUCTION

19. + ? — Radical agitators exaggerate when they assert that the　F　O　N
bulk of the wealth in this country is owned by a very small
portion of the population.

20. + ? — As a general rule, our economic system distributes wealth　F　O　N
and income among the various individuals in proportion
to their ability, energy, and usefulness to society.

21. + ? — Social control of industry will destroy personal initiative.　F　O　N

22. + ? — The American standard of living would decline appre-　F　O　N
ciably if private ownership of industry were abolished.

23. + ? — Economic planning for the good of our entire population　F　O　N
is impossible within the framework of capitalism.

24. + ? — Public business enterprises are generally unsuccessful.　F　O　N

25. + ? — Most labor trouble is due to the work of radical agitators.　F　O　N

26. + ? — Trade unions do more harm than good to our industrial　F　O　N
progress.

27. + ? — Rabbis should support the right of labor to engage in col-　F　O　N
lective bargaining through unions of their own choosing.

28. + ? — The use of injunctions in labor disputes should cease.　　F　O　N

29. + ? — The sit-down strikes are contrary to law and order.　　　F　O　N

30. + ? — We must either democratize our industrial structure or　F　O　N
recognize the bankruptcy of the democratic ideals of the
American people.

31. + ? — The ownership of the radio, the press, and the cinema by　F　O　N
profit-seeking corporations accounts, to a considerable extent, for the perversion of American taste and the lowering
of political intelligence in this country.

32. + ? — It is more difficult for the poor than for the rich to get　F　O　N
justice in our courts.

	FREQUENCY OF PREACHING OR TEACHING

ATTITUDE

33. + ? — Our system of economic individualism has degraded human character and has appealed to the most selfish impulses of man.   F O N

34. + ? — Prostitution is, in the main, due to character deficiencies and would not be materially curtailed by the improvement of economic conditions for the masses.   F O N

35. + ? — In the interest of human culture the capitalist system should, on the whole, be preserved.   F O N

36. + ? — A Socialist system would provide better opportunities for the average person to exercise worth-while personal initiative than the capitalist system.   F O N

37. + ? — The maintenance of an adequate health level for the entire community should be made the responsibility of the state.   F O N

38. + ? — Public utilities, railroads, and coal mines should be owned and operated by governmental units.   F O N

39. + ? — Consumers cooperatives are detrimental to the country's prosperity.   F O N

40. + ? — Governmental appropriations for relief must be substantially increased in order to enable the unemployed to live on a minimum level of decency.   F O N

41. + ? — Methods calculated to set workers against the present order should be rejected.   F O N

42. + ? — The Supreme Court should be deprived of its power to invalidate legislation enacted for the economic protection of the population.   F O N

43. + ? — A farmer-labor party is needed to bring about much-needed changes in our political and social structure.   F O N

VIEWS ON EDUCATION

44. + ? — Laws demanding special loyalty oaths for teachers constitute a threat to good teaching.   F O N

45. + ? — Teachers should not be allowed to organize in labor unions.   F O N

46. + ? — Licenses to teach in the public school should be refused to socialists.   F O N

47. + ? — Teachers who are known to be members of the Communist party should be dismissed from service.   F O N

48. + ? — No school, college, or university should teach anything that is found to result in its students' doubting or questioning the Bible as containing the word of God.   F O N

49. + ? — Compulsory military training in our schools and colleges is in the best interests of the country.   F O N

50. + ? — It is the obligation of society to conduct a systematic program of adult education centering on the major economic and social problems of today.   F O N

51. + ? — Where a community is incapable of providing adequate educational facilities to youths, the state should appropriate funds for that purpose.   F O N

52. + ? — The Federal Government should apportion funds for the improvement of educational facilities throughout the nation.   F O N

FREQUENCY
OF
PREACHING
OR
ATTITUDE   TEACHING

53. + ? — Designation of periods during school hours for religious F   O   N
instruction by denominational teachers contradicts the
principle of non-sectarianism of the public school.

54. + ? — Bible reading should be included in the Public School   F   O   N
curriculum.

55. + ? — In the interests of sound education for our young, teachers F   O   N
should be encouraged to fight against sub-standard living
conditions in the home.

56. + ? — Economies in public education should in times of crises F   O   N
be made only as a last resort.

CIVIL LIBERTIES

57. + ? — Those who criticize our Constitution are unpatriotic.   F   O   N

58. + ? — We should exclude from the United States those who seek F   O   N
to establish a communist order.

59. + ? — We should exclude from the United States those who wish F   O   N
to establish a fascist government.

60. + ? — In the interests of public morality rabbis should favor cen- F   O   N
sorship of the movies, art, and literature.

VIEWS ON PEACE AND INTERNATIONALISM

61. + ? — Whatever his individual view is with regard to the justice F   O   N
of a war or the right of the government to declare it, the
rabbi should come to the aid of a person whose conscience
forbids him to participate in war.

62. + ? — The manufacture and sale of arms and munitions should F   O   N
be entirely in the hands of the Federal Government.

63. + ? — A strongly armed America is the best way of keeping   F   O   N
America out of war.

64. + ? — America should defend the right of its citizens to carry on F   O   N
foreign trade even at the risk of becoming embroiled in
a war.

65. + ? — It is the duty of the American government to protect   F   O   N
American business interests abroad even to the extent
of making use of our armed forces.

66. + ? — The government should prohibit American business, in-   F   O   N
dustry, and finance to make loans to governments at war.

67. + ? — America should keep strictly aloof from dealing with   F   O   N
European problems.

68. + ? — America should take the initiative in bringing about inter- F   O   N
national disarmament.

69. + ? — The American government ought to intercede in behalf   F   O   N
of Jews and other minority groups who are victims of
oppression.

70. + ? — American participation in the World Court should be   F   O   N
rejected as a violation of our national sovereignty.

VIEWS ON SEX

71. + ? — In the interests of the race it is justifiable to demand a F   O   N
higher standard of sex morality from women than from
men.

ATTITUDE

72. + ? — Extra-marital sex relations between mature individuals is   F   O   N
the legitimate concern of society only if such relations are
likely to result in offspring.

73. + ? — Birth control should be opposed as contrary to the spirit   F   O   N
of Judaism.

74. + ? — The best interests of society would be served if women   F   O   N
could dedicate themselves solely to the care of families.

75. + ? — In general, divorce laws in this country need liberalizing.   F   O   N

76. + ? — It is in the interest of moral advance to facilitate woman's   F   O   N
efforts to enter professions.

77. + ? — Sex problems should not be discussed from the pulpit.   F   O   N

VIEWS ON RACE

78. + ? — A Federal anti-lynching law should be enacted.   F   O   N

79. + ? — The Jim Crow system in the South violates the principle   F   O   N
of the brotherhood of man.

80. + ? — In view of the different standards of living, different salary   F   O   N
scales for Negro and White teachers in the South are
justified.

81. + ? — Orientals should be admitted to American citizenship.   F   O   N

82. + ? — It is in the interest of good government to maintain special   F   O   N
qualifications for Negro suffrage in the South until such
time as their cultural level will rise appreciably.

83. +? — The belief in the superiority of the white race is scientifi-   F   O   N
cally sound.

SECTION II

DIRECTIONS:—(1) Please indicate your stand with regard to the various issues
listed below by putting a check √ in the space on the left next to the phrase
which *best corresponds* to your belief. Even if you find a number of statements,
relating to any particular issue, satisfactory mark only the best single one. Mark
one space only. If you believe, for example, in number 2, below, that the highest
type of prayer is "a petition for the establishment of social justice," place a check
in the space adjoining this phrase.

(2) In the right hand margin (Frequency of Preaching or Teaching) are the letters
F, O, N. If in your sermons, writings, personal contacts, teaching adult groups, etc.,
you frequently advocate the position indicated by your answer in the left margin
encircle F, if you advocate this position only occasionally encircle O, if never encircle N.

VIEWS ON RELIGION, MORALS, JUDAISM AND JEWISH PROBLEMS

1. Prayers are worth while principally because:
    ....(a) they literally bring divine aid to the suppliant   F   O   N
    ....(b) they give the suppliant the feeling of divine sup-
port for his efforts
    ....(c) they provide psychological release to suppliant
    ....(d) they are helpful in maintaining Jewish group
unity
    ....(e) they help to raise human life to a higher moral
level

ATTITUDE

2. The highest type of prayer is a petition for:
................(a) the welfare of one's own person or the person's   F   O   N
          associates
................(b) the fulfillment of God's purpose on earth
................(c) the establishment of social justice
................(d) communion with God

3. The conception of sin that calls for greatest emphasis in our age is:
.... (a) omission or disregard of the precepts of Shulḥan   F   O   N
          'Aruk
................(b) an act which emanates from one's base impulses
................(c) an act which results in harm to society as a whole
................(d) an act harmful to neighbors, business associates,
          and friends
................(e) support of or acquiescence to accepted institutions
          which are socially harmful

4. The conception of salvation that calls for most emphasis in our
   age is:
................(a) happiness in the world to come   F   O   N
................(b) the achievement of an integrated personality
................(c) participation in social movements which make for
          social progress

5. The nature of God is best expressed in the notion of:
................(a) first cause   F   O   N
................(b) literal creator and active ruler of the universe
................(c) the sum total of forces and tendencies which make
          for greater intelligence, beauty, and goodness
................(d) the unitary creative impulse which expresses itself
          in organic evolution and human progress
................(e) the symbol of all that we consider good and true

6. Religion is:
................(a) man-made and therefore will disappear in time as   F   O   N
          a result of man's growing intelligence and changes
          in his aspirations and desires
................(b) an institution through which man attempts to
          realize the highest spiritual values of life and since
          life is undergoing constant change, even *funda-
          mental* religious standards of conduct must be con-
          tinually reconstructed
................(c) a divine institution whose standards of conduct are
          not subject to change, but their application must
          be adjusted to conditions as they are
................(d) a divine institution, and the standards of conduct
          which it has set up are not subject to change

7. The primary consideration in determining the morality of a specific course of action is to examine:
................(a) how it conforms to the moral traditions of human-   F   O   N
          ity
................(b) how it conforms to the moral dictates of the indi-
          vidual's conscience
................(c) the consequences of the act upon the individual
          and society

8. On the whole organized religion as it now functions:
................(a) is an important force in improving social, eco-   F   O   N
          nomic, and cultural conditions

ATTITUDE

...............(b) is a slight factor in the improvement of human life but can be made into an important factor by changing the content of the religious message and the function of the religious teacher

...............(c) must necessarily remain a slight factor in view of the texture of contemporary social life

...............(d) is detrimental to the best interests of man

9. The spirit of Judaism demands:

...............(a) the fundamental abolition of our inherited indus-   F   O   N
trial system which is based on private ownership of the means of production and the urge for private profit

...............(b) the correction of certain evils of our industrial system leaving private ownership and the private profit incentive intact

...............(c) neutrality on the question of economic reconstruction

...............(d) support of our present economic institutions which, on the whole, are calculated to secure the best form of life possible

10. The most important function of the Jewish ministry today is:

...............(a) to afford comfort and support in face of individual   F   O   N
temptation and difficulties without taking sides on important social issues

...............(b) to teach those moral ideals and religious insights which have a bearing on contemporary social problems

...............(c) to advocate the replacement of our inherited institutions by a cooperative society

11. The Bible is:

...............(a) literally the word of God   F   O   N

...............(b) the word of God in the sense that it reflects in a superior degree human striving after wisdom and goodness

...............(c) a record of the moral and religious evolution of the Jews

12. The Jewish people denote a:

...............(a) racial entity   F   O   N

...............(b) nationality

...............(c) religious community

13. The obstacles in the path of the upbuilding of Palestine by Jews can best be overcome by:

...............(a) convincing England that her interests would be   F   O   N
best served by supporting Jews rather than Arabs

...............(b) appealing to the sense of justice of mankind

...............(c) fighting it out with the Arabs

...............(d) attempting to arrive at an understanding with the masses of the Arab people which would permit Jewish immigration and provide for maintenance of national values

14. Our activities in Palestine should aim at:

...............(a) making Palestine a Jewish National State   F   O   N

...............(b) making Palestine a bi-national state of Jews and Arabs

ATTITUDE
...............(c) dividing Palestine into separate Arab and Jewish
            countries

VIEWS ON ECONOMICS AND ECONOMIC RECONSTRUCTION

15. Insurance against sickness, accident, unemployment, death and
    old age should be primarily:
    ....(a) left to individuals interested   F   O   N
    ....(b) made the ultimate responsibility of the individual
                states
    ....(c) made the responsibility of the Federal Government
16. Provisions for the welfare of helpless members of society should
    be the:
    ....(a) concern exclusively of private charities   F   O   N
    ....(b) concern primarily of private charities but assisted
                by the government
    ....(c) concern primarily of the government but assisted
                by private institutions
    ....(d) concern exclusively of the government
17. A sound policy for America to follow is to:
    ....(a) leave our economic order much as it is   F   O   N
    ....(b) leave individual ownership in the means of pro-
                duction intact but correct the defects of the
                present system by regulation of industry and pro-
                visions for social security
    ....(c) gradually socialize our economy to the point where
                our essential industry and banking system will be
                owned and controlled by the state
    ....(d) work toward complete socialization of production
                and distribution
    ....(e) centralize power to bring about political and eco-
                nomic changes in the hands of an honest, energetic,
                and intelligent leader

VIEWS ON EDUCATION

18. It is the duty of publicly supported educational institutions to:
    ....(a) remain neutral with respect to the problems of   F   O   N
                social reconstruction
    ....(b) preserve our inherited institutions
    ....(c) stimulate students to think about the problems of
                social reconstruction
    ....(d) lead students to identify themselves with social
                movements which aim at the creation of a collec-
                tivist commonwealth
19. It is the duty of society to make freely available to the youth:
    ....(a) an elementary education   F   O   N
    ....(b) a high school education
    ....(c) a college education

VIEWS ON PEACE AND INTERNATIONALISM

20. The United States should join the League of Nations:
    ....(a) immediately   F   O   N
    ....(b) when the League proves itself to be a force for
                peace; in the meantime our government should
                extend active assistance to the League

ATTITUDE

...............(c) never; but should be willing to assist as a non-member in important matters involving world good

...............(d) never; and should be aloof

SECTION III

DIRECTIONS:—(1) Complete each statement by underlining the *italicized* word or phrase which most closely approximates your opinion.

(2) In the right hand margin (Frequency of Preaching or Teaching) are the letters F, O, N. If in your sermons, writings, personal contacts, teaching adult groups, etc., you frequently advocate the position indicated by your answer in the left margin encircle F, if you advocate this position only occasionally encircle O, if never encircle N.

1. I believe that for the problems of Jewish adjustment
   - (a) The self removal of Jews from prominent places in business, politics and intellectual endeavor constitutes *no solution, a minor solution, a major solution.*   F O N
   - (b) Good will conferences between Jewish and Gentile leaders constitute *no solution, a minor solution, a major solution.*   F O N
   - (c) Zionism constitutes *no solution, a minor solution, a major solution.*   F O N
   - (d) A militant fight against anti-Semitism constitutes *no solution, a minor solution, a major solution.*   F O N
   - (e) A scheme of general education which aims at raising the intelligence level of the population constitutes *no solution, a minor solution, a major solution.*   F O N
   - (f) Improved religious teaching constitutes *no solution, a minor solution, a major solution.*   F O N
   - (g) A socialist economy constitutes *no solution, a minor solution, a major solution.*   F O N
   - (h) Emergence of an international spirit constitutes *no solution, a minor solution, a major solution.*   F O N

2. I believe it proper to withhold freedom of speech from:
   - (a) Communists—*always, never, during periods of social and economic crisis, during war time.*   F O N
   - (b) Fascists—*always, never, during periods of social and economic crisis, during war time.*   F O N
   - (c) Those who advocate violent seizure of governmental power —*always, never, during periods of social and economic crisis, during war time.*   F O N
   - (d) Those who advocate disobedience among the armed forces of the Nation—*always, never, during periods of social and economic crisis, during war time.*   F O N
   - (e) Strike agitators—*always, never, during periods of social and economic crisis, during war time.*   F O N
   - (f) Advocates of a general strike—*always, never, during periods of social and economic crisis, during war time.*   F O N
   - (g) Critics of the Constitution—*always, never, during periods of social and economic crisis, during war time.*   F O N
   - (h) Advocates of disobedience of mobilization orders—*always, never, during social and economic crises, during war time.*   F O N
   - (i) Critics of our fundamental economic, social, and religious institutions—*always, never, during periods of social and economic crisis, during war time.*   F O N

ATTITUDE

3.   (a) I would support the government of the United States in   F   O   N
           war—
           under all circumstances, in case the antagonist is a Com-
           munist power, in case the antagonist is a Fascist power, in
           case American territory is invaded, never.
       (b) I would refuse to support the government of the United   F   O   N
           States in war—
           under all circumstances, in case the antagonist is a Com-
           munist power, in case the antagonist is a Fascist power, in
           case American territory is invaded, never.
       (c) I would actively oppose the government of the United   F   O   N
           States in war—
           under all circumstances, in case the antagonist is a Com-
           munist power, in case the antagonist is a Fascist power, in
           case American territory is invaded, never.

4. I believe that in bringing about war
       (a) The human instinct of pugnacity is *no factor, a minor,*   F   O   N
           factor, a major factor.
       (b) Capitalist institutions are *no factor, a minor factor, a major* F   O   N
           factor.
       (c) Imperialist competition for markets is *no factor, a. minor* F   O   N
           factor, a major factor.
       (d) Fascist militarism is *no factor, a minor factor, a major*   F   O   N
           factor.
       (e) Missionary zeal of the communists is *no factor, a minor fac-* F   O   N
           tor, a major factor.
       (f) Private manufacture and sale of munitions is *no factor,*   F   O   N
           a minor factor, a major factor.
       (g) Loans to foreign powers are *no factor, a minor factor, a*   F   O   N
           major factor.

SECTION IV

PERSONAL AND CONGREGATIONAL DATA

Age..   Place of Birth..

Marital Status: Single........................   Married........................   Widowed........................
                Separated........................   No. of children........................
My annual income from salary and other sources is below $2500, $2500–$3999, $4000–
$5999, $6000–$10,000 above $10,000 (Underline the figure that most closely approxi-
mates your income).
Total number of years of schooling (after High School) ....
DEGREE   INSTITUTION   MAJOR STUDY

....

....

....

I have been in the Rabbinate........................years.
I completed my rabbinical studies at..

I read regularly the following periodicals: ....

....

....

The congregation in which I serve is at: City........................., State...........................

My Congregation is Orthodox, Conservative, Reform, Other.....................................
(Underline or write in appropriate word)

The bulk of the membership of my congregation are *foreign born, American born of foreign parentage, American born of American parentage.* (Underline appropriate phrase.)

Rank the income groups in your congregation in order of their size by placing the number 1 in the parenthesis next to the most numerous income group, number 2 next to the second most numerous group, 3 next to the third most numerous group, etc.

    ( ) less than $2000 per annum, ( ) $2000–$5000, ( ) $5000–$10,000
    ( ) above $10,000.

Rank the occupational groups in your congregation in order of their size by placing the number 1 in the parenthesis adjoining the most numerous occupational group, number 2 next to the second most numerous group, etc.

    ( ) Industrial workers, ( ) Clerical employees, ( ) Professionals,
    ( ) Managerial, ( ) Proprietal, ( ) Commercial other than proprietal, ( ) Agricultural.

The relations between Jews and Gentiles of the same cultural and economic status in my community are *good, bad, indifferent.* (Underline one.)

Both Jewish and non-Jewish charities in my city are provided for by a shared community chest. *Yes No* (Underline).

Underline the appropriate expression in *italics* for each of the following statements (a) to (g).

In my experience—

    (a) The level of intelligence of the congregation constitutes *no factor, a minor factor, a major factor* in limiting freedom of preaching and teaching.

    (b) Local biases constitute *no factor, a minor factor, a major factor* in limiting freedom of preaching and teaching.

    (c) Conservatism on economic issues constitutes *no factor, a minor factor, a major factor* in limiting freedom of preaching and teaching.

    (d) Pressure groups such as the American Legion, the D.A.R. constitute *no factor, a minor factor, a major factor* in limiting freedom of preaching and teaching.

    (e) The Press constitutes *no factor, a minor factor, a major factor* in limiting freedom of preaching and teaching.

    (f) The vested interests of some members of the congregation constitute *no factor, a minor factor, a major factor* in limiting freedom of preaching and teaching.

    (g) Consideration of the feelings of Gentiles constitutes *no factor, a minor factor, a major factor* in limiting freedom of preaching and teaching.

The following other factors constitute major obstacles in the way of freedom of preaching:

....

....

....

In the space provided below make any comments you care to on the issues raised directly or indirectly by the questionnaire.

APPENDIX B

CHARTS TO DETERMINE POSITIONS ON GENERAL ISSUES

CHART I

KEY TO RESPONSES IN TERMS OF NATURALISM *vs.* SUPERNATURALISM

	POINT OF VIEW	
Topic	*Naturalistic*	*Supernaturalistic*
1. Changing and unchanging in religion.	Religion a passing phase.	
	Fundamentals subject to reconstruction.	Fundamentals not subject to reconstruction.
2. Concept of God.	Forces making for good creative impulse.	First cause. Literal creator.
3. Nature of Bible.	Figuratively word of God. Record of moral and religious evolution.	Literal word of God.
4. Belief in biblically recorded miracles.	Not essential to Judaism.	Essential to Judaism.
5. Biblical story of creation.	Myth.	Not myth.
6. Hostility of Judaism to science contradicting Bible.	No.	Yes.
7. Doctrine of personal immortality.	Not essential to Judaism.	Essential to Judaism.
8. Preferential status of observing Jews in the hereafter.	No.	Yes.
9. The function of prayer.	Gives feeling of divine aid. Provides psychological release. Provides Jewish unity. Raises moral level of life.	Actually brings divine aid.
10. Highest type of prayer.	For welfare of person or associates. For establishment of social justice.	For fulfillment of God's purpose. For communion with God.
11. Concept of sin.	Act emanating from base impulse. Act harmful to society. Act harmful to neighbors, friends, etc. Support or acquiescence to socially harmful institutions.	Disregard of Shulḥan 'Aruk.

214

CHART 1 (*Continued*)

KEY TO RESPONSES IN TERMS OF NATURALISM *vs.* SUPERNATURALISM

| Topic | POINT OF VIEW | |
	Naturalistic	Supernaturalistic
12. Concept of salvation.	Integrated personality. Participation in progressive social movements.	Happiness in the hereafter.

CHART II

KEY FOR APPRAISAL OF RESPONSES IN TERMS OF ATTITUDE TOWARD JEWISH NATIONALISM

| Topic | POINT OF VIEW | |
	Pro-Nationalistic	Non- or Anti-Nationalistic
1. Judaism possible without Jews.	No.	Yes.
2. Place of Hebrew and Palestine in Jewish life.	Essential.	Not essential.
3. Nature of Jewish people.	A race; a nation.	A religious community.
4. Zionism as salvation to Jewish problem.	Major solution.	No solution. Minor solution.

CHART III

KEY FOR APPRAISAL OF RESPONSES WITH REGARD TO RECOGNITION OF LINKAGE OF JEWISH DESTINY WITH THE DESTINY OF MANKIND

| Topic | POINT OF VIEW | |
	Recognition of Linkage	Nonrecognition of Linkage
1. Hope for Jewish adjustment in collectivism and world unity.	Yes.	No.
2. Discontinuance of Jewish participation in radical social movements in their own interests.	No.	Yes.
3. General education as solution to Jewish problem.	Major solution.	No solution. Minor solution.
4. A socialist economy as solution to Jewish problem.	Major solution.	No solution. Minor solution.
5. Internationalism as solution to Jewish problem.	Major solution.	No solution. Minor solution.

CHART IV

KEY FOR APPRAISING ATTITUDES ON SOCIAL RESPONSIBILITY FOR INDIVIDUAL WELFARE

Topic	POINT OF VIEW	
	Recognition of Responsibility	Nonrecognition of Responsibility
1. State responsibility for maintenance of adequate health level.	Yes.	No.
2. Increase relief outlays to level necessary to minimum decency.	Yes.	No.
3. Insurance against sickness, accident, unemployment, death, and old age.	Responsibility of states. Responsibility of Federal Government.	Concern of individuals.
4. Provision for helpless members of society.	Government assisted by charities. Exclusively concern of government.	By private charities. By private charities assisted by government.

CHART V

KEY FOR APPRAISING ATTITUDES TOWARD LABOR

Topic	POINT OF VIEW	
	Pro-Labor Bias	Anti-Labor or No-Labor Bias
1. Spirit of Judaism pro-labor.	Yes.	No.
2. Rabbinic support for the cause of collective bargaining.	Yes.	No.
3. Labor trouble due to radical agitators.	No.	Yes.
4. Trade unions do more harm than good to industrial progress.	No.	Yes.
5. Elimination of use of injunction in labor disputes.	Yes.	No.
6. Sit-down strikes contrary to law and order.	No.	Yes.

CHART VI

KEY FOR APPRAISING ATTITUDES ON COLLECTIVISM

Topic	POINT OF VIEW	
	Pro-Collectivist	Anti- or Non-Collectivist
1. Concentration of wealth in hands of few is a fact.	Yes.	No.
2. Wealth is distributed according to merit.	No.	Yes.
3. Socialized industry is detrimental to initiative.	No.	Yes.

CHART VI (*Continued*)

KEY FOR APPRAISING ATTITUDES ON COLLECTIVISM

	POINT OF VIEW	
Topic	*Pro-Collectivist*	*Anti- or Non-Collectivist*
4. Abolition of private ownership will result in decline of standard of living.	No.	Yes.
5. Economic planning is impossible under capitalism.	Yes.	No.
6. Public business enterprises are unsuccessful.	No.	Yes.
7. Profit motive in radio, cinema, and press degrade public intelligence and taste.	Yes.	No.
8. Economic individualism degrades character.	Yes.	No.
9. Human culture demands preservation of capitalism.	No.	Yes.
10. Socialist system affords more opportunity for common man than capitalism.	Yes.	No.
11. Socialization of utilities, railroads, and mines.	Yes.	No.
12. Consumer cooperatives are detrimental to prosperity.	No.	Yes.
13. Employment of class appeal in social change is justified.	Yes.	No.
14. Need for a farmer-labor party.	Yes.	No.
15. Sound policy for America is:	Limited socialization. Complete socialization of production and consumption.	Leave economy as is. Corrected capitalism. Centralization of power.

CHART VII

KEY TO APPRAISAL OF RESPONSES WITH RESPECT TO RECOGNIZED SCOPE OF SOCIAL RESPONSIBILITY FOR EDUCATION

	POINT OF VIEW	
Item	*Broad Concept*	*Narrow Concept*
1. Society should make freely available.	Secondary education. College education.	Elementary education.
2. Social responsibility for adult education.	Yes.	No.
3. Economies in public education should be made as last resort only.	Yes.	No.
4. Equalization of educational opportunities by state.	Yes.	No.
5. Federal support of education.	Yes.	No.

CHART VIII

KEY TO APPRAISAL OF RESPONSES IN TERMS OF ATTITUDE TOWARD
CONTROL OF TEACHERS' OPINIONS

	POINT OF VIEW	
Item	*Opposed to Control of Teachers' Opinions*	*Favorable to Control of Teachers' Opinions*
1. Loyalty oaths are threat to good teaching.	Yes.	No.
2. Permissibility of unionization of teachers.	Yes.	No.
3. Refusal of teaching licenses to socialists.	No.	Yes.
4. Dismissal of communist teachers.	No.	Yes.

CHART IX

KEY TO APPRAISAL OF RESPONSES IN TERMS OF ATTITUDES TOWARD
EMPLOYMENT OF EDUCATION IN SOCIAL RECONSTRUCTION

	POINT OF VIEW	
Item	*Favorable to Employment of Education in Social Reconstruction*	*Opposed to Employment of Education in Social Reconstruction*
1. Encouragement of teachers to fight against sub-standard living conditions.	Yes.	No.
2. The duty of publicly supported schools is:	To develop social intelligence. To make students identify themselves with social movements aiming at collectivism.	To be neutral on social issues. In support of existing institutions.

CHART X

KEY TO APPRAISAL OF RESPONSES WITH RESPECT TO PROVISION FOR RELIGIOUS
EDUCATION WITHIN THE FRAMEWORK OF THE PUBLIC SCHOOL

	POINT OF VIEW	
Item	*Opposed to Provision for Religious Training*	*Favorable to Provision for Religious Training*
1. Safeguarding belief in literal truths of Bible.	No.	Yes.
2. Designation of special period for religious instruction.	No.	**Yes.**
3. Inclusion of Bible reading in curriculum.	No.	Yes.

CHART XI

KEY TO APPRAISAL OF RESPONSES IN TERMS OF LIBERALISM
ON THE ISSUE OF CIVIL LIBERTIES

	POINT OF VIEW	
Topic	*Liberal*	*Anti-Liberal*
1. Criticism of the Constitution unpatriotic.	No.	Yes.
2. Exclusion from the United States of advocates of communism.	No.	Yes.
3. Exclusion from the United States of advocates of fascism.	No.	Yes.
4. Rabbinic support of censorship of movies, art, and literature.	No.	Yes.
5. Withhold freedom of speech from communists.	Never.	Always.
6. Withhold freedom of speech from fascists.	Never.	Always.
7. Withhold freedom of speech from advocates of violent seizure of government.	Never.	Always.
8. Withhold freedom of speech from advocates of military disobedience.	Never.	Always.
9. Withhold freedom of speech from strike agitators.	Never.	Always.
10. Withhold freedom of speech from advocates of general strikes.	Never.	Always.
11. Withhold freedom of speech from critics of the Constitution.	Never.	Always.
12. Withhold freedom of speech from advocates of disobedience of mobilization orders.	Never.	Always.
13. Withhold freedom of speech from critics of fundamental institutions.	Never.	Always.

CHART XII

KEY TO APPRAISAL OF RESPONSES CONCERNING THE QUESTION
OF RELATION BETWEEN SEXES

| | POINT OF VIEW | |
Issue	Liberal Response	Anti-Liberal Response
1. Birth control contradictory to spirit of Judaism.	No.	Yes.
2. Discussion of sex problems from pulpit.	Yes.	No.
3. Prostitution in the main due to character deficiencies.	No.	Yes.
4. Double standard of sex morality.	No.	Yes.
5. Extra-marital relations between adults not likely to result in offspring not of social concern.	Yes.	No.
6. Social desirability of women's limitation to care of family.	No.	Yes.
7. Social desirability of facilitating women's entry into professions.	Yes.	No.
8. Liberalization of divorce laws.	Yes.	No.

CHART XIII

KEY TO APPRAISAL OF RABBIS' RESPONSES ON ISSUES OF RACE RELATIONS

| | POINT OF VIEW | |
Issue	Egalitarian Response	Non- or Anti-Egalitarian Response
1. Enactment of Federal Anti-Lynching Law.	Yes.	No.
2. Contradiction between Jim Crow practice and principle of brotherhood of man.	Yes.	No.
3. Different standard of wages for white and Negro teachers in the South.	No.	Yes.
4. Admissibility of Orientals to citizenship.	Yes.	No.
5. Special qualifications for Negro voters in the South.	No.	Yes.
6. Scientific soundness of belief in white superiority.	No.	Yes.

CHARTS XIV THROUGH XX—COMBINATIONS OF RESPONSES TO PAIRS OF PROPOSITIONS

CHART XIV

COHERENT, NON-COHERENT, AND APPARENTLY INCONSISTENT COMBINATIONS
OF RESPONSES TO PAIRS OF PROPOSITIONS WITHIN THE AREA OF THEOLOGY[1]

	Coherent Combinations	Non-Coherent Combinations	Apparently Inconsistent Combinations
a. Propositions paired with 1, Section I			
2-I	++, ––, –1?2, ?1?2	–1+2, ?1+2	+1–2, +1?2, ?1–2
7-I	+1–7, –1+7, ??	––, –1?7, ?1–7	++, +1?7, ?1+7
8-I	++, ––, ??	–1+8, –1?8, ?1–8	+1–8, +1?8, ?1–8
9-I	+1–8, ??, –1+9, –1?9	–1–9, ?1–9	++, +1?9, ?1+9
5-II	+1b, –1a, –1c, –1d, –1e	+5a–5b, ?1b	+5c, +5d, +5e, ?1a, ?1c, ?1d, ?1e
6-II	+1c, +1d –1a, –1b	–1c, –1d, ?1c, ?1d	+1a, +1b, ?1a, ?1b
11-II	+1a, –1b, –1c	–1c, ?1a	+1b, +1c, ?1b, ?1c
b. Propositions paired with 2, Section I			
7-I	+2–7, –2+7, ??	––, –2?7, ?2–7	++, +2?7, ?2+7
1-II	+2a, –2b, –2c, –2d, –2e	+2b, +2c, +2d, +2e, –2a, ?2a, ?2b, ?2c, ?2d, ?2e	Same
5-II	+2b–2a, –2c, –2d, –2e	+2a, +2c, +2d, +2c, ?2a, ?2b	–2, ?2c, ?2d, ?2e
6-II	+2c, +2d, –2a, –2b	+2b, –2c, –2d, ?2c, ?2d	+2a, ?2a
11-II	+2a, –2b, –2c	?2b, ?2c	+2b, +2c, –2a, ?2a
c. Propositions paired with 5, Section I			
11-II	+5a, +5b, –5b–5c, –5, ?5b, ?5c	+5c	–5a, ?5a
d. Propositions paired with 6, Section I			
4-I	++, ––, ??	+6–4, +6?4, ?6–4	–6+4, –6?4, ?6+4
4-II	+6a, –6b–6c ?6b, ?6c	+6b, +6c–6a ?6a	None

CHART XIV (*Continued*)

COHERENT, NON-COHERENT, AND APPARENTLY INCONSISTENT COMBINATIONS OF
RESPONSES TO PAIRS OF PROPOSITIONS WITHIN THE AREA OF THEOLOGY[1]

	Coherent Combinations	Non-Coherent Combinations	Apparently Inconsistent Combinations
e. Propositions paired with 8, Section I			
9–I	+8–9, –8–9, ??	++, +8?9, ––, –8?9, ?8+9, ?8–9	None
3–II	+8a, –8b, –8c, –8d, –8e, ?8b, ?8c, ?8d, ?8c	+8b, +8c, +8d, +8e	–8a, ?8a
4–II	+8a, –8b, –8c, ?8b, ?8c	+8b, +8c, –8a, ?8a	None
f. Propositions paired with 9, Section I			
7–I	++, ––, ??	+9–7, +9?7, –9?7, ?9+7, ?9–7	–9+7
g. Propositions paired with 5, Section II			
6–I	b+6, c–6, c?6, d–6, d?6, e–6, e?6	a+6, a–6, a?6, b–6, b?6, c+6, d+6, e+6	None
h. Propositions paired with 11, Section II			
5–II	11a5a, 11a5b, 11b5c, **11b5d,** 11b5c, 11c5c, 11c5d, 11c5e	11b5a, 11c5a	11a5c, 11a5d, 11a5c, 11b5b, 11c5b
6–II	11a6c, 11a6d, 11b6c, 11c6a, 11c6b	11b6a	11a6c, 11a6b, 11b6c, 11b6d, 11c6c, 11c6d

[1] Key interpretation of Charts XIV to XX: Roman numerals refer to sections of questionnaire; Arabic numerals refer to items in sections; plus signs (+), minus signs (–), question marks (?), and particular responses refer to true and false statements; letters refer to particular choices in the case of multiple-choice statements.

CHART XV

COHERENT, NON-COHERENT, AND APPARENTLY INCONSISTENT COMBINATIONS OF
RESPONSES TO PAIRS OF PROPOSITIONS WITHIN THE AREA OF
PHILOSOPHY OF JEWISH LIFE[1]

	Coherent Combinations	Non-Coherent Combinations	Apparently Inconsistent Combinations
a. Propositions paired with 10, Section I			
11–I	+10–11, +10?11, –10+11, ?10+11, ??	–10?11, ?10–11, ++, ––	None
12–II	+10c, –10a, –10b, ?10a, ?10b	–10a, +10b, –10c, ?10c	None
b. Propositions paired with 11, Section I			
12–II	+11b, –11c, ?11c	+11a, –11c, –11a, ?11a	–11b, ?11b ?11a
c. Propositions paired with 13, Section I			
1c–III	+13No1c, +13Mi1c, –13Maj1c, ?13Maj1c	+13Maj1c, –13No1c, –13Mi1c, ?13No1c, ?13Mi1c	None

[1] For key to interpretation see footnote to Chart XIV.

CHART XVI

COHERENT, NON-COHERENT, AND APPARENTLY INCONSISTENT COMBINATIONS OF
RESPONSES TO PAIRS OF PROPOSITIONS WITHIN THE AREA OF
ECONOMIC RECONSTRUCTION

	Coherent Combinations	Non-Coherent Combinations	Apparently Inconsistent Combinations
a. Propositions paired with 14, Section I			
17–I	+14–17, –14+17, ??	–+, +14?17, ––, –14?17, ?14+17, ?14–17	None
35–I	++, ––, ??	+14–35, +14?35, –14+35, ?14+35, ?14–35, –14?35	None
41–I	++, ––, ??	+14–41, +14?41, –14+41, –14?41, ?14+41, ?14–41,	None

CHART XVI (*Continued*)

COHERENT, NON-COHERENT, AND APPARENTLY INCONSISTENT COMBINATIONS OF
RESPONSES TO PAIRS OF PROPOSITIONS WITHIN THE AREA OF
ECONOMIC RECONSTRUCTION

	Coherent Combinations	Non-Coherent Combinations	Apparently Inconsistent Combinations
42–I	+14–42, –14+42	++, +14?42, –– –14?42, ?14+42, ?14–42	None
43–I	+14–43, ??, –14+43	+14?43, ––, –14?43, ?14+43, ?14–43,	++
b. Propositions paired with 21, Section I			
33–I	+21–33, –21+33, ??	++, +21?33, –– –21?33, ?21+33, ?21–33	None
38–I	+21–38, –21+38 ??	–21–36, –21?38, +21–38	++, +21?38, ?21+38
43–I	+21–43, –21+43 ?21+43, ??	++, +21?43, –– –21?43, ?21–43	None
c. Propositions paired with 23, Section I			
33–I	++, ––, ??	+23–33, +23?33, –23?33, ?23+33, ?23–33	–23+33
36–I	++, ––, ??	+23?36, –23+36, –23?36, ?23+36, ?23–36	+23–36
43–I	++, ––, ?23+43, ??	+23–43, –23?43, –23+43, –23?43, ?23–43	None
17–II	+23c, –23d, –23a, –23b, ?23d, ?23e	+23a, –23c, –23a, ?23a, ?23b, ?23c	+23a, +23b, –23d
d. Propositions paired with 25, Section I			
27–I	+25–27, –25+27, ??	++, +25?27, ––, –25?27, ?25+27, ?25–27	None
28–I	+25–28, –25+28	+25?28, ––, 25?28, ?25+28, ?25–28	++
41–I	++, ––, ??, ?25+41	–25+41, –25?41, ?25–41	+25–41, +25?41
17–II	+a, +b, –e, –c, –d	+c, –a, –b, –e, ?a, ?b, ?c, ?e	+d, ?d

CHART XVI (*Continued*)

COHERENT, NON-COHERENT, AND APPARENTLY INCONSISTENT COMBINATIONS OF
RESPONSES TO PAIRS OF PROPOSITIONS WITHIN THE AREA OF
ECONOMIC RECONSTRUCTION

	Coherent Combinations	*Non-Coherent Combinations*	*Apparently Inconsistent Combinations*
e. Propositions paired with 27, Section I			
17–I	++, ––, ??	+27–17, +27?17, –27?17, ?27–17	–27+17, ?27+17
43–I	++, ––, ??	+27–43, +27?43, –27+43, –27?43, ?27+43, ?27–43	None
f. Propositions paired with 28, Section I			
27–I	++, ––, ??	+28–27, +28?27, –28+27, –28–27, ?28+27, ?28–27	None
17–I	++, ––, ??	+28–17, +28?17, –28+17, ?28?17, ?28+17, ?28–17	None
43–I	++, ––, ??	+28–43, +28?43, –28+43, –28?43, ?28+43, ?28–43	None
g. Propositions paired with 29, Section I			
25–I	++, ––, ?29–25, ??	+29–25, +29?25, –29+25, –29?25, ?29+25	None
27–I	+29–27, +29?27, –29+27, ?29+27, ??	++, ––, –29?27, ?29–27	None
28–I	+29–28, –29+28, ??	–29–28, –29?28, ?29+28, ?29–28	++, +29, ?28
41–I	++, ––, ?29–41, ??	+29–41, +29?41, –29+41, –29?41, ?29+41	None
h. Propositions paired with 33, Section I			
34–I	+33–34, +33?34, –33+34, ?33+34, ??	++, ––, –22?34, ?33+34	None
36–I	++, ––, ??, ?33–36	+33–36, +33?36, –33+36, –33?36, ?33+36	None

CHART XVI (*Continued*)

COHERENT, NON-COHERENT, AND APPARENTLY INCONSISTENT COMBINATIONS OF
RESPONSES TO PAIRS OF PROPOSITIONS WITHIN THE AREA OF
ECONOMIC RECONSTRUCTION

	Coherent Combinations	Non-Coherent Combinations	Apparently Inconsistent Combinations
43–I	++, ——, ??	+33–43, +33?43, −33+43, −33?43, ?33+43, ?33−43	None
17–II	+33c, +33d, −33a, −33b, ?33b, ?33e	+33b, +33a, −33c, −33d, −33e, ?33c, ?33d	+33a, ?33a
i. Propositions paired with 35, Section I			
21–I	++, ——, ??	+35–21, +35?21, −35?21, ?35+21, ?35−21	−35+21
36–I	+35–36, −35+36, ??	+35?36, −35−36, ?35+36, ?35−36, −35?36	++
43–I	+35–43, −35+43, ?35+43, ??	++, +35?43, ——, −35?43, ?35−43	
17–II	+35a, −35b, −35c, −35d	?35c, ?35d, ?35e, +35e, −35a, −35b, −35e, ?35a, ?35b	+35c, +35d
j. Propositions paired with 36, Section I			
43–I	++, ——, ??	+36–43, +36?43, −36+43, −36?43, ?36+43, ?36−43	None
17–II	+35c, +36d, −36a, −36b	+36e, −36e, ?36a, ?36b, ?36c, ?36d, ?36e	+36a, +36b, −36c, −36d
k. Propositions paired with 38, Section I			
43–I	++, ——, ??	+38–43, +38?43, −38+43, −38?43, ?38+43, ?38−43	None
17–II	+38c, +38d, −38a, −38b	+38a, −38e, ?38a, ?38b, ?38e	+38a, +38b, −38c, −38d, ?38c, ?38d

CHART XVI (*Continued*)

COHERENT, NON-COHERENT, AND APPARENTLY INCONSISTENT COMBINATIONS OF
RESPONSES TO PAIRS OF PROPOSITIONS WITHIN THE AREA OF
ECONOMIC RECONSTRUCTION

	Coherent Combinations	*Non-Coherent Combinations*	*Apparently Inconsistent Combinations*
l. Propositions paired with 41, Section I			
35–I	++, ––, ??	+41–35, +41?35, –41+35, –41?35, ?41+35, ?41–35	None
43–I	??, +41–43, –41+43	+41?43, ––, –41?43, ?41+43, ?41–43	++
17–II	+41a, +41b, –41c, –41d	+41c, +41d, +41e, –41a, –41b, –41c, ?41a, ?41b, ?41c, ?41d, ?41e	None
m. Propositions paired with 43, Section I			
27–I	++, ––, ??	+43–27, +43?27, –43+27, –43?27, ?43+27, ?43–27	None
17–II	+43c, +43d, –43a, –43b	+43c, –43c, –43d, –43c, ?43a, ?43b, ?43c, ?43d, ?43e	+43a, +43b

CHART XVII

COHERENT, NON-COHERENT, AND APPARENTLY INCONSISTENT COMBINATIONS OF
RESPONSES TO PAIRS OF PROPOSITIONS WITHIN THE AREA OF EDUCATION

	Coherent Combinations	*Non-Coherent Combinations*	*Apparently Inconsistent Combinations*
a. Propositions paired with 44, Section I			
47–I	+44–47, –44+47, ??	++, +44?47, ––, –44?47, ?44+47, ?44–47	None
48–I	+44–48, –44+48, ??	++, +44?48, ––, –44?48, ?44+48, ?44–48	None

CHART XVII (*Continued*)

COHERENT, NON-COHERENT, AND APPARENTLY INCONSISTENT COMBINATIONS OF
RESPONSES TO PAIRS OF PROPOSITIONS WITHIN THE AREA OF EDUCATION

	Coherent *Combinations*	*Non-Coherent* *Combinations*	*Apparently* *Inconsistent* *Combinations*
b. Propositions paired with 45, Section I			
27–I	+45–27, –45+27, ??	+45?27, –45?27, ?45+27, ?45–27, –––	++
c. Propositions paired with 48, Section I			
1–I	++, ––, ??	–1?48, ?1+48, ?1–48	+1–48, +1?48, –1+48
2–I	++, ––, ??	+2–48, +2?48, –2?48, ?2–48	–2+48, ?2+48
7–I	+48–7, –48+7, ??	––, –48?7, ?48–7	++, +48?7, ?48+7
8–I	++, ––, ??	+8–48, +8?48, –8+48, –8?48, ?8–48	None
9–I	+48–9, –48+9, ??	–48–9, –48?9, ?48–9	++, +48?9, ?48+9
d. Propositions paired with 51, Section I			
21–I	+21–51, –21+51, ??	++, +21?51, ––, –21?51, ?21+51, ?21–51	None
e. Propositions paired with 18, Section II			
17–II	aa, 18a17b, 18b17a, bb, cc, 18c17d, 18d17c, 18d17d	18a17c, 18a17d, 18a17e, 18b17e, 18c17e, 18d17e	18b17c, 18b17d, 18c17a, 18d17a, 18d17b

CHART XVIII

COHERENT, NON-COHERENT, AND APPARENTLY INCONSISTENT COMBINATIONS OF
RESPONSES TO PAIRS OF PROPOSITIONS WITHIN THE AREA OF
CIVIL LIBERTIES

	Coherent Combinations	Non-Coherent Combinations	Apparently Inconsistent Combinations
Propositions paired with 58, Section I			
14–I	++, ––, ??	+14–58, +14?58, –14+58, –14?58, ?14–58, ?14+58	None
44–I	+44–58, –44+58, –44?58, ??	++, +44?58, ––, ?44+58, ?44–58	None
17–II	+58a, +58b, –58c, –58d, ?58a, ?58b	+58c, +58d, –58a, –58b, +58e, –58e, ?58c, ?58d, ?58e	None
2a–III	+58 Always –58 Never	+58war, +58crisis, –58war, –58crisis, ?58 Always, ?58 Never, ?58war, ?58crisis	+58 Never –58 Always

CHART XIX

COHERENT, NON-COHERENT, AND APPARENTLY INCONSISTENT COMBINATIONS OF
RESPONSES TO PAIRS OF PROPOSITIONS WITHIN THE AREA OF
PEACE AND INTERNATIONALISM

	Coherent Combinations	Non-Coherent Combinations	Apparently Inconsistent Combinations
a. Propositions paired with 61, Section I			
63–I	+61–63, –61+63, ?61+63, ?61–63, ??	++, +61?63, ––, –61?63	None
66–I	++, ––, ??, ?61–66	+61–66, +61?66, –61?66, –61+66, ?61–66	None
b. Propositions paired with 64, Section I			
66–I	+64–66, –64+66, ??	+64?66, –64?66, ?64+66, ?64–66	++, ––

CHART XIX (*Continued*)

COHERENT, NON-COHERENT, AND APPARENTLY INCONSISTENT COMBINATIONS OF
RESPONSES TO PAIRS OF PROPOSITIONS WITHIN THE AREA OF
PEACE AND INTERNATIONALISM

	Coherent Combinations	*Non-Coherent Combinations*	*Apparently Inconsistent Combinations*
c. Propositions paired with 67, Section I			
69–I	+67–69, –67+69, ??	+67?69, ––, –67?69, ?67–69	++, ?67+69
d. Propositions paired with 70, Section I			
20–II	+70d, –70a, –70b	–70c, –70d, ?70d	+70a, +70b, +70c, ?70a, ?70b, ?70c
e. Propositions paired with 20, Section II			
67–I	a–67, b–67, d+67	c+67, c–67, c?67, d–67, d?67	a+67, a?67, b+67, b?67

CHART XX

COHERENT, NON-COHERENT, AND APPARENTLY INCONSISTENT COMBINATIONS OF
RESPONSES TO PAIRS OF PROPOSITIONS WITHIN THE AREA OF
RELATION BETWEEN SEXES

	Coherent Combinations	*Non-Coherent Combinations*	*Apparently Inconsistent Combinations*
Propositions paired with 71, Section I			
34–I	++, ––, ??	+34–71, +34?71, –34+71, –34?71, ?34–71	None
72–I	+71–72, –71+72, ??	+71?72, ––, –71?72, ?71–72	++, ?71+72
74–I	++, ––, –71?74, ?71–74, ??	+71–74, +71?74, –71?74, ?71+74	None

INDEX

Abravanel, Isaac, 72
Academic training, of rabbinate, 45
Age, of rabbinate, 43
Albo, 72
American Institute, 194
American Jewish Year Book, 53
American Legion, 179 f.
Anti-Semitism, 95, 185, 192, 204, 211
Arabs, 99
Art, 144 f., 190. *See* Censorship
Augsburg Synod, 16, 17

Ben Zimra, David, 72
Beth Ha-midrash, 24
Bible, the, *See* Religion; Theology
Birth control. *See* Sex problems
Birthplace, of congregations, 56 f.; of rabbinate, 41 f.
Business interests. *See* War

Capitalism, 113 f., 122 f., 137, 189, 194, 204, 212. *See* Collectivism
Catholicism, 9, 34, 72
Censorship, 139 f., 144 f., 190, 206
Central Conference of American Rabbis, 2, 4, 19, 20, 29, 32 f., 194, 196
Chicago Hebrew Theological Seminary, 47 f.
Cinema, 144, 190, 204. *See* Censorship
Civil liberties, 2, 139 f., 175, 178, 190, 194, 206, 219, 229
Codes. *See* Religion; Theology
Coherence of thought, of rabbinate, 167 f., 191, 221 f.
Collective bargaining. *See* Labor
Collectivism, 194, 204, 216. *See* Economic reconstruction
Commission on Social Justice, 29 f., 33
Committee on Church and State, 34
Committee on International Peace, 37
Committee on Social Justice of the Rabbinical Assembly, 35 f.
Communism, 140, 205, 211. *See* Civil liberties
Community chests, 2
Conference of the Union of Orthodox Jewish Congregations of America, 37 f.

Congregational schools, 2
Congregations, of rabbinate, 53 f., 212 f.
Conservative Rabbinical Assembly, 194
Constitution, the, 140, 206, 211, 219. *See* Civil liberties
Cooperatives, 115, 205

Daughters of the American Revolution, 179
Declaration of World Peace, 195
Disciples of the Wise, 1, 196

Economic reconstruction, 2, 29 f., 110, 113 f., 173, 178, 189 f., 204, 210, 223 f. *See* Religion
Economic status, of congregations, 58 f.; of rabbinate, 50 f.
Economics, 115 f., 204, 210
Education, 2, 109, 117 f., 131 f., 135, 137, 174, 178, 190, 205, 210, 211, 217, 218, 227 f. *See* Religion; Social reconstruction
Emancipation, 12 f.
Enlightenment. *See* Emancipation

Farmer-labor party, 127 f., 190, 205. *See* Collectivism
Fascism, 140, 206, 211. *See* Civil liberties
Freedom of pulpit, 179 f., 192. *See* Religion
Freedom of speech, 139 f., 190, 211. *See* Civil liberties
Finkelstein, Louis, 71, 73
Frankel, Zachariah, 22
French Constituent Assembly, 12

Gallup poll, 149
Geiger, 16
Geographical distribution, of congregations, 54 f.
Ginsberg, Louis, 22, 71, 73
Government control, 115, 126 f., 189, 205, 210. *See* Civil liberties; Collectivism; Economic reconstruction

Halakah, 49. *See* Religion
Hasidism, 18

231